JCMS Annual Review of the European Union in 2005

D1493797

Edited by
Ulrich Sedelmeier
and
Alasdair R. Young

General Editors: William Paterson and Jim Rollo

Blackwell Publishing

First published 2006 by Blackwell Publishing Ltd

British Library Cataloguing-in-Publication Data applied for
ISBN 1-4051-4516-1

Set in the United Kingdom by Photoscript, Deddington, Oxon
Printed and bound in Singapore by Seng Lee Press Pte Ltd

The publisher's policy is to use permanent paper from mills
that operate a sustainable forestry policy, and which has been
manufactured from pulp processed using acid-free and
elementary chlorine-free practices.
Furthermore, the publisher ensures that the text paper and cover board
used have met acceptable environmental accreditation standards.

For further information on Blackwell Publishing, visit our website:
http://www.blackwellpublishing.com

CONTENTS

JCMS 2006 Volume 44 Annual Review pp. 1–5

Editorial: Crisis, What Crisis? Continuity and Normality in the European Union in 2005

ULRICH SEDELMEIER
London School of Economics and Political Science

ALASDAIR R. YOUNG
University of Glasgow

The themes of crisis, continuity and normality have dominated the European Union (EU) in 2005. A widespread sense of crisis engulfed the EU in the wake of the negative referendums on the Constitutional Treaty in France and the Netherlands, as well as the initial failure to agree on the financial perspective for 2007–13 during the Luxembourg presidency. The crisis is real and the failure of the Constitutional Treaty is significant, as we acknowledge by devoting the keynote article of this *Annual Review* to the subject, and as is reflected in almost all of our contributors commenting on its impact in their policy areas. Yet beyond these eye-catching events, the less visible developments are equally telling about the EU in 2005; and these developments are more evocative of continuity and normality. In a sense the very source of the crisis can be interpreted as a sign of the EU as a maturing polity. As Paul Taggart argues in the keynote article, popular rejections of change are 'normal' politics.

Moreover, although there was much gnashing of teeth over the French and Dutch votes in the immediate aftermath, the EU went on to have quite a successful year, taking major, difficult decisions in a variety of policy domains, not least with respect to its relations with neighbouring countries. This is particularly striking, as Sandra Lavenex and Frank Schimmelfennig point out, because of widespread anticipation of 'enlargement fatigue' in the wake of the 2004 enlargement. Rather, during 2005 the EU opened accession negotiations with Turkey and Croatia and recognized Macedonia as a candidate country. It also cleared the path to starting negotiations on stabilization and association agreements with Serbia and Montenegro, and with Bosnia and Herzegovina.

Likewise, despite ongoing speculation about whether Bulgaria and Romania will join in 2007 as envisaged, and unkind commentary that their accession will turn 'enlargement fatigue' in 'enlargement disgust', Member State representatives in the various formations of the Council of Ministers – in which Bulgarian and Romania representatives have participated since signing their accession treaties – already consider their membership as a normal fact of everyday working life.

More generally, enlargement to 25 Member States does not appear to have led to the paralysis of decision-making that the Constitutional Treaty was, at least in part, intended to alleviate, although – as Desmond Dinan notes – the Commission has struggled more than other institutions to absorb officials from the new members. As the contributions by David Howarth, Amy Verdun and Derek Hearl discuss with different emphases, the March European Council relaunched the Lisbon process and agreed reform of the Stability and Growth Pact. While the outcomes may not have been spectacular, they represented difficult decisions that are unlikely to have been any more spectacular if the EU still had only 15 Member States. Further, after the French and Dutch referendums the Member States agreed on the financial perspectives for 2007–13. This was a protracted and unseemly affair, as David Howarth, Derek Hearl and Richard Whitman describe, but not markedly more so than previous wrangling over the EU's budget.

Aside from these landmark decisions, the process of EU policy-making continued apace, like a duck's legs paddling vigorously beneath the surface of the water. As Jörg Monar reports, the EU took a number of important decisions in the field of justice and home affairs, including agreeing minimum standards for granting and withdrawing refugee status. In addition, as Jörg Monar and Richard Whitman note, the London bombings on 7 July galvanized co-operation on terrorism. Although Dave Allen and Michael Smith note that the negative referendum results in France and the Netherlands have had adverse implications for the common foreign and security policy and European security and defence policy, most immediately by derailing preparations to create a European external action service, the EU continued to be active in the wider world, undertaking new missions in Aceh (Indonesia), the Palestinian Authority, Iraq, the Democratic Republic of Congo and in Darfur (Sudan).

Although there continue to be problems in the EU's external actions, not least with respect to trade, these are quite traditional problems, which have not obviously been exacerbated by enlargement. There is a similar story with internal policies. David Howarth, for example, contends that the Council and Parliament directive on cross-border mergers essentially codifies existing different national practices. The controversial services and REACH directives also continued their painful progress through the EU's decision-making process.

Perhaps surprisingly enlargement has, according to Desmond Dinan, compounded the problems of an already weak Commission. In an attempt to counter the image of over-regulation from Brussels, the Commission even sought to scrap a number of proposals not deemed essential, although in this it faced opposition from the European Parliament. Nonetheless, the Commission launched a number of significant policy initiatives, including an enlargement strategy and a policy plan on legal migration. It also imposed a €60 million fine against the pharmaceutical company AstraZeneca for abuse of dominant position. The European Parliament, according to Dinan, has been emboldened in the wake of enlargement and was unfazed, perhaps inappropriately so, by the French and Dutch referendum results.

The European Court of Justice made a number of significant rulings. In *Mangold* it held that non-discrimination on grounds of age must in fact be regarded as a general principle of Community law, which Michael Dougan argues seems to broaden the scope of the principle of direct effect, but not without limits. Dougan and Monar, from different perspectives, both discuss two significant cases concerning justice and home affairs: *Pupino*, which held that national laws should be interpreted in the light of unimplemented framework decisions; and *Commission* v. *Council*, which established that just because an EU measure includes criminal law provisions, such as providing criminal penalties for violations, it does not fall under Title VI of the Treaty of European Union, but can be pursued exclusively under the first pillar.

As at the EU level, there was a high degree of continuity in the political and economic developments of the Member States. Although there were several important elections in the Member States, as Nick Sitter and Karen Henderson point out, these resulted in few changes of government, the most notable being in Germany, where a CDU-led grand coalition replaced the SPD–Green coalition. As Amy Verdun discusses, economic growth in the euro area slowed slightly in 2005 and continues to be weaker than the average performance of other advanced economies. By contrast, as Debra Johnson describes, almost half of the non-euro area Member States grew more quickly in 2005 than in 2004, and all but Malta grew faster than the euro area average.

Thus at both the EU and Member State levels, 2005 showed a remarkable degree of business as usual despite the upheavals of the French and Dutch rejections of the Constitutional Treaty. That said, the view expressed in the immediate aftermath of the referendums, notably by the Luxembourg presidency (Hearl) and the European Parliament (Dinan), that the referendum results were mere hiccups and that the EU should move to a plan B to 'rectify' the negative results, akin to the earlier cases of Danish and Irish referendums on the Treaties of Maastricht and Nice respectively, fell rapidly by the wayside.

To acknowledge that the EU is a maturing polity with continued dynamism despite the ratification crisis does not simply translate into advocating a 'business as usual' approach. Given the apparent continuing (relative) effectiveness of EU decision-making despite enlargement, the failure to ratify the Constitutional Treaty may matter most in terms of the legitimacy of EU decision-making, by not extending the Parliament's influence. This is somewhat ironic as it was plebiscitory democracy that derailed the process.

'Continuity' and 'normality' are also central to our reorganization of this *Annual Review* as the new editors. Continuity has been possible thanks to the excellent work of the previous editors and contributors that has established the *Annual Review* as a leading source of information for researchers, teachers and practitioners. At the same time, we endeavour to build on what has come before to make it even more user-friendly. To this end we have sought to make the *Annual Review* even more useful as a research tool and as a resource for those teaching on the EU by asking the contributors to provide an overview of key reading in their respective areas, such as prime documents or secondary literature, published during the year. In addition, given the ready availability of much basic information on the EU, with our contributors we are aiming to move away from the *Annual Review* being a publication of record that seeks to cover, often only in passing, all the developments in a particular policy area towards a more reflective guide through the thicket of readily available information.

This more reflective nature of the *Annual Review* is evident not only in continuing the tradition of a keynote article, which provides a timely and in-depth analysis of one of the key developments of the previous year, but in the addition of a review article on the 'state of EU studies' in which leading experts in the field provide an authoritative 'state of the art' of a central debate in EU studies. We are particularly pleased to have secured Beate Kohler-Koch and Berthold Rittberger as authors of the inaugural review article. Their analysis of the 'Governance Turn in EU Studies' sets a high standard for this new feature of the *Annual Review* which we hope subsequent volumes will continue to establish as one of the most authoritative contributions to conceptual debates in EU studies.

We have also undertaken a more prosaic reorganization of the content of the *Annual Review* in order to reflect the normality of an enlarged EU. We have, therefore, done away with the division between 'old' and 'new' members as an organizing principle. As the result of exchanges with Nick Sitter and Karen Henderson, we have incorporated what had been two chapters into one jumbo chapter covering political developments in all the Member States. While this reorganization implies a less explicit coverage of political developments in candidate countries than in previous issues, those developments that have a bearing on accession are now covered in a new contribution on the EU's relations with the 'wider Europe'. With regard to economic developments in the Member States, we divided the focus (and thus the labour) along the euro area/non-euro area divide, ably covered by Amy Verdun and Debra Johnson respectively.

We have replaced the previous contributions on 'external relations' and 'enlargement' with contributions on 'relations with the wider Europe' – for which we are happy to have gained Sandra Lavenex and Frank Schimmelfennig – and 'the rest of the world,' which remains in the capable hands of Dave Allen and Mike Smith. This reorganization reflects both the shorter queue of candidate countries and the continued development of the EU's policies towards its various neighbours (including beyond Europe).

The new line-up of contributors reflects our goal to diversify the geographical spread of contributors – both country of origin and home institution – to reflect the broader reach of UACES and *JCMS*. While the UK still dominates, we are happy to have increased the contingent of contributors from the other side of the Atlantic, from the continent, as well as from outside the current membership (although unfortunately the new Member States remain a blind spot). We are grateful to the 'old hands' who stayed on and welcome the new authors who embark on this venture with us and thank them all for keeping within the tight deadlines of the *Annual Review*.

We would also like to thank our predecessor, Lee Miles, for handing over such a vigorous going concern and for helping to ease us into our new roles. We are grateful to UACES, particularly Jo Shaw, and the *JCMS* editors, Willie Paterson and Jim Rollo, for entrusting us with this endeavour and for providing their moral and material support for our ideas for the *Annual* Review. We must also thank Blackwells for agreeing to extend the page extent of the *Annual Review* in order to accommodate our desired changes. We are also indebted to our copy editor, Mary Robinson, for handling all aspects of production and project management and giving us the confidence to go forwards.

JCMS 2006 Volume 44 Annual Review pp. 7–25

Keynote Article: Questions of Europe – The Domestic Politics of the 2005 French and Dutch Referendums and their Challenge for the Study of European Integration*

PAUL TAGGART
University of Sussex

Introduction

For those interested in European integration, 2005 will clearly be regarded as the year in which the voters of two of the European Union's (EU's) founding states rejected the European Constitutional Treaty. After the success and the symbolic importance of the 2004 enlargement, it comes as a spectacular contrast for 2005 to be the year that French and the Dutch voters said 'no' to the next big European initiative. From what was clearly a major success in 2004 we have what looks like a substantial rejoinder to the next big European initiative in 2005.

Looked at from 'above', from the EU studies community with its primary concern with the EU level of governance, the referendums look like road-blocks in the path of European integration, or as the expression of popular dissatisfaction with the larger project. Certainly the two results have appeared to halt the European Constitutional Treaty's ratification (at least in its present form) and therefore have had important ramifications for the future of European integration. The implications for the future concern not only the Constitutional Treaty itself but also other key aspects, most notably enlargement and the Lisbon strategy for economic modernization (Whitman, 2005, pp. 685–6). The reaction by many in the EU studies community has been to describe the 2005 referendum results as amounting to a crisis for the EU if not for the European

* I would like to thank the editors for their help in preparing this article. In addition I would like to extend my thanks to Tim Bale, James Hampshire, Robert Harmsen, Francis McGowan and Sally Marthaler for assistance and advice on an earlier draft and for ideas and help.

project in general (e.g. Mény, 2005; Hobolt, 2006). Putting together the two referendum results there is also a temptation to see them as marking a rising tide of popular euroscepticism.

Looked at in the round, as part and parcel of both EU politics and European politics, the 2005 referendum results, however, look like politics as usual. They are less threatening than they seem to the wider process of European integration and stem from very different circumstances. They are only two of the four national referendums held on the Constitutional Treaty. They are much like the representative democratic politics that underpin the Member States of the EU; iterative processes that involve messy compromises, coalition-building and, frequently, defeats and set-backs. The referendums in France and the Netherlands gave a verdict on a largely top-down initiative set in train at the Laeken European Council. That initiative sought to secure legitimacy through creating a semi-inclusive and semi-deliberative convention that came up with a treaty constructed to satisfy disparate interests and that then had to reckon with a procedure that involved 25 different ratification processes, including, in some cases, a resort to direct democracy. That there was no wholesale endorsement in all 25 states should come as no surprise if we understand the way this sort of politics usually operates in Europe. What is surprising is that we appear so surprised.

This contribution explores what the negative referendum results of 2005 mean in the context of European politics and how the reaction to them tells us much about how we treat the issue of European integration as commentators and researchers. The article argues that we need more systematically to integrate the study of European domestic politics with the study of the politics of the European integration process. This is not simply to reiterate the argument that comparative politics offers us tools that are useful for understanding European institutions (Hix, 2005), but rather to suggest that, as the European project permeates domestic institutions and as plebiscitary pressures seem to drive the European project to seek domestic legitimation, we can no longer understand the process of European integration in isolation from domestic politics. The uncomfortable reality seems to be that a full understanding of European politics in its widest sense means an understanding of at least 26 distinct and often messy processes.

The two referendums demonstrate how many European events cannot be regarded as the exclusive preserve of EU-level or domestic processes. For scholars of European integration, therefore, the events of 2005 provide two challenges: one practical and one theoretical. The practical challenge lies in how to focus on a European integration process that is becoming more and more plural; one that may give rise to different reactions. The larger, theoretical challenge lies in integrating into theories of European integration domestic politics and doing so with a sensitivity to the growing interdependence of EU politics and domestic politics.

In order to make this case, the article first deals with the more theoretical conceptualization of models of democratic process and suggests that the increased use of referendums marks a tendency towards resorting to plebiscitary politics in the European integration project. After considering the way in which referendums have been dealt with in European studies, the article analyses the French and Dutch referendum results, highlighting key differences between the arguments, forces, campaigns and 'no' votes that reinforce both the importance of not treating them as indicative of common factors and the need to integrate effectively the study of domestic European political processes with European integration. The final section explores the challenge that this integrated approach poses for the study of contemporary Europe.

I. Models of Democracy and the Growth of Plebiscitary Politics

The French and Dutch referendum results of 2005 could be read as popular, plebiscitary, populist reactions to an elite-led project. Doubts about the democratic credentials of the EU have led to a persistent debate about the 'democratic deficit' and this has therefore set the terms for many in seeing the referendum results as popular consequences for an unpopular polity.

In the debate about the 'democratic deficit' of the European project there is a tendency to treat both domestic and European democracy in a monolithic fashion and to act as if there is only one democratic model at play in contemporary Europe. This tendency leads to different conclusions. Moravcsik (2002) suggests that in fact the EU institutional processes, if measured by the yardstick of national democracies, actually function rather more effectively and in a more transparent fashion than national democratic institutions and processes. Mény (2003) takes a somewhat different line, arguing that the European level of democracy has an underdeveloped aspect of popular sovereignty and an overdeveloped constitutionalism. Consequently we need to construct new models for the European level that bolster popular sovereignty, and therefore 'Europe has to invent a new democratic system, a system which as yet has no name' (Mény, 2003, p. 13).

It is more useful not to treat the European project as part of an integrated Europe requiring integrated models of democracy (Weiler, 1999). We can then draw on an already well-developed range of democratic models (Held, 1996). There are at least two different models of democracy, and particularly of the democratic process, at play in the European project. On one side we have the representative model of politics which emphasizes the importance of representation, of representative institutions, such as parliaments, and of deliberation through those institutions as a means of resolving political conflicts. On the other side there is the model of direct democracy where citizens are treated as sovereign and as such play a direct role in decision-making either through institutions of direct democracy such as referendums and ballot initiatives, or through deliberative processes such as conventions or town-hall meetings. It is important that we understand these as distinct models. They are normative – not empirical – models that emphasize the way democracy should be structured. They have different dynamics, employ different institutional arrangements, have different legitimating logics and give rise fundamentally to different forms of politics. Both models have been implicitly at play in the development of the European project.

A quick tour of the institutions of European integration illustrates the role of the different models. The European Parliament serves of course, as the benchmark of representative democracy with European-level representatives, the role of executive oversight and the possibility of a European-wide party system in the party groups. Its direct election in 1979 was explicitly a measure to address the (representative) democratic deficit. And, for all the qualifications we can raise about its limited role and the unusual nature of the party groups, the Parliament is clearly acting like other representative assemblies, increasingly asserting its democratic legitimacy and making use of the political processes of legislation and oversight (Hix *et al.,* 2003). Even the European Council and the Council of Ministers fit into the model as indirectly representative institutions either made up of government ministers, or appointed by and accountable to directly elected bodies. In terms of the criteria for states joining the EU, representative politics is seen as the benchmark of democracy.

The Convention served as a hybrid of representative models with a strong presence of directly elected assembly members, but with a clear aspiration to a deliberative method of operation, even if this was more in conception than operation (Maurer, 2003; Crum, 2004; Lucarelli and Radaelli, 2004). And the use of referendums to ratify European treaties, accession or membership of the euro marks the clearest example of the institutionalization of direct democratic practices. Table 1 lays out referendum on European integration issues in European states since 1970.

The use of referendums as part of the European integration process represents a marked shift towards plebiscitary politics in certain areas. It appears that, in important domains, there is a move towards a model of direct democracy and away from representative democracy. The use of referendums is admittedly sporadic, but they are being used at key moments of European integration. They are being used for membership (either EU or euro) and for treaty ratification. In both types of cases, plebiscitary politics is being used to make fundamental decisions. The nature of European integration has meant that

Table 1: European Referendums on European Integration Issues

Year	Country	Referendum Topic
1972	France	Enlarge EC
	Ireland	EC membership
	Norway	EC membership
	Denmark	EC membership
	Switzerland	Free trade with EC
1975	UK	EC membership
1986	Denmark	Ratify SEA
1987	Ireland	Ratify SEA
1989	Italy	Legalize MEPs' powers
1992	Denmark	Ratify TEU (Maastricht)
	Ireland	Ratify TEU (Maastricht)
	France	Ratify TEU (Maastricht)
	Switzerland	EEA membership
	Liechtenstein	EEA membership
1993	Denmark	Ratify TEU and Amsterdam
1994	Austria	EU membership
	Finland	EU membership
	Sweden	EU membership
	Norway	EU membership
1998	Ireland	Ratify Amsterdam
	Denmark	Ratify Amsterdam
2000	Switzerland	Bilateral agreement with EU
	Denmark	EMU membership
2001	Switzerland	Restart EU accession talks
	Ireland	Ratify Nice
2002	Ireland	Ratify Nice
2003	Malta	EU membership
	Slovenia	EU membership
	Hungary	EU membership
	Lithuania	EU membership
	Slovakia	EU membership
	Poland	EU membership
	Czech Republic	EU membership
	Estonia	EU membership
	Sweden	EMU membership
	Latvia	EU membership
2005	Spain	Ratify Constitutional Treaty
	France	Ratify Constitutional Treaty
	Netherlands	Ratify Constitutional Treaty
	Luxembourg	Ratify Constitutional Treaty

Source: Shu (2005).

treaties represent quasi-constitutional moments for the polity (Wessels, 2005), and the question of membership also constitutes, for the states, a juncture of great importance.

Nineteen out of the present 25 Member States have held referendums on issues of European integration (see Table 1). While some states clearly use them more often and place more emphasis on their use, what is evident is that, across the EU, many political systems that do not otherwise resort easily to referendums have used this device for the European issue.

Most of the institutions, processes and politics in the EU system are characterized by reference, implicitly or explicitly, to models of representative politics. There is a certain tension about the difficulty of fitting national models of representative politics to a complex system where the institutional engine of integration, the Commission, is appointed and not elected and where national political elites do not tend to take the European issue to their electorates regularly or systematically. The growth of plebiscitary politics is therefore not seen much in the day-to-day operation of the EU, but is becoming more in evidence at key decision moments.

The growth of plebiscitary politics gives rise to two fundamental paradoxes in the use of referendums by EU Member States. The first paradox is that EU Member and candidate States have increasingly used referendums in recent years. Of the 40 referendums held on issues of European integration since 1972, nine preceded the Maastricht Treaty and the other 31 have been held since 1992 (Shu, 2005). There is an increasing tendency to ratify decisions on European integration through referendums. This means that referendums have become more popular as the European integration project has become less popular. The Maastricht Treaty process and the politics around it marked the demise of the 'permissive consensus' – the assumption that elites could push forward integration safe in the knowledge of mass support, or at least acquiescence. The demise of the permissive consensus, at least as something that could be assumed, seems to have marked the emergence of the move to plebiscitary politics to legitimate that which would previously have been legitimated through consensus.

The decline of the permissive consensus can be traced roughly to the early 1990s and is evident in a number of ways. First, the Danish initial rejection of Maastricht started a series of European referendum rejections where mass opinion seems to have gone against elite expectations. Put simply, six referendums in EU Member States on European issues have resulted in 'no' votes since 1992, whereas no referendums in Member States before then resulted in rejections. Second, there has been increasing contestation of the European issue among European political parties (Szczerbiak and Taggart, forthcoming). Public opinion has not, at an aggregate level, changed in its level of support for or opposition to European integration. What has changed is that political actors' assumption of consensus has collapsed, and that this has opened up the space for explicit contestation over the European issue by many political actors at both mass and elite levels.

The second paradox is that the increasing use of referendums on European integration marks a very different democratic logic to that found in the Member States themselves. EU Member States are universally characterized by representative democratic institutions. The criteria for membership and, perhaps more importantly for my argument here, the character of politics among the European states that make up the EU is essentially that of representative politics. The move towards the plebiscitary politics of referendums and direct democracy is therefore a departure from normal practice for the states of the EU.

European Referendums and European Studies

If we consider how European referendums have been dealt with by those who study them, it is clear that they have largely been treated as processes apart from the wider processes of European integration. The consideration of referendums in European political processes has seen four different types of approach. One tends to see them in relation to the broader normative issue of direct democracy. This sort of literature uses empirical cases to explore the normative benefits and deficiencies of direct democracy, and to have a primary concern with referendums as a case of direct democracy rather than with the characteristics of referendums themselves (Qvortrup, 2002; Setala, 1999). A second approach focuses on analysing the outcomes of particular referendums, treating each as a single case study. This has become something of a growth industry given the importance of referendums in the European politics of the Maastricht Treaty, euro membership, EU membership and now the Constitutional Treaty (e.g. Butler and Kitzinger, 1976; Siune *et al.*, 1994; Garry *et al.*, 2005; Ivaldi, 2006).[1]

A third body of literature on European referendums explicitly uses the European cases to develop wider hypotheses about the dynamics of referendums in general. In some cases these have used particular cases to develop such hypotheses. A case in point has been the Danish referendums on the Maastricht Treaty which produced the literature examining the extent to which, as Franklin originally suggested, referendums were largely treated as opportunities by voters to punish or support incumbent governments (Franklin, 2002; Franklin *et al.*, 1994; Svensson, 2002; Siune *et al.*, 1994). The fourth area of research is the work brought together by Szczerbiak and myself which uses

---

[1] See also the series of referendum briefing papers from the European Parties Elections and Referendums Network at «http://www.sussex.ac.uk/sei/1-4-2.html».

the concurrence of the nine accessions referendums to develop and test models of turnout and outcomes in European referendums (Szczerbiak and Taggart, 2005). This is an attempt to provide a robust synchronic comparison of a set of European referendums with implications for both European studies and the wider study of referendums.

What unites the general comparative work is the sensitivity towards domestic conditions. The debate between Franklin (2002) and Svensson (2002) uses the Danish case to tease out an important change to the original thesis about referendums being simply about government support. The comparative study of the 2004 accession referendums clearly demonstrated the importance of cues from domestic actors as well as the general domestic context, for determining the way in which Europe was contested (or not contested) as an issue, and even for determining levels of turnout in European referendums (Szczerbiak and Taggart, 2005).

In normative terms, the move to plebiscitary politics in European integration, as embodied in the increased use of referendums, represents a move, in one domain, towards the direct democratic model. In analytical terms it represents a move that means that we need to be particularly sensitive to the nature of domestic political conditions in those Member States employing referendums in their European policies.

II. The Domestic Politics of the (Dutch and French) Results

A consideration of the particularities of the French and Dutch referendums is instructive. They should be seen as two of four European referendums on the Constitutional Treaty and contrasted with the positive popular votes in Spain in February and Luxembourg in July (see Harmsen, 2005; Hausemer, 2005). Resisting the temptation to view both negative results from 'above' and see them in terms of a unified 'no' vote to Europe, allows us to consider what was discussed, how the issue of Europe was framed and what were the constellations of pro and anti forces, as well as the range of reasons that lay behind the 'no' votes. Doing this reveals two very different processes that may sometimes be about almost entirely separate constitutional treaties. The domestic politics of both the European issue and the referendum processes were very different, and we need to pay attention to this to understand what the two different rejections amount to collectively.

The French Referendum: Contesting Models of Europe and the French Economy

The French debate over the Constitutional Treaty was a case in which the European issue was discussed at length. While many factors of domestic politics impinged on the debate, it is clear that the nature, future and national implications of European integration were debated (see Ivaldi, 2006). It is also the case that there were important domestic contextual factors in France that structured the debate and which played an important role in the outcome.

The referendum appears to be have been decided on in France for four main reasons. The first was that Chirac was keen to prevent his centre-right rival, Nicolas Sarkozy, from stealing his thunder by proposing a referendum. The second reason was that Chirac was aware that a referendum would be difficult and divisive for his opponents in the *Parti Socialiste*. The third is that the announcement by UK Prime Minister Tony Blair, committing the UK to a referendum on the Constitutional Treaty, put pressure on Chirac to do the same. And finally, there appeared to be the sense that any referendum would be won and therefore would be in the interests of the government proposing it. What is remarkable about these factors is that they largely stem from considerations related to domestic politics. In the one factor of the Blair announcement there is an example of an international process, but the pressure came about because of the domestic politics of the UK where Blair's announcement appeared to be calculated to diffuse the European issue in the upcoming general election.

Understanding both the timing and the nature of the French referendum process requires some attention being paid to the nature of the French polity. The nature of the French party system and the conflict between and within the parties had a vital influence on the timing, conduct and outcome of the referendum. The divisions within the *Parti Socialiste,* which were revealed by the party's own referendum held in December 2004; the campaign for a 'no' vote by prominent Socialists such as Laurent Fabius; and the exploitation of the Socialists' difficulties by Chirac all influenced the timing of the referendum (Hainsworth, 2006, p. 99). The referendum was originally planned for late 2005, but on the heels of the positive Spanish referendum and the Socialist Party's internal divisions, Chirac moved it forward to 29 May. This partly reflected a calculation that the referendum process would be particularly difficult for Chirac's divided socialist opponents. Internal party conflict and the inter-party competition between the centre-right and left in France are therefore key ingredients from the very beginning in the story of the French referendum (see Drake, 2005).

Support for the Constitutional Treaty came from the mainstream right in the shape of the *Union pour un Mouvement Populaire* (UMP) and *Union pour la Démocratie Française* (UDF). The *Parti Socialiste* was in support officially (although there were clearly strong elements of opposition within the party) and similarly the Greens were officially supportive but with a divided membership. Opposition to the Treaty came from the right in the form of the *Front National,* the *Mouvement National Républicain*, de Villiers' *Mouvement pour la France* and Pasqua's *Rassemblement pour la France*, and from the hunting lobby as represented by *Chasse, Pêche, Nature et Traditions*. On the left, opposition came from the extreme left in the form of the *Parti Communiste Français*, the Trotskyist *Ligue Communiste Révolutionnaire* and *Lutte Ouvrière*, as well as from the mainstream left in Chevènement's *Mouvement Républicain et Citoyen* and from Laurent Fabius. The issue of the Constitutional Treaty was therefore one which divided the political parties and did so at both the centre and the periphery.

The debate in France ranged over a number of issues and what is perhaps most remarkable about it is the quantity as much the content, as there was a welter of book publications, and newspaper and television debate over the Constitutional Treaty. One issue that had a particular resonance in French domestic politics was the issue of Turkish accession. This was exploited effectively by de Villiers (Ivaldi, 2006, p. 55). Another issue that came to play a role was the 'Bolkestein directive'[2] on services and the internal market which was seen by many in France as indicative of the liberal direction of the EU under an Anglo-Saxon economic model which raised the prospect of the influx of 'Polish plumbers' into France. The third issue of importance was the general state of the French economy, and particularly the impact of some negative trends in unemployment which were published during the campaign.

The result in France was that on a turnout of 69.3 per cent, 54.7 per cent of the votes cast were against the Constitutional Treaty. According to a *Eurobarometer* survey (Commission, 2005a), the most common reason for supporting the Treaty given by those voting for it was that it was seen as essential in order to pursue the 'European construction' (39 per cent). The second largest category comprised those who argued that they had always been in favour of the 'European construction' (16 per cent) (Commission, 2005a). Support for the Constitutional Treaty seems therefore most commonly to be support for the EU rather than a defence of the Treaty itself.

According to *Eurobarometer*, the five reasons most frequently cited for opposing the Treaty were: the Treaty had a negative economic effect on French employment (31 per cent); the economic situation/too much French unemployment (26 per cent); the Treaty was 'too (economically) liberal' (19 per cent); opposition to President Chirac/the national government/certain political parties (18 per cent); and 'not enough social Europe' (16 per cent). What is notable in the reasons given by rejectionists is that there is a particular national

---

[2] The services directive (often named after its originator, Frits Bolkestein) in its attempt to liberalize services across the EU raised the concerns of labour who saw this as encouraging lower standards and wage levels. The 'Polish plumber' became a spectre symbolizing the potential influx of foreign workers in the French referendum campaign. This symbol was a concrete representation, for potential opponents, of the coming together of concerns about the sort of Europe that was being built on domestic economic concerns.

construction to the debate over the European project as being seen as a threat to jobs and a wider social agenda (Ivaldi, 2006, p. 61). The opponents of the Constitutional Treaty are defending a particular European vision, and it is hard not to see that particular construction of the European debate as a national one. The impression of nationalism is compounded by the high numbers of those who saw a 'no' vote as a way of attacking incumbent politicians/government/ parties.

Looking exclusively at the French debate and the outcome of the referendum on the Constitutional Treaty, three things stand out. First, the nature of party competition, both within and between parties, played a key role in the timing and conduct of the campaign. Second, the configuration of 'anti' forces on the question of the Constitutional Treaty was very diverse and drew upon some very different objections to aspects of the Constitutional Treaty and the European project itself. Third, insofar as we can identify broad overarching themes in the way in which the issue of Europe was debated in the French campaign, defence of a vision of a 'social Europe' was clearly important for the left (Marthaler, 2005, pp. 232–3), while the right's opposition built on the themes of sovereignty and fears about French identity, as well as an embrace of anti-globalization themes by some (Ivaldi, 2006, p. 61).

This is not to say that EU level factors did not impinge on the French campaign and its outcome. Issues such as the debate over the 'Bolkestein directive' helped to galvanize French public opinion against the Treaty. Moreover, the Treaty itself, which was widely distributed and discussed, was hardly incidental to the result. Simply relying on European-level factors, however, does not sufficiently explain the outcome, and encourages misleading generalizations.

The Dutch Referendum: Anti-Establishment Sentiment and an Anti-European Result

While the French had previously held a referendum on the Maastricht Treaty, the referendum on the Constitutional Treaty in the Netherlands was an extremely unusual event in Dutch politics as it was the first ever referendum. Harmsen (2005, p. 3) suggests that the use of a referendum was so alien to the Dutch political system that its outcome can largely be attributed to the failure of the elite to recognize the very different type of process to which it gave rise. The disjuncture between domestic political processes and this aspect of a wider European process therefore threw up important difficulties.

The Dutch decision to hold a referendum appears to be the consequence of an ongoing debate about consultative referendums and initiatives to use them. One of the Dutch members of the Convention, Frans Timmermans, as early as October 2002 brought a resolution to Parliament to have a referendum on the

Constitution, which was passed. After the national election the pro-referendum parties lost their majority, but an NGO campaign in favour of a referendum in combination with the support of the Liberals and other parties ensured that the referendum idea remained alive and set in train the process that led to the referendum on the Constitutional Treaty (Nijeboer, 2005). As with the French decision, the assumption of a positive result was an important contextual factor in the decision.

The Dutch referendum was held on 1 June, only a matter of days after that in France. The negative result was noteworthy both for compounding the French result and because the Netherlands was another founding Member State with a relatively unified political establishment that was both pro-European and pro-Constitutional Treaty and a public that has shown sustained support for the European integration project.

The referendum campaign was slow to get started, but once started the dynamic worked against the 'yes' side. The 'yes' campaign was slow to mobilize, assuming that the campaign would be won in the final phase. It was also prone to gaffes and seemed to be attempting to scare the public into supporting the Treaty by presenting a rejection as leading to various disastrous scenarios for Europe (Harmsen, 2005). But by the end of the campaign, there was extensive debate and a clear sense that momentum was moving away from support for the Treaty.

Those opposed to the Treaty were more effective despite their heterogeneous make-up. The constellation of forces was a 'patchwork of protest', bringing together the radical left in the shape of the Socialist Party, the populist right as represented by the Pim Fortuyn List and the Groep Geert Wilders, and the traditional protestant parties in the Christian Union and the Political Reformed Party (Harmsen, 2005). The arguments against the Constitutional Treaty therefore came from a variety of positions. From the left there were was a focus on the threat to the Dutch social model and, in particular, the threat to the Dutch 'crown jewels' of liberal policies on gay marriage, drugs and euthanasia. This was combined with fears about the Netherlands' position in the EU and sense that it was in danger of losing its national identity. On the right, Wilders, a refugee from the Liberal Party, campaigned on issues such as Turkish accession amounting to an Islamicist Europe and on fears about immigration and the threat to Dutch national identity.

The pro-side of the equation was supported by the political establishment. In contrast to the French situation, there was virtual unanimity with government parties and most of the opposition supporting the Treaty. This unanimity may have reinforced a certain complacent inertia on the part of the advocates of the Treaty which led them to become active only in the latter part of the campaign. Binnema and Crum (2006) argue that the result indeed represented a specific moment of Dutch anti-political sentiment rather than a surge of euroscepticism.

The final 'no' vote was 61.5 per cent; it consisted of a range of opinions, with no single overwhelming reason for the rejection. According to *Eurobarometer* (Commission, 2005b), the four most common reasons for voting 'no' were: a lack of information (32 per cent); loss of national sovereignty (19 per cent); opposition to the national government/certain political parties (14 per cent); and Europe being too 'expensive' (13 per cent). Compared to the French reasons we can therefore observe that there were fundamentally different considerations at play; a significant part of the Dutch opposition sought a lower spending European project, while an equally significant part of the French opposition sought a Europe prepared to focus on social concerns and therefore presumably spending more.

The Referendums in Comparative Perspective

Looking at the campaigns and the voting in the two referendums, it is clear that there were very different patterns of support and opposition in the two cases. In France there was opposition to the Constitutional Treaty from within the heart of the party system, with opposition from the Socialists and particularly from Fabius. In the Dutch case there was little opposition to the Treaty from the mainstream parties. The issues that drove the two campaigns were also different. Although there were similarities, the issues with resonance and salience were very different.

In addition, it is clear that the 'European issue' is constructed in very different ways in the two systems, and reasons for voting 'no' were very different in the two cases. Certainly there is an important parallel in that those who voted 'yes' in both France and the Netherlands tended to see the European Constitutional Treaty as a test of the European project as a whole, and they were in favour of that. But the differences in the 'no' voters' reasons seem to suggest that there is no unified wave of eurosceptic sentiment.

One similarity that existed in both campaigns was that prominent pro campaigners in both countries looked as if they were trying to bounce the public into supporting something not because what they were voting for was a good thing, but because of the negative consequences of not voting 'yes'. This was the case with Chirac's television appearance in which he made a last-ditch appeal to the French people's historic responsibility to the European project and to the need to secure the future of Europe (Hainsworth, 2006, p. 105). In the Dutch case the Justice Minister advocated support for the Treaty to prevent the possible violent collapse of Europe in the manner of Yugoslavia (Harmsen, 2005, p. 8). In retrospect it is easy to read these as counter-productive strategies likely only to appeal to those already in support and missing the point that opposition was coming from those with very different, and often very domestic agendas. It also played into a populist narrative of elites conspiring to force the people to vote a certain way in a process that is supposedly in the hands of the people.

The argument here is that treating the European referendums solely as disaggregations of a wider European process gives us a distorted picture of the position in 2005. But, just as we should not treat the referendums simply as part of the European integration process, equally we should not treat them simply as part of domestic politics. The need and challenge is properly to integrate our understanding of European integration with our understanding of European domestic politics.

III. The Study of European Politics and the Politics of European Integration

While the French and Dutch referendums emphasize the importance for analysts of the European integration process of incorporating effectively the dynamics of domestic politics, they also provide a challenge for those of us trying to characterize those domestic politics. Put simply, the nature of the debate and the structuring of the politics of Europe in that debate may be evidence that it is increasingly difficult (if it was ever possible) to talk in universal terms about a single contest over European integration. The way Europe is contested varies fundamentally according to the context in which it takes place.

The debate about the use of comparative politics approaches in the study of European integration has been focused mainly on the utility of using those approaches to analyse the process of European integration. The argument has been made that the concepts that have been used to study European politics at the domestic level can usefully be applied to the European Union. This has of course much to do with the assertion that we can understand the EU as a political system like many others (Hix, 2005) or as a multi-levelled governance system (Hooghe and Marks, 2001) in which the component levels need to be understood in their own terms. The debate has therefore been about moving the EU as an object of international relations to one of comparative politics.

The terms of the debate about approaches to studying the EU have not, however, substantially breached the academic divide between those who conduct research on the EU and those who study the domestic politics in European states. There still remains something of an academic Berlin Wall between those who study European domestic processes and those who study the process of European integration. The challenge lies in actually integrating those two fields of study. The fault, if we should indeed use such language, lies on both sides of the academic fence. For those used to studying domestic processes, European integration is often in danger of being treated as a bolt-on extra and something that need not substantially concern analysts of domestic politics. I suspect that much of the reason for this is not that the EU is not treated as important, but rather that the fit between the politics of Europe and European politics is fundamentally an awkward one that does not allow for easy synthesis (Hix, 1999). Nevertheless some have managed to integrate the two (e.g. Marks and Steenbergen, 2004). For those whose primary interest is at the EU level, the machinations of parties and domestic politics have often seemed both distant and of little relevance for the process of European integration. These referendum results, like some earlier, have demonstrated that this is not true.

The challenge for academics is not unlike that for contemporary European politicians who have to operate at both EU and domestic levels. The challenge is the possibility of not treating the EU as an exogenous factor in domestic politics and not considering domestic politics exogenous when considering the process of European integration. But the very success of the European project creates difficulties. It means that those studying the EU need to be sensitive to 25 different domestic political processes, as well as to complexities of the institutional architecture of the enlarged EU itself.

Conclusion

It is extremely tempting to argue for a simple, monocausal explanation of the fate of the European project in the hands of the French and Dutch referendums. To see a wave of popular discontent with the European project as manifested in two moments of popular politics in France and the Netherlands would be a nice straightforward narrative and one that clearly is easy to tell. But it is to miss the real picture and, perhaps even more importantly, it is to miss the challenge that lies before us as observers of the European project. It is frustrating to have to make the suggestion that the picture is more complicated than the simple story.

It is not new to say that the European polity can be regarded as multi-levelled (Hooghe and Marks, 2001) or that the lessons of comparative politics can be usefully applied in understanding the EU (Hix, 2005). What is new is that, with the Dutch and French referendums of 2005, we have in stark relief a vision of a political process that, in resorting to plebiscitary politics, has regularized the possibility of domestic political processes to have a profound impact on European integration. We have different domestic politics creating 'no' votes for very different reasons. The danger, as this article has tried to suggest, is that we still analytically view these events from the top down and therefore see illusions of similarity where there are substantial differences. The referendum results have illustrated how integrating domestic and European politics in a way that ignores key domestic differences, paints a picture of the European project that is liable to be distorted. With the increasing resort to plebiscitary politics to legitimate the European integration project, it becomes vital that we meet the challenge of fully integrating the domestic politics of Europe into our understandings of the European integration process. It is possible that these two results might halt the move to plebiscitary politics, but it is also the case that the move away from plebiscitary politics it not as easy as the move towards it.

The argument here is that referendums are an illustration of what is occurring broadly in the politics of European integration. The use of referendums and an associated move towards a plebiscitary politics do not constitute the whole case for re-examining how we look at European politics but they do illustrate why we should do this. If we understand the fact that we now have to deal with a plural Europe, with at least 26 political processes that all have the potential to operate in distinct ways, we will be less surprised by moments of decision that do not chime with a sense of a unified monolithic Europe.

To understand the EU as an international organization rather than as a set of political processes may well be a convenient escape hatch for the understanding of this newly complex, plural and sizeable project, but it does not aid us in understanding how the politics of European integration work. This is not because of the well-rehearsed disagreements between international relations and comparative politics approaches to understanding the EU, but simply because at the heart of the current puzzle is a process that is not an institutionalized part of other international organizations, such as the World Trade Organization or North Atlantic Treaty Organization. For our purposes there can be little purchase in seeing the EU as an international organization as it does not get us any further in explaining the causes and effects of domestic political processes on this organization. Other international organizations do not, with the regularity or constitutionality of the EU, seek popular endorsement be it through indirect elections, direct elections and referendums.

Enlargement may well be the one unequivocally successful European policy area, but it does provide a fundamental challenge for those determined to stay cognizant of the changing dynamics of European integration. The challenge for scholars of European integration is as much empirical as analytical. Effectively understanding the domestic political processes of all Member States in the same way as we as we understand the EU level, and integrating that with domestic processes is a profound challenge in an EU of 25 members. There is a lot of data to collate as the EU enlarges. The project, as it gets larger, becomes more important but also more difficult to unpack. As the scale increases we also have to deal with the EU as an increasingly pluralized polity. This is not simply in terms of functional areas that the EU deals with (Wallace, 2001), but also in terms of the nature of the politics and processes that comprise the wider European project. To add to the mix, we have also seen how there are multiple normative models of democracy at play in this same set of institutions and processes. As analysts of the EU we naturally seek to find simple, sweeping and all-embracing answers to the complexity and the scale of the contemporary project but, while the search for patterns and regularities is a useful heuristic exercise, sometimes we simply need to recognize that the answers in a complex plural polity may well themselves be plural and complex.

The difficulty of dealing with this complexity is compounded by the specific way the European issue is conceptualized in academic analysis and mobilized in practical politics. One of the revealing things about the reaction to referendum rejections is the way in which it reveals how unusually the European issue is dealt with in both practical politics and academic analysis. The fact that many European politicians feel that European integration is an issue that can be dealt with through the medium of direct democracy and through the simple device of citizens' 'yes' or 'no' answer demonstrates that they see it as a policy that is unlike any other. If it were a more usual policy, such as education, housing or welfare, we would not expect it to advance through moments of 'yes' and 'no'. The idea of development through iteration, discussion, debate and decisions that we would expect in any other important policy area seems abandoned when the European integration project resorts to plebiscitary politics. European integration is an unusual issue, but it is not as different as some would have us believe.

The events of 2005 in Europe, despite the protestations of many in the European studies community, do not amount to a crisis for European integration. They do represent a challenge for the European project as there are both symbolic and substantive effects of two founding EU nations rejecting the attempt to constitutionalize Europe through a new treaty. But, just as importantly, the events of 2005 highlight the difficulties for the way we as observers understand Europe. The tendency towards compartmentalization in the studies of domestic European politics and the EU has obscured the real relevance of the events of 2005 for European politics as a whole. The key challenge is to integrate these different areas of study to make full sense of the way in which Europe is headed.

References

Binnema, H. and Crum, B. (2006) 'Euroscepticism as a Carrier of Elite-Mass Incongruence: The Case of the Netherlands'. Paper presented at the 'Resisting Europe: Euroscepticism and National Civic Cultures' International Colloquium, Brussels, 16–17 March.

Butler, D.E and Kitzinger, U. (1976) *The 1975 Referendum* (Basingstoke: Macmillan).

Commission of the European Communities (2005a) 'The European Constitution: Post-Referendum Survey in France'. *Flash Eurobarometer,* No. 171.

Commission of the European Communities (2005b) 'The European Constitution: Post-Referendum Survey in the Netherlands'. *Flash Eurobarometer,* No. 172.

Crum, B. (2004) 'Politics and Power in the European Convention'. *Politics*, Vol. 24, No. 1, pp. 1–11.

Drake, H. (2005) 'Jacques Chirac's Balancing Acts: The French Right and Europe'. *South European Society & Politics,* Vol. 10, No. 2, pp. 297–313.

Franklin, M.N. (2002) 'Learning from the Danish Case: A Comment on Palle Svensson's Critique of the Franklin Thesis'. *European Journal of Political Research,* Vol. 41, No. 6, pp. 751–7.

Franklin, M.N., Marsh, M. and Wlezien, C. (1994) 'Attitudes towards Europe and Referendum Votes: A Response to Siune and Svensson'. *Electoral Studies,* Vol. 13, No. 2, pp. 117–21.

Garry, J., Marsh, M. and Sinnott, R. (2005) '"Second Order" Versus "Issue Voting" Effects in EU Referendums: Evidence from the Irish Nice Treaty Referendums'. *European Union Politics*, Vol. 6. No. 2, pp. 223–42.

Hainsworth, P. (2006) 'France Says No: The 29 May 2005 Referendum on the European Constitution'. *Parliamentary Affairs,* Vol. 59, No. 1, pp. 98–117.

Harmsen, R. (2005) 'The Dutch Referendum on the Ratification of the European Constitutional Treaty, 1 June 2005'. European Parties Elections and Referendums Network Referendum Briefing Paper, No.13, University of Sussex. Available at «http://www.sussex.ac.uk/sei/1-4-2.html».

Hausemer, P. (2005) 'Luxembourg's Referendum on the European Constitutional Treaty, 20 July 2005'. European Parties Elections and Referendums Network Referendum Briefing Paper, No.14, University of Sussex. Available at «http://www.sussex.ac.uk/sei/1-4-2.html».

Held, D. (1996) *Models of Democracy,* 2nd edn (Cambridge: Polity).

Hix, S. (1999) 'Dimensions and Alignments in European Union Politics: Cognitive Constraints and Partisan Responses'. *European Journal of Political Research,* Vol. 35, No. 1, pp. 69–106.

Hix, S. (2005) *The Political System of the European Union,* 2nd edn (Basingstoke: Palgrave).

Hix, S., Raunio, T. and Scully, R. (2003) 'Fifty Years on: Research on the European Parliament'. *Journal of Common Market Studies*, Vol. 41, No. 2, pp. 191–202.

Hobolt, S. (2006) 'Direct Democracy and European Integration'. *Journal of European Public Policy*, Vol. 13, No. 1, pp. 153–66.

Hooghe, L.and Marks, G. (2001) *Multi-Level Governance and European Integration* (Lanham, MD: Rowman and Littlefield).

Ivaldi, G. (2006) 'Beyond France's 2005 Referendum on the European Constitutional Treaty: Second-Order Model, Anti-Establishment Attitudes and the End of the Alternative European Utopia'. *West European Politics*, Vol. 29, No. 1, pp. 47–69.

Lucarelli, S. and Radaelli, C.M. (2004) 'The European Convention: A Process of Mobilization?'. *South European Society & Politics*, Vol. 9, No. 1, pp. 1–23.

Marks, G. and Steenbergen, M.R. (eds) (2004) *European Integration and Political Conflict* (Cambridge: Cambridge University Press).

Marthaler, S. (2005) 'France's Referendum on the EU Treaty, May 2005'. *Representation*, Vol. 41, No. 3, pp. 228–36.

Maurer, A. (2003) 'Less Bargaining – More Deliberation: The Convention Method for Enhancing EU Democracy'. *Internationale Politik und Gesellschaft*, No. 1, pp. 167–90.

Mény, Y. (2003) '*De la démocratie en Europe:* Old Concepts and New Challenges'. *Journal of Common Market Studies*, Vol. 41, No. 1, pp. 1–13.

Mény, Y. (2005) 'Europe Bewildered, France Adrift'. *EUSA Review*, Vol. 18, No. 4, pp. 4–5.

Moravcsik, A. (2002) 'In Defence of the "Democratic Deficit": Reassessing Legitimacy in the European Union'. *Journal of Common Market Studies*, Vol. 40, No. 4, pp. 603–24.

Nijeboer, A. (2005) 'The First Dutch Referendum: A Pre-Ballot Assessment'. Notre Europe Policy Paper No. 14, Paris.

Qvortrup, M. (2002) *A Comparative Study of Referendums: Government by the People* (Manchester: Manchester University Press).

Setala, M. (1999) *Referendums and Democratic Government: Normative Theory and the Analysis of Institutions* (Basingstoke: Palgave).

Shu, M. (2005) 'Referendums and European Integration'. PhD dissertation, University of Bristol.

Siune, K., Svensson, P. and Toonsgaard, O. (1994) 'The European Union: The Danes Said "No" in 1992 but "Yes" in 1993 – How and Why?'. *Electoral Studies*, Vol. 13, No. 2, pp. 99–111.

Svensson, P. (2002) 'Five Danish Referendums on the European Community and European Union: A Critical Assessment of the Franklin Thesis'. *European Journal of Political Research*, Vol. 41, No. 6, pp. 733–50.

Szczerbiak, A. and Taggart, P. (2005) (eds) *EU Enlargement and Referendums* (London: Routledge).

Szczerbiak A. and Taggart, P. (forthcoming) (eds) *Opposing Europe: The Comparative Party Politics of Euroscepticism*, 2 vols (Oxford: Oxford University Press).

Wallace, H. (2001) (ed.) *Interlocking Dimensions of European Integration* (Basingstoke: Palgrave).

Weiler, J.H. H. (1999) *The Constitution of Europe* (Cambridge: Cambridge University Press).

Wessels, W. (2005) 'Keynote Article: The Constitutional Treaty – Three Readings from a Fusion Perspective'. *Journal of Common Market Studies (Annual Review)*, Vol. 43, pp. 11–36.

Whitman, R. (2005) 'No and After: Options for Europe'. *International Affairs*, Vol. 81, No. 4, pp. 673–87.

JCMS 2006 Volume 44 Annual Review pp. 27–49

Review Article:
The 'Governance Turn' in EU Studies*

BEATE KOHLER-KOCH
University of Mannheim

BERTHOLD RITTBERGER
Kaiserslautern University of Technology

Introduction

Research on governance and the European Union is a veritable growth industry. A quick glance at the Social Science Citation Index (SSCI) suffices to witness an explosion of EU governance research in the past decade. While the SSCI rarely reported more than ten articles a year on EU governance in the mid-1990s, in the late 1990s and early 2000s there were between 40 and 50 articles per year. Against this background, this article pursues a conceptual, substantive and empirical stock-taking exercise. First, the origins of the concept of governance in the academic discourse and in different political science sub-disciplines are traced, before the article turns to the causes of the 'governance turn' in EU studies. The second section presents the key features of the concept of 'EU governance' and flags two strands of research – work on the EU as a 'regulatory state' and research on 'new modes of governance' – which have not only contributed to our understanding of EU governance, but have also spurred on the governance research agenda. Third, two central themes of EU governance research are highlighted by asking whether and how EU governance arrangements have impacted upon or even transformed national patterns of governance, and vice versa. Fourth, the article considers the normative concerns that are intimately linked to EU governance research: does governance beyond the state provide solutions to pressing policy problems

* For comments and suggestions on this article, we wish to thank Fabrice Larat, Dirk De Bièvre, Thomas Schneider, Arndt Wonka and the editors of the *Annual Review*.

which cannot be solved by states unilaterally? Can governance beyond the nation-state be democratically legitimate?

This article draws on a survey of recent and ongoing research in EU Member States and countries of the wider Europe undertaken as part of the 'Network of Excellence' on 'Efficient and Democratic Governance in a Multi-Level Europe'(CONNEX), funded under the EU's sixth research framework programme. The objective of this study was to increase transparency among national and disciplinary research communities and make available the wealth of knowledge for further research. About 1,600 research projects and 30 country reports have been documented and are accessible online (see «http://www.connex-network.org/govdata»). A summary evaluation reflecting on the state of the art and relevant background conditions in comparative perspective will be published by the end of 2006 (Kohler-Koch and Larat, forthcoming).

I. Governance: The Journey of a Concept

While governance has become a popular research focus in EU studies, there is still confusion about the conceptualization of the term. 'The concept of governance is notoriously slippery; it is frequently used among both social scientists and practitioners without a definition all agree on' (Pierre and Peters, 2000, p. 7). Schneider (2004, p. 25) even argues that the conceptual vagueness of the term is the 'secret of its success'.

Conceptualizing Governance

Cutting through the clutter of different definitions and conceptualizations, Pierre (2000, p. 3) distinguishes between two broad meanings of the concept. The first refers to 'the empirical manifestation of state adaptation to its external environment as it emerges in [the] late twentieth century'. From this perspective, governance can be considered both a process and a state whereby public and private actors engage in the intentional regulation of societal relationships and conflicts. Governance is thus different from government, the latter stressing hierarchical decision-making structures and the centrality of public actors, while the former denotes the participation of public and private actors, as well as non-hierarchical forms of decision-making.

The second meaning refers to governance as the 'conceptual or theoretical representation of [the] co-ordination of social systems' (Pierre, 2000, p. 3). Pierre argues that two major sets of research problems and questions emanate from this latter meaning of governance. The first adopts a 'state-centric' perspective as it points to the 'steering' capacity of the state and its institutions, as well as to its relationship with non-state – private – interests and actors.

The second set of research problems and questions chooses a society-centred point of departure, focusing on the 'co-ordination and various forms of formal or informal types of public–private interaction' (Pierre, 2000, p. 3), which are manifested in different types of networks and public–private partnerships.

To these two meanings of governance, we add a third, prescriptive meaning of governance *viz.* 'good governance'. The notion of 'good governance' has become prominent in economic development discourse since the late 1980s. The World Bank and the Development Assistant Committee of the Organization for Economic Co-operation and Development have been leading advocates of propagating sound fiscal management and administrative efficiency as a precondition to sustainable growth and development (World Bank, 1997). The concept gained popularity among donor countries and institutions and was soon used in a broader political understanding. The benchmark of 'good governance' was expanded to include legitimacy derived from a democratic mandate of those in power, the rule of law, free market competition and a greater involvement of non-governmental organizations (NGOs). NGOs would not just participate in designing and implementing development strategies closer to the needs of the people and mobilizing endogenous economic and social resources, but also activate civil society and boost grass roots democracy (Weiss, 2000). The notion of 'good governance' was also embraced by the EU and considered a crucial ingredient of EU–ACP co-operation relations (Smith, 2003, pp. 122–44; Beck and Conzelmann, 2004).

The 'good governance' discourse in the context of development, however, was formerly quite detached from critical reflections on the state of EU institutions. The notion of 'good governance' in the EU context first became prominent through the release of the Commission's White Paper on 'European Governance' (Commission, 2001) in which it lists several principles underpinning 'good governance', such as openness, participation and effectiveness.

These themes continue to inform the discussion on governance, in particular in the field of political science, the lead discipline in the governance debate. The article goes on to a discussion of the development of the governance debate in the fields of international relations (IR) and comparative politics (CP) before it turns to the 'governance turn' in EU studies.

Governance and International Relations

The advent of governance in the field of IR is seen first and foremost as a reaction to processes of economic globalization 'societal denationalisation' (Zürn, 1998). Denationalization connotes that the capacity of national political systems to achieve desired policy outcomes is put under strain as the boundaries of social transactions increasingly transcend the confines of the state (see also Scharpf, 1999, p. 84). Others, however, argue that this perspective is incomplete as it sidelines the role of 'politics'.

A crucial factor that made governance the focus of international politics was the end of the cold war and the concomitant termination of an ideological power struggle. Hence, these changes in the international system elevated the notion of effective and efficient 'problem-solving' to a guiding principle which was to be pursued through a system of international governance (Kohler-Koch, 1993). The hitherto dominant strand in the IR literature, which engaged in an inquiry into the conditions under which co-operation in an anarchic system would be possible, was complemented by a new strand of research, emphasizing questions of the effectiveness and problem-solving capacity of different forms of international (institutionalized) co-operation (Jachtenfuchs, 2003; Rosenau and Czempiel, 1992), underlining the central role of the state in producing and sustaining international order or 'governance'.

This literature has been complemented by an emerging discussion of the role of private actors, such as transnational business corporations and NGOs, in fulfilling a large variety of governance functions, from international economic regulation to providing security through private military forces (Büthe, 2004; Cutler *et al.*, 1999; Hall and Biersteker, 2002).

Governance and Comparative Politics

The 'governance turn' has also left its firm imprint in CP in general, and the theory of the state in particular. For the theory of the state, the guiding question is 'why and how complex societies succeed in establishing various central mechanisms of control and co-ordination' (Schneider, 2004, p. 26). In the German debate on the state's steering capacity, the theory of the state was starkly influenced by a functionalist, systems-theoretic strand – connected to names such as Talcott Parsons and Niklas Luhmann – which made inroads into the political science literature, highlighting 'steering' as a systemic function, dissociated from the actual actions of concrete actors (Willke, 1983).

The rapidly evolving research in the field of policy analysis triggered a shift from a functionalist focus to an actor-centred conception of 'steering', which presumes goal-oriented activities by actors who do the steering and objects that are being steered (Mayntz, 1987; Mayntz and Scharpf, 1995). The notion of intentional, actor-driven steering of societal (sub-)systems presumed an idea of a 'problem-solving' state in which politics is characterized by its orientation towards realizing the 'public good' rather than the pursuit of particularistic interests. The central premises that state actors are the central or, as in the neo-corporatist tradition, at least prominent actors in the policy process, that there is a clear distinction between steering subjects and objects, and that a centralized authority implementing and enforcing decisions predominantly by 'command and control' instruments was gradually abandoned in favour of concepts that are open to more co-operative forms of governing (Mayntz, 2005). Once the state's capacity to steer is hampered by economic globalization, 'what other means does the state have of imposing its will on society and the economy?' (Pierre, 2000, p. 5).

To bolster the problem-solving effectiveness of national policies under these conditions, hierarchical modes of decision-making are complemented by horizontal, co-operative forms of policy formulation and implementation. In the 'co-operative state' (Mayntz, 1987) there are a plethora of decision-making arrangements among public and private actors, ranging from horizontal and vertical joint decision-systems among public authorities, to policy networks of state and non-state actors, to voluntary or mandated forms of private self-regulation. In the 'co-operative state', the distinction between steering objects and subjects is blurred. As a consequence, rule structures and their impact on decision-making processes and outcomes became the focus of most research, complementing that on different forms and instruments of steering (Manytz, 2005, p. 13). The increasing importance and relevance of the European and international levels of decision-making exacerbate this situation as they increase the fragmentation of the 'steering subject'.

While in Germany, the 'governance turn' was intimately linked to a theoretical development within the realm of the theory of the state (Schneider, 2004), the governance debate in Anglo-American scholarship was more strongly influenced by changes in policy co-ordination and administration. The focus on governance was fuelled starkly by the financial crisis of the state, which prompted a wide range of public sector reforms and the development of new instruments of governance. This change in state capacity and the shift towards governance was accompanied and even intensified by an 'ideological shift from politics towards the market' (Pierre and Peters, 2000, p. 55), epitomized by the Reagan and Thatcher administrations. Governance, in this sense, 'signifies a change in the meaning of government, referring to a *new* process of governing; or a *changed* condition of ordered rule; or the *new* method by which society is governed' (Rhodes, 2003, p. 65, emphasis in original).

The 'Governance Turn' in EU Studies

Since the 1960s, research on the EU grappled predominantly with how to explain European integration, the process whereby national sovereignty is transferred from the domestic to the European level (Diez and Wiener, 2004, pp. 6–10; Jachtenfuchs, 2001, p. 246). While the first phase of EU research took the EU polity as the dependent variable, the 'governance turn' in EU studies takes the EU polity as a given and 'look[s] at the impact of the Euro-polity on national and European policies and politics' (Jachtenfuchs, 2001, p. 50). The 'governance turn' in European studies has conceptual, empirical and 'institutional' groundings.

Conceptually, 'policy-making' in the EU became a new focus of attention. It was in the late 1980s and early 1990s that European studies began to import concepts from the field policy analysis – policy cycles and policy networks – to illuminate the process of policy formulation and implementation in the EU (see, for example, Schumann, 1993). On the 'empirical' plane, this development coincided with and was stimulated by a significant increase in European-level policy-making competencies in the wake of the Single European Act and the single market programme.

It was in this context that questions of EU 'government' and governance – policy-making and co-ordination – began to challenge 'European integration' as the first and foremost focus of scholarly research in EU studies. The specific thematic orientation of the research has changed over time. Governance and the regions were a favourite topic in the 1990s, relating either to the debate on the 'regionalization' of Europe and the new role of the regions in EU governance, or to the investigation of new modes of governance, such as the implementa-tion of the 'partnership principle' and the ensuing effects on learning, civil society participation and improvements in problem-solving capacities. With the 2004 accessions the topic has again gained prominence. Research focuses on managing trans-border regional co-operation and supporting regional inter-est representation in EU decision-making. First-pillar issues still dominate the agenda of policy-oriented governance research; only very recently have several research projects been dedicated to exploring the governance of the common foreign, security and defence policy and policing.

The focus of governance research also varies between countries. For ex-ample, in the new Member States (and the wider Europe) the broader aspects of integration and accession-related transformation dominate. Institutionally, several research programmes and research institutions accompanied and fuelled the 'governance turn' in European studies. The Mannheim Centre for European Social Research (MZES) was the hub of a large-scale research project on 'Governance in the European Union' funded by the German Science Foundation (1996–2002) and is currently also the host institution for Connex. The UK's Economic and Social Research Council (ESRC) funded the 'One Europe or Several?' (1999–2003) programme, which adopted an even broader '"pan-European" frame of reference' (Wallace, 2003, p. 2). The Norwegian Arena (Centre for European Studies) programme, which was launched in 1994, has also made and continues to make a profound contribution to the study of EU governance.

In sum, the 'governance turn' in EU studies resembles developments in both the field of policy analysis and in IR. First, it has an elaborate process dimension that explores the patterns, instruments and conditions of policy formulation and implementation and the diversity of actor constellations. Second, it reflects the different aspects of 'system transformation' (at both EU and national levels) and its likely impact on problem-solving capacity and democratic accountability. The article now turn to these two sets of issues.

II. Understanding EU Governance

In the course of the past decade, a plethora of analyses have come to see the EU as a system of governance characterized by 'a unique set of multi-level, non-hierarchical and regulatory institutions, and a hybrid mix of state and non-state actors' (Hix, 1998, p. 39). Concepts that sought to grasp the alleged *sui generis*-nature of the EU polity mushroomed during this period: 'multi-level governance' (Marks *et al.,* 1996), the 'regulatory state' (Majone, 1996a), and 'network governance' (Eising and Kohler-Koch, 1999; Kohler-Koch, 1999).

Dominant Features of EU Governance

As a concept, EU governance requires some considerable 'stretching' to include all areas of EU policy-making activity. Some of the concept's central features, such as its multi-level nature, apply to the whole EU 'pillar' structure. Other core features, such as the key role of supranational actors in the 'community method' (see below), the dominance of regulatory politics or public–private policy networks are characteristic of only the first pillar. Over the years policy co-operation developed in additional areas, including economic and monetary affairs, security and defence, as well as police and judicial co-operation. Here the policy-making process that brought about integration is characterized by 'intensive transgovernmentalism'. In the case of the single currency it resulted in delegating institutional powers to a function-specific agency, the European Central Bank. In no other areas has a centralized and hierarchical institutional process been introduced. Rather, 'intensive transgovernmentalism' prevails. This breeds special forms of policy co-ordination involving national and Community officials that allow Member State governments to retain consider-able control but still transform the ways in which states traditionally go about doing their business (Wallace, 2005, pp. 80, 87–9).

The 'community method', however, is crucial and, in practice, the dominant feature of EU governance. Scharpf (2003) has dubbed this method the 'joint-decision mode', characterized by a strong role for the European Commission in the formulation and execution of Community legislation, with the European Parliament (EP) gaining power and influence. All legislation is adopted by the Council of Ministers by qualified majority or unanimous vote. During the preparation, formulation and implementation of policies, the Commission and EP consult or even co-opt private groups and organizations to give information and expertise. Furthermore, 'comitology committees' of national civil servants and outside experts work out compromise solutions for implementation (Joerges and Vos, 1999) to smooth transposition and compliance at the national and sub-national level.

Another prominent feature of EU governance is its multi-level nature. Marks (1993, p. 392; Marks *et al.,* 1996) developed the concept of 'multi-level governance' (MLG), which is a 'system of continuous negotiation among nested governments at several territorial tiers'. MLG posits that decision-making authority is not monopolized by the governments of the Member States but is diffused to different levels of decision-making – the sub-national, national and supranational levels. Aiming at a general theory of MLG, Hooghe and Marks (2001, p. 4) emphasized that governance is interconnected, not nested: 'while national arenas remain important arenas for the formation of national government preferences, the multi-level governance model rejects the view that subnational actors are nested exclusively within them. Instead, subnational actors operate in both national and supranational arenas ... National governments ... share, rather than monopolize, control over many activities that take place in their respective territories'. 'Multi-level' thus signifies the interdependence of actors operating at different territorial levels – local, regional, national, supranational – while 'governance' refers to the growing importance of non-hierarchical forms of policy-making such as dynamic networks which involve public authorities as well as private actors (Hooghe and Marks, 2001).

These two features – the multi-level nature of the EU 'political system' and the growing importance of private actors in the policy process – are also among the defining characteristics of the concept of 'network governance' (Eising and Kohler-Koch, 1999; Kohler-Koch, 1999). Network governance is distinct from other forms of governance, such as corporatism, pluralism and statism. In a system of network governance 'the "state" is vertically and horizontally segmented and its role has changed from authoritative allocation "from above" to the role of an "activator" '. Governing the EU involves bringing together the relevant state and societal actors and building issue-specific constituencies' (Eising and Kohler-Koch, 1999, p. 5). Furthermore, given the dominance of regulatory policy-making and the marginality of redistributive conflicts in the EU, network governance is characterized by an orientation towards problem-solving instead of individual utility-maximization (Eising and Kohler-Koch, 1999, p. 6).

To these three dominant features – the 'community method', MLG and 'network governance' – is added a fourth – 'detached political contestation'. While the EU is developing into an ever more powerful centre of decision-making, we are witnessing a 'hollowing out' of policy competition between political parties at the domestic level (Mair, 2006). The EU impinges directly on national policy-making by limiting the policy space available for national party competition, by reducing the range of available policy instruments through supranational delegation and by circumscribing the policy repertoire fuelled by the politics of negative integration (Mair, 2006). Still, the EU is heavily under-politicized since the majority of the large mainstream political parties in the domestic arena sideline EU issues in national electoral contests. Party competition takes place within national boundaries and is the driving force for accentuating or bridging national cleavage structures; it frames political options and thereby 'gives them a face'. There is (still) no equivalent in the wider European political space. Elections to the EP do not generate transnational preferences, nor do they give contested issues a European profile, they are – as Reif and Schmitt (1980) famously put it – 'second-order national contests'. Thus, the 'European' aspects of EP elections affect voting behaviour only marginally (Hix, 2005, pp. 192–6).

The Advent of the Regulatory State and its Impact on Governance

One strand of research indicative of the 'governance turn' in EU studies, characterizes the EU as a 'regulatory state' (Majone, 1996a, b). This presupposes that the EU polity has achieved a considerable degree of maturity as a political system that has come to exercise 'classical' functions of political systems, such as the production of public policy, with regulatory politics as the central pillar of the EU's political activity. The literature has advanced a set of compelling reasons why the EU is geared towards regulatory policy-making (Majone, 1996a, b; Jachtenfuchs, 2001). Part of the argument is historic: the ambition to create a single European market demanded a considerable degree of regulatory activity to eliminate trade barriers, to stimulate competition and to correct or compensate for market failures. The other part of the argument is structural: regulatory policies require only weak legitimation since the (potential) (re-) distributive effects are not immediately visible.

The demand for regulatory policies is driven by both public and private actors. While 'intergovernmentalists' emphasize the centrality of Member State governments and intergovernmental bargaining (Garrett,1992; Moravcsik, 1998), 'weak' intergovernmentalism (Scharpf, 1999) stresses the centrality of a wider set of public actors, Member States and EU institutions; and 'supra-nationalists' (such as Stone Sweet, 2004) stress the centrality of private actors, organized interests in particular, in alliance with supranational actors, such as the Commission and the European Court of Justice (ECJ). The supply of regulation has furthered functional and administrative differentiation and, because of the Commission's dependence on external expertise and 'stake-holder' support, the proliferation of sectoral policy networks. While there is broad agreement in the literature that policy networks play a role in the agenda-setting and implementation stage, with private actors – experts and organized interest groups – playing a prominent role (Eising and Kohler-Koch, 2005), the actual decisions are still taken according to the hierarchical mode of decision-making. Börzel (2005, p. 87), therefore, calls for a distinction between governing *in* networks, which she considers rare in the EU, and governance *with* networks, a characteristic feature of the EU where private actors are heavily involved in the preparation and implementation of policies.

The demand for regulation, however, is not always met by the supply. Scholars and practitioners alike identify a performance crisis of EU governance. This crisis has its roots, at least partially, in the startling success of European integration, which now directly affects core activities of the state, 'employment policy, social policy, migration, criminal prosecution, and education' (Héritier, 2003, p. 105). Given variations in national regulatory regimes, the salience of the issues and the diverse preferences of domestic actors, 'one-size-fits-all' solutions are hardly applicable. As a response to this dilemma, EU Member States have introduced 'new modes governance'.

'New Modes of Governance'

The introduction of 'new modes of governance' (NMGs) was a reaction to the imminent risk of deadlock in Community decision-making. The evolution of the scholarly discourse is closely connected with the 'open method of co-ordination' (OMC), which was established by the Maastricht Treaty as an instrument destined for co-ordinating national economic policies through the use of recommendations and guidelines (Hodson and Maher, 2001). Research on the OMC has mushroomed since it was officially established by the May 2000 Lisbon European Council (Borrás and Greve, 2004; Héritier, 2003).

What are the defining characteristics of NMGs? First, they depart from the Community method of legislating through regulations and directives (Eberlein and Kerwer, 2004, p. 123; Knill, 2005), relying on 'soft law,' which is not legally binding and has no legal sanctioning mechanisms against non-compliance (voluntarism). Second, NMGs are negotiated between public and private actors at different levels of decision-making while the effective policy choice is left to each individual Member State (subsidiarity). Third, all relevant actors are included in the process of defining policy goals and instruments. That is, no distinction is made between steering subjects and steering objects (Héritier, 2003, p. 105).

Yet, caution is necessary when presenting NMGs as the magic solution to the EU's performance problem. The effectiveness and problem-solving capacity of NMGs vary according to the type of policy and actor preference constellations at hand. Héritier (2003, p. 124) argues that redistributive policies and 'deeply entrenched problems' are unlikely candidates for the successful application of NMGs, although 'distributive, co-ordinative, network goods problems as well as diverse, discrete, and high complexity/uncertainty issues are more amenable to a "treatment" by new modes of governance'.

Research on NMGs takes two broad directions (see Eberlein and Kerwer, 2004, pp. 124–6). One focuses on the motivations of EU actors to propose the application of NMGs. For instance, much has been written about the Commission's self-interested or legitimacy-driven motivations for pursuing 'good governance' (Joerges et al., 2001). The second comprises a great variety of empirical work that seeks to assess the significance of NMGs. A considerable number of studies have tested whether there has actually been a significant shift from the 'community method' to NMGs across a wide range of policy areas. While there is ample evidence of such a shift (Eberlein and Kerwer, 2004, p. 125), some studies show that the application of NMGs in individual policy areas is still scant compared to the application of traditional 'command and control' instruments (Jordan et al., 2005; Rittberger and Richardson, 2003). Moreover, the application of NMGs, such as the OMC, is not restricted only to 'uncontroversial cases in which there is a high level of consensus. On the contrary, they are almost always introduced after legislative deadlocks' (Eberlein and Kerwer, 2004, p. 125). Other studies have looked at the impact of NMGs on actor behaviour. By emphasizing 'benchmarking', 'peer review', and 'best practice' MNGs engender the assumption that participating actors can learn from assessment and comparison. This assumption has been borne out by several studies (Eberlein and Kerwer, 2004, pp. 125–6; Lenschow, 2005, pp. 66–7).

In addition, because NMGs stress participation, transparency and learning, they are of particular interest to democratic theory. De la Porte and Nanz (2004) have, for instance, analysed the OMC's 'democratic dimension' from the perspective of deliberative democracy. Others have found that, despite the rhetoric and high aspirations, MNGs do not necessarily produce participatory decision-making (Goetschy, 2003).

III. The Transformation of the Nation-State through European Governance

The introduction of MLG into EU studies 'signifies the end of the separate treatment of European and national politics' (Lenschow, 2005, p. 56) and thus contributes to a widening of the conceptual lens by pointing at the consequences of European integration for domestic political institutions and policy processes captured by the concept of 'Europeanization' (Featherstone and Radaelli, 2003). Definitions of Europeanization abound (Radaelli, 2000; Olsen, 2002) pointing at a plethora of potential avenues and mechanisms through which 'Europe' triggers or produces 'domestic adaptations' (Lenschow, 2005, p. 59). From a governance perspective, research on Europeanization takes EU-level govern-ance arrangements as the independent variable in order to explain domestic transformations, which can be assessed in terms of changes in domestic policies, discourses, institutions, or actor capabilities, to mention only a few.

A review of Europeanization research offers evidence that public *policies* are more likely to be affected than national *politics* or *polities* and 'that some poli-cies are more impermeable than others to "Europe"' (Radaelli, 2004, p. 14). But comparing the domestic impact of EU governance yields inconclusive results. We know little about the relationship between different modes of governance and forms of domestic change, i.e. when and under which conditions we are likely to observe inertia, retrenchment, absorption, accommodation or trans-formation of domestic governance arrangements. Even though the literature on Europeanization has improved our understanding of the impact of 'Europe' on many facets of domestic public policy, we observe that knowledge scarcely travels beyond smaller sets of comparisons to generate general propositions except for the insight that EU regulations do not produce conformity but rather a 'differential Europe' (Héritier *et al.*, 2001).

The dominant perspective in the Europeanization literature, however, remains 'top-down' or 'unidirectional', conceiving Europeanization as a process 'by which domestic policy areas are becoming increasingly subject to European policy-making' (Börzel, 1999, p. 574). Research challenging this 'unidirectional' focus is, however, slowly taking root, adding a 'bottom-up' perspective (Börzel, 2002; Knodt, 1998; Kohler-Koch, 1998), or even seeking a more encompassing perspective that highlights, *inter alia*, the interrelationship between EU governance and national governance arrangements (Kohler-Koch, 2000, 2003).

Research on the links between EU and national governance has produced some interesting insights. First, it enables the researcher to conceive of the European level as an opportunity structure that domestic actors may, depend-ing on their interests and resources, be able to exploit to further their own interests and, in turn, shape EU-level and national governance arrangements (see Kohler-Koch, 2000). Héritier (1996) has shown, for instance, that the expansion of regulatory policies in the EU can often be traced to the initiative of a domestic 'first mover' who seeks to transfer a particular national regulatory style to the European level.

Second, conceptualizing EU and national governance as an interactive and highly contextualized process draws attention to the importance of the temporal dimension. If we adopt a 'snapshot' perspective (Pierson, 1998), domestic adjustments to new modes of governance are often considered to have failed, yet over time adjustment costs may change due to exogenous changes in the overall setting of national governance and hence render domestic adjustment feasible in the medium to long run (Lang, 2003).

Third, the EU system of network governance carries structural characteristics which are closer to neo-corporatist systems (such as Germany) than to statist, i.e. hierarchically organized state-centred systems (such as France). The EU system of partnership arrangements is thus more easily 'absorbed' by neo-corporatist than by statist systems of governance (Lenschow, 1999; Schmidt, 1999).

IV. Problem-solving and the Legitimacy of Governance

The 'governance turn' in EU studies is also marked by a new strand of research inquiring into the consequences of the transformation of EU and national governance for their problem-solving effectiveness and democratic legitimacy. Van Kersbergen and van Warden (2001, p. 39; 2004) ask forcefully, 'can policy making in complicated, abstruse and intransparent multi-level network structures still be controlled by traditional checks and balances, such as the ... dualism between government and parliament, by federalism, or by judicial review at the national level?'. Furthermore, what are the consequences of these new forms of governance for the problem-solving capacity of political systems? Does multi-level network governance not forfeit governability, 'the capacity for resolute decision-making?' These two themes – the problem-solving capacity and democratic legitimacy of EU governance – continue to be at the centre of scholarly debate.

The Problem-solving Capacity of EU Governance

Research on the problem-solving capacity of EU governance is closely tied to Fritz Scharpf (1988) and his earlier work, based on an analysis of policy-making in the German federalist system, which expressed scepticism about the EU's capacity for consensual policy-making. This scepticism became epitomized in the concept of the 'joint decision trap' and has been echoed and partially refined in research on policy-making in different types of multi-level governance systems (Benz, 2004).

However, effective and efficient problem-solving beyond the nation-state through EU-wide rules is a well-documented empirical fact (Eichener, 1997; Grande and Jachtenfuchs, 2000; Scharpf, 1999). The likelihood of the creation of EU-level rules and regulations is closely tied to the distinction between 'negative' and 'positive' integration (Tinbergen, 1965). While negative integration refers to those activities that lead to the removal of barriers to trade or of obstacles to undistorted competition, positive integration refers to 'the reconstruction of a system of economic regulation at the level of the larger unit' (Scharpf, 1999, p. 45). Scharpf (1999, p. 50) argues that negative integration has been the 'main beneficiary of supranational European law'. The ECJ and the Commission have developed negative integration into a powerful tool aimed at removing national measures that distort the free movement of goods, services, capital and people. These activities are underpinned by the interests of market actors to further transnational trade (Stone Sweet, 2004).

By contrast, the potential for the EU's supranational actors to bring about measures of positive integration is much more limited (see, however, Stone Sweet, 2004), since such measures 'generally require explicit approval by the Council of Ministers and, increasingly, by the European Parliament' (Scharpf 1999, p. 1) and thus a high-level consensus among the actors involved. The EU's problem-solving capacity is therefore 'limited by the need to achieve action consensus among a wide range of divergent national and group interests' (Scharpf, 1999, p. 71). Effective solutions, however, are still possible and even probable where they are supported by underlying constellations of national interests. There is even ample evidence of 'races to the top', especially when business expects to profit from high product quality standards. In contrast, social or environmental policies that affect the costs of production with no improvement in product quality are much less likely to be adopted on a European basis. Conflicts of interest between governments with advanced and less advanced economies and divergent policy traditions or institutional structures are likely to make agreement difficult if not impossible (see Scharpf, 1999, pp. 107–16).

An actor-centred institutionalist approach, however, does not necessarily predict poor system performance. Some scholars even argue that the institutional peculiarities of the EU system of governance – its high degree of institutional fragmentation, fluidity and the absence of clear-cut hierarchies – are conditions conducive for problem-solving. The EU's 'poly-centric' system of governance engenders a particular problem-solving mode – deliberation – which has co-operation-friendly action orientation and carries a high problem-solving capacity (Cohen and Sabel, 1997).

EU Governance and the Question of Democratic Legitimacy

If governance beyond the nation-state can be effective and efficient, then legitimacy based on outputs is sufficient. This, in a nutshell, is the argument put forward by the proponents of the regulatory state. In order not to jeopardize Pareto-optimal solutions, decision-making must be vested in the hands of independent regulatory agents and should be excluded from the adversarial power-play of parliamentary, majoritarian politics (Majone, 2000, 2002). Since regulatory policies make up the bulk of the EU's policy output, proponents of the regulatory state thus see proposals to 'politicize' the Commission, for instance, by giving the EP an enhanced role in the Commission's investiture, with a dose of scepticism, as such reforms would reduce the credibility of its decisions and hence jeopardize democratic (output) legitimacy.

This perspective faces two main criticisms. First, high levels of performance can be equated with output legitimacy only if 'the people' and not experts define policy objectives. Second, many authors dismiss the basic assumption that 'the EU is a glorified regulatory agency, a "fourth branch of government", much like regulatory agencies at the domestic level in Europe, such as telecoms agencies, competition authorities, central banks, or even courts' (Follesdal and Hix, 2005, p. 7).

While the regulatory state concept emphasizes the output side of the democratic legitimacy equation, MLG emphasizes the input side. MLG displays a considerable degree of ambivalence concerning its potential to enhance the EU's democratic quality (Bache and Flinders, 2004; Hooghe and Marks, 2001; Kohler-Koch and Rittberger, forthcoming; Peters and Pierre, 2004). First, when authority is shared vertically between supranational, national and sub-national institutions, executive and parliamentary jurisdiction varies substantially and hence impinges on democratic accountability. Second, the shift from hierarchy and formal procedures to networking and informality – while allowing for extensive input – undermines the democratic principles of political equality and control.

In the European multi-level system the executive is crossing levels of jurisdiction easily, whereas the territorial reach of parliaments is more limited. In a 'penetrated system of governance' (Kohler-Koch, 1998, pp. 15–16) democratic representation and political accountability become deficient when organized through territorially bound parliaments. In recent years, national parliaments have made efforts to exert more influence, but are caught up in a 'negotiation–accountability dilemma' (Benz, 2003, p. 88). Since stricter control over governments reduces flexibility and success in Council negotiations, parliaments, or rather majority factions in national parliaments, refrain from exerting formal veto powers and choose informal ways to hold their governments accountable. According to Benz (2003), this strategy sets in motion a 'de-institutionalization' of EU decision-making, which 'results in opaque processes that the public are hardly able to control. It makes accountability of representatives difficult and, hence, deteriorates the democratic quality of representative structures. Thus, despite (or because of) the important role of parliaments in EU policy-making, the system fails to conform to the standard of democratic accountability' (Benz, 2003, p. 101).

Most scholars see the distinctiveness of MLG not just in the vertical diffusion of authority across levels of government but even more so in the horizontal dispersion of authority in which jurisdictions are task-specific, intersecting and flexible (Hooghe and Marks, 2003, p. 237) and in which public and private actors have a 'shared responsibility for resource allocation and conflict resolution' (Schmitter, 2002, p. 55). Empirical evidence supports the theory that the inclusive nature of network governance has the positive effect of being more open to new interests and innovative ideas (Héritier, 1999, p. 275), but provides a mixed account of the more ambitious expectations concerning 'participatory governance' and democratic upgrading. The implementation of the treaty-based 'partnership' principle in EU policies often does not attain the stipulated inclusiveness, openness and transparency. Since the rules and practice of participation do not guarantee equality between actors, the involvement of a multitude of private actors is still far from promoting EU democracy (Swyngedouw *et al.*, 2002, p. 128). The deficits of network governance are aggravated by the multi-level character of EU governance: 'The relations between actors involved … are not sufficiently exposed to public scrutiny, or to the scrutiny of the legitimate, democratic, and representative bodies' (Papadopoulos, 2005, p. 10). Furthermore, scholars claim that the celebrated 'informality' of MLG entails a potential for inequality and thereby risks violating a fundamental norm of democratic governance (Peters and Pierre, 2004).

Conclusion

The 'governance turn' has improved our knowledge about the particularities of the EU system of governance: a unique set of multi-level and regulatory institutions, as well as a hybrid mix of state and non-state actors in a non-hierarchical system of network governance. Furthermore, the governance perspective stresses the causes and effects of 'system transformation'; the repercussions of EU integration on both domestic systems and the EU system of governance and the effect of this transformative impact on the efficiency and democratic legitimacy of European rule.

Yet, despite the omnipresence of 'governance' in the study of the EU, governance is still ambiguous and under-specified as a concept, let alone as a theory. But, as the term 'governance perspective' suggests, governance research on the EU comprises works with a shared interest in the transformation of governance beyond the state through normative and empirical-analytical lenses. Thus conceived, the governance perspective is not wedded to a particular theory or method of inquiry.

This dual normative and empirical focus has produced a plethora of analyses on the effectiveness, efficiency and democratic legitimacy of EU governance. However, looking at the rich and differentiated picture of research (as presented and reflected in the CONNEX database), it can be deduced that the wealth of descriptive and causal knowledge accumulated all over Europe has – as yet – not fed back into the conceptual debate on EU governance. We close on the hopeful note that the institutionalization of research networks such as CONNEX, not least with the support of the EU, will improve mutual awareness and thus engender scientific progress.

References

Bache, I. and Flinders, M. (2004) 'Themes and Issues in Multi-level Governance'. In Bache, I. and Flinders, M. (eds) *Multi-level Governance* (Oxford: Oxford University Press).

Beck, D. and Conzelmann, T. (2004) 'Zwischen Sanktionierung und Dialog. Die Durchsetzung von *Good Governance* in der Entwicklungspartnerschaft von EU und AKP'. In Pappi, F.U., Riedel, E., Thurner, P.W. and Vaubel, R. (eds) *Die Institutionalisierung Internationaler Verhandlungen,* Mannheimer Jahrbuch für Europäische Sozialforschung, No. 8 (Frankfurt: Campus).

Benz, A. (2003) 'Compounded Representation in EU Multi-Level Governance'. In Kohler-Koch, B. (ed.) *Linking EU and National Governance* (Oxford: Oxford University Press).

Benz, A. (2004) 'Multilevel Governance – Governance in Mehrebenensystemen'. In Benz, A. (ed.) *Governance – Regieren in komplexen Regelsystemen. Eine Einführung* (Wiesbaden: VS Verlag).

Borrás, S. and Greve, B. (2004) (eds) *The Open Method of Co-ordination in the European Union,* Special issue of the *Journal of European Public Policy,* Vol. 11, No. 4.

Börzel, T. (1999) 'Towards Convergence in Europe? Institutional Adaptation to Europeanization in Germany and Spain'. *Journal of Common Market Studies,* Vol. 37, No. 4, pp. 573–96.

Börzel, T. (2002) 'Member State Responses to Europeanization'. *Journal of Common Market Studies,* Vol. 40, No. 2, pp. 193–214.

Börzel, T. (2005) 'European Governance – nicht neu, aber anders'. In Schuppert, G.F. (ed.) *Governance-Forschung. Vergewisserung über Stand und Entwicklungslinien* (Baden-Baden: Nomos).

Büthe, T. (2004) 'Governance Through Private Authority: Non-State Actors in World Politics'. Review Article, *Journal of International Affairs*, Vol. 58, No. 1, pp. 281–90.

Cohen, J. and Sabel, C. (1997) 'Directly-Deliberative Polyarchy'. *European Law Journal*, Vol. 3, No. 4, pp. 313–42.

Commission of the European Communities (2001) 'European Governance: A White Paper'. COM(2001) 428, available at «http://europa.eu.int/comm/governance/white_paper/index_en.htm».

Cutler, C., Haufler, V. and Porter, T. (1999) (eds) *Private Authority and International Affairs* (Albany: State University of New York Press).

De la Porte, C. and Nanz, P. (2004) 'OMC – A Deliberative-Democratic Mode of Governance? The Cases of Employment and Pensions'. *Journal of European Public Policy*, Vol. 11, No. 2, pp. 267–88.

Diez, T. and Wiener, A. (2004) 'Introducing the Mosaic of Integration Theory'. In Wiener, A. and Diez, T. (eds) *European Integration Theory* (Oxford: Oxford University Press).

Dyson, K. and Goetz, K. (2003) (eds) *Germany, Europe and the Politics of Constraint* (Oxford: Oxford University Press).

Eberlein, B. and Kerwer, D. (2004) 'New Governance in the European Union: A Theoretical Perspective'. *Journal of Common Market Studies*, Vol. 42, No. 1, pp. 121–42.

Eichener, V. (1997) 'Effective European Problem-Solving: Lessons from the Regulation of Occupational Safety and Environmental Protection'. *Journal of European Public Policy*, Vol. 4, No. 4, pp. 591–608.

Eising, R. and Kohler-Koch, B. (1999) 'Governance in the European Union: A Comparative Assessment'. In Kohler-Koch, B. and Eising, R. (eds) *The Transformation of Governance in the European Union* (London: Routledge).

Eising, R. and Kohler-Koch, B. (2005) 'Interessenpolitik im europäischen Mehrebenesystem'. In Eising, R. and Kohler-Koch, B. (eds) *Interessenpolitik in Europa* (Baden-Baden: Nomos).

Featherstone, K. and Radaelli, C. (2003) (eds) *The Politics of Europeanization* (Oxford: Oxford University Press).

Follesdal, A. and Hix, S. (2005) 'Why There is a Democratic Deficit in the EU: A Response to Majone and Moravcsik'. *European Governance Papers (EUROGOV)* No. C-05-02, available at «http://www.connex-network.org/eurogov/pdf/egp-connex-C-05-02.pdf».

Garrett, G. (1992) 'International Co-operation and Institutional Choice: The European Community's Internal Market'. *International Organization*, Vol. 45, pp. 539–64.

Goetschy, J. (2003) 'The European Employment Strategy, Multi-Level Governance and Policy Co-ordination'. In Zeitlin, J. and Trubek, D. (eds) *Governing Work and Welfare in a New Economy: European and American Experiments* (Oxford: Oxford University Press).

Grande, E. and Jachtenfuchs, M. (2000) (eds) *Wie problemlösungsfähig ist die EU? Regieren im europäischen Mehrebenensystem* (Baden-Baden: Nomos).

Hall, R.B. and Biersteker, T. (2002) *The Emergence of Private Authority in Global Governance* (New York: Cambridge University Press).

Héritier, A. (1996) 'The Accommodation of Diversity in European Policy Making and its Outcomes: Regulatory Policy as a Patchwork'. *Journal of European Public Policy,* Vol. 3, No. 2, pp. 149–67.

Héritier, A. (1999) 'Elements of Democratic Legitimation in Europe. An Alternative Perspective'. *Journal of European Public Policy,* Vol. 6, No. 2, pp. 269–82.

Héritier, A. (2003) 'New Modes of Governance in Europe: Increasing Political Capacity and Policy Effectiveness?'. In Börzel, T. and Cichowski, R. (eds) *The State of the European Union, Vol. 6: Law, Politics, and Society* (Oxford: Oxford University Press).

Héritier, A., Knill, C., Lehmkuhl, D., Teutsch, M. and Douillet, A.C. (2001) *Differential Europe. The European Impact on National Policymaking* (Lanham, MD: Rowman & Littlefield).

Hix, S. (1998) 'The Study of the European Union II: The "New Governance" Agenda and its Rivals'. *Journal of European Public Policy,* Vol. 5, No. 1, pp. 38–65.

Hix, S. (2005) *The Political System of the European Union,* 2nd edn (Basingstoke: Palgrave).

Hodson, D. and Maher, I. (2001) 'The Open Method as a New Mode of Governance'. *Journal of Common Market Studies,* Vol. 39, No. 4, pp. 719–46.

Hooghe, L. and Marks, G. (2001) *Multi-Level Governance and European Integration* (Lanham, MD: Rowman & Littlefield).

Hooghe, L. and Marks, G. (2003) 'Unraveling the Central State, But How? Types of Multi-level Governance'. *American Political Science Review,* Vol. 97, No. 2, pp. 233–43.

Jachtenfuchs, M. (2001) 'The Governance Approach to European Integration'. *Journal of Common Market Studies,* Vol. 39, No. 2, pp. 245–64.

Jachtenfuchs, M. (2003) 'Regieren jenseits der Staatlichkeit'. In Hellmann, G., Wolf, K.D. and Zürn, M. (eds) *Die neuen Internationalen Beziehungen: Forschungsstand und Perspektiven in Deutschland* (Baden-Baden: Nomos).

Joerges, C. and Vos, E. (1999) (eds) *EU-Committees: Social Regulation, Law and Politics* (Oxford: Hart).

Joerges, C., Mény, Y. and Weiler, J.H.H. (2001) (eds) 'Mountain or Molehill? A Critical Appraisal of the European Commission White Paper on Governance'. European University Institute, Jean Monnet Working Paper No. 6/01.

Jordan, A., Wurzel, R. and Zito, A. (2005) 'The Rise of "New" Policy Instruments in Comparative Perspective: Has Governance Eclipsed Government?'. *Political Studies,* Vol. 53, No. 3, pp. 477–96.

Kersbergen, K. van and Waarden, F. van (2001) 'Shifts in Governance: Problems of Legitimacy and Accountability'. White Paper on the theme 'Shifts in Governance' as part of the Strategic Plan 2002–05 of the Netherlands Organization for Scientific Research.

Kersbergen, K. van and Waarden, F. van (2004) ' "Governance" as a Bridge between Disciplines: Cross-Disciplinary Inspiration Regarding Shifts in Governance and Problems of Governability, Accountability and Legitimacy'. *European Journal of Political Research*, Vol. 43, No. 2, pp. 143–71.

Knill, C. (2005) 'Die Politiken der EU'. In Holzinger, K., Knill, C., Peters, D., Rittberger, B., Schimmelfennig, F. and Wagner, W. (eds) *Die Europäische Union. Theorien und Analysekonzepte* (Paderborn: Schöningh).

Knodt, M. (1998) *Tiefenwirkung europäischer Politik. Eigensinn oder Anpassung regionalen Regierens?* (Baden-Baden: Nomos).

Kohler-Koch, B. (1993) 'Die Welt regieren ohne Weltregierung'. In Böhret, C. and Wewer, G. (eds) *Regieren im 21. Jahrhundert. Zwischen Globalisierung und Regionalisierung* (Opladen: Leske+Budrich).

Kohler-Koch, B. (1998) 'Europäisierung der Regionen: Institutioneller Wandel als sozialer Prozess'. In Kohler-Koch, B. (ed.) *Interaktive Politik in Europa. Regionen im Netzwerk der Integration* (Opladen: Leske+Budrich).

Kohler-Koch, B. (1999) 'The Evolution and Transformation of European Governance'. In Kohler-Koch, B. and Eising, R. (eds) *The Transformation of Governance in the European Union* (London: Routledge).

Kohler-Koch, B. (2000) 'Europäisierung: Plädoyer für eine Horizonterweiterung'. In Kohler-Koch, B. and Knodt, M. (eds) *Deutschland zwischen Europäisierung und Selbstbehauptung* (Frankfurt: Campus).

Kohler-Koch, B. (2003) 'Interdependent European Governance'. In Kohler-Koch, B. (ed.) *Linking EU and National Governance* (Oxford: Oxford University Press).

Kohler-Koch, B. and Eising, R. (1999) (eds) *The Transformation of Governance in the European Union* (London: Routledge).

Kohler-Koch, B. and Larat, F. (forthcoming) *A Decade of Research on EU Multilevel Governance*.

Kohler-Koch, B. and Rittberger, B. (forthcoming) 'Introduction: Debating the Democratic Legitimacy of the European Union'. In Kohler-Koch, B. and Rittberger, B. (eds) *Debating the Democratic Legitimacy of the European Union* (Lanham, MD: Rowman & Littlefield).

Lang, J. (2003) 'Policy Implementation in a Multi-Level System: The Dynamics of Domestic Response'. In Kohler-Koch, B. (ed.) *Linking EU and National Governance* (Oxford: Oxford University Press).

Lenschow, A. (1999) 'Transformation in European Environmental Governance'. In Kohler-Koch, B. and Eising, R. (eds) *The Transformation of Governance in Europe* (London: Routledge).

Lenschow, A. (2005) 'Europeanization of Public Policy'. In Richardson, J. (ed.) *European Union. Power and Policy-making*, 3rd edn (London: Routledge).

Mair, P. (2006) 'Political Parties and Party Systems'. In Graziano, P. and Vink, M. (eds) *Europeanization: New Research Agendas* (Basingstoke: Palgrave).

Majone, G. (1996a) *Regulating Europe* (London: Routledge).

Majone, G. (1996b) 'Redistributive und sozialregulative Politik'. In Jachtenfuchs, M. and Kohler-Koch, B. (eds) *Europäische Integration*, 1st edn (Opladen: Leske+Budrich).

Majone, G. (2000) 'The Credibility Crisis of Community Regulation'. *Journal of Common Market Studies,* Vol. 38, No. 2, pp. 273–302.

Majone, G. (2002) 'Delegation of Regulatory Powers in a Mixed Polity'. *European Law Journal,* Vol. 38, No. 3, pp. 319–39.

Marks, G. (1993) 'Structural Policy and Multilevel Governance in the EC'. In Cafruny, A. and Rosenthal, G. (eds) *The State of the European Community* (Boulder, CO: Lynne Rienner).

Marks, G., Hooghe, L. and Blank, K. (1996) 'European Integration from the 1980s: State-centric *v.* Multi-level Governance'. *Journal of Common Market Studies,* Vol. 34, No. 3, pp. 341–78.

Mayntz, R. (1987) 'Politische Steuerung und gesellschaftliche Steuerungsprobleme – Anmerkungen zu einem theoretischen Paradigma'. *Jahrbuch zur Staats- und Verwaltungswissenschaft,* Vol. 1, pp. 89–110.

Mayntz, R. (2005) 'Governance Theory als fortentwickelte Steuerungstheorie?'. In Schuppert, G.F. (ed.) *Governance-Forschung. Vergewisserung über Stand und Entwicklungslinien* (Nomos: Baden-Baden).

Mayntz, R. and Scharpf, F.W. (1995) (eds) *Gesellschaftliche Selbstregelung und politische Steuerung* (Frankfurt: Campus).

Moravcsik, A. (1998) *The Choice for Europe. Social Purpose and State Power from Messina to Maastricht* (Ithaca: Cornell University Press).

Olsen, J.P. (2002) 'The Many Faces of Europeanization'. *Journal of Common Market Studies,* Vol. 40, No. 5, pp. 921–52.

Papadopoulos, Y. (2005) 'Political Accountability in Network and Multi-Level Governance'. Paper presented at the Connex Stocktaking Conference on 'Multilevel Governance in Europe. Structural Funds, Regional and Environmental Policy', Athens, 5–7 May.

Peters, B.G. and Pierre, J. (2004) 'Multi-level Governance and Democracy: A Faustian Bargain?'. In Bache, I. and Flinders, M. (eds) *Multi-level Governance* (Oxford: Oxford University Press).

Pierre, J. (2000) 'Introduction: Understanding Governance'. In Pierre, J. (ed.) *Debating Governance. Authority, Steering, and Democracy* (Oxford: Oxford University Press).

Pierre, J. and Peters, B.G. (2000) *Governance, Politics and the State* (Basingstoke: Macmillan).

Pierson, P. (1998) 'The Path to European Integration: A Historical-Institutionalist Analysis'. In Sandholtz, W. and Stone Sweet, A. (eds) *European Integration and Supranational Governance* (Oxford: Oxford University Press).

Radaelli, C. (2000) 'Whither Europeanization? Concept Stretching and Substantive Change'. *European Integration Online Papers,* Vol. 4.

Radaelli, C. (2004) 'Europeanization: Solution or Problem?'. *European Integration Online Papers,* Vol. 8.

Reif, K. and Schmitt, H. (1980) 'Nine National Second-order Elections: A Systematic Framework for the Analysis of European Election Results'. *European Journal of Political Research,* Vol. 8, No.1, pp. 3–44.

Rittberger, B. and Richardson, J. (2003) 'Old Wine in New Bottles? Commission Proposals and the Use of Environmental Policy Instruments'. *Public Administration,* Vol. 81, No. 3, pp. 575–606.

Rhodes R. (2003) 'What is New about Governance and Why does it Matter'. In Hayward, J. and Menon, A. (eds) *Governing Europe* (Oxford: Oxford University Press).

Rosenau, J. and Czempiel, E.-O. (1992) (eds) *Governance without Government: Order and Change in World Politics* (Cambridge: Cambridge University Press).

Scharpf, F.W. (1988) 'The Joint Decision Trap. Lessons from German Federalism and European Integration'. *Public Administration,* Vol. 66, No. 3, pp. 239–78.

Scharpf, F.W. (1999) *Governing in Europe. Effective and Democratic?* (Oxford: Oxford University Press).

Scharpf, F.W. (2003) 'Problem-Solving Effectiveness and Democratic Accountability in the EU'. Max-Planck-Institut für Gesellschaftsforschung, Working Paper No. 1/2003, available at «http://www.mpi-fg-koeln.mpg.de/pu/workpap/wp03-1/wp03-1.html».

Schmidt, V.A. (1999) 'National Patterns of Governance under Siege: The Impact of European Integration'. In Kohler-Koch, B. and Eising, R. (eds) *The Transformation of Governance in the European Union* (London: Routledge).

Schmitter, P.C. (2002) 'Participation in Governance Arrangements: Is there any Reason to Expect it will Achieve "Sustainable and Innovative Policies in a Multilevel Context"?'. In Grote, J. and Gbikpi, B. (eds) *Participatory Governance. Political and Societal Implications* (Opladen: Leske+Budrich).

Schneider, V. (2004) 'State Theory, Governance and the Logic of Regulation and Administrative Control'. In Warntjen, A. and Wonka, A. (eds) *Governance in Europe* (Baden-Baden: Nomos).

Schumann, W. (1993) 'Die EG als neuer Anwendungsbereich für die Policy-Analyse: Möglichkeiten und Perspektiven der konzeptionellen Weiterentwicklung'. In Héritier, A. (ed.) *Policy-Analyse. Kritik und Neuorientierung,* PVS Sonderheft No. 24 (Wiesbaden: Westdeutscher Verlag).

Smith, K.E. (2003) *European Union Foreign Policy in a Changing World* (Cambridge: Polity).

Stone Sweet, A. (2004) *The Judicial Construction of Europe* (Oxford: Oxford University Press).

Swyngedouw, E., Page, B. and Kaika, M. (2002) 'Sustainability and Policy Innovation in a Multi-Level Context: Crosscutting Issues in the Water Sector'. In Heinelt, H. (ed.) *Participatory Governance in Multi-Level Context. Context and Experience* (Opladen: Leske+Budrich).

Tinbergen, J. (1965) *International Economic Integration,* 2nd edn (Amsterdam: Elsevier).

Wallace, H. (2003) 'Contrasting Images of European Governance'. In Kohler-Koch, B. (ed.) *Linking EU and National Governance* (Oxford: Oxford University Press).

Wallace, H. (2005) 'An Institutional Anatomy and Five Policy Modes'. In Wallace, H., Wallace, W. and Pollack, M. (eds) *Policy-Making in the European Union,* 5th edn (Oxford: Oxford University Press).

Weiss, T.G. (2000) 'Governance, Good Governance and Global Governance: Conceptual and Actual Challenges'. *Third World Quarterly,* Vol. 21, No. 5, pp. 795–814.

Willke, H. (1983) *Entzauberung des Staates. Überlegungen zu einer gesellschaftlichen Steuerungstheorie* (Königstein: Athenäum).

World Bank (1997) *World Development Report – The State in a Changing World* (Oxford: Oxford University Press).

Zürn, M. (1998) *Regieren jenseits des Nationalstaates. Denationalisierung und Globalisierung als Chance* (Frankfurt: Suhrkamp).

JCMS 2006 Volume 44 Annual Review pp. 51–5

The Luxembourg Presidency: Size Isn't Everything

DEREK HEARL
Eastern Mediterranean University

Introduction

1 January 2005 saw the beginning, not only of the Grand Duchy of Luxembourg's 11th EU presidency, but also the fourth time that its Prime Minister, Jean-Claude Juncker had been at the EU helm – more often than any other single individual.

The first presidency semester of 2005 was always going to be a challenging one. The various dossiers that were carried over included two especially difficult and complex issues: the comprehensive mid-term review of the 'Lisbon process' and what was to prove the poisoned chalice of the EU's 'financial perspective' (long-term budget) for the years 2007–13. In addition, there was the ongoing ratification of the proposed European Constitution, as well as a number of potentially sensitive foreign policy dossiers.

Nevertheless, there were grounds for optimism. Luxembourg has considerable experience at holding the presidency and a generally enviable track record of success. Juncker, the EU's longest-serving head of government, had a reputation as an effective EU 'fixer', combining linguistic and negotiating skills with a dogged Europeanism. While the prime minister inevitably dominated the Luxembourg presidency, the Foreign Minister, Jean Asselborn, and the Minister of Justice, Luc Frieden, both made particularly important contributions.

Obviously the Grand Duchy's professional permanent civil service is far too small to be able to shoulder the burden of an EU presidency without significant augmentation and assistance. The country tries to deal with this problem by bringing home Luxembourgers working abroad, particularly embassy staff and academics, for the duration of a presidency and called upon additional help and support from the Council Secretariat and other EU bodies.

On the other hand, its small size gives the administration a number of advantages. Internal communication links between departments are very short, both literally and figuratively. In addition, as promotion opportunities are fewer, administrative continuity and institutional memory increases; often the same official might still work in the same department, and perhaps even in the same job, as when the country last held the presidency.

Further, politicians and officials tend to know each other personally, relationships are typically close and informal, resulting in levels of trust enabling the former to allow the latter considerable autonomy in decision-making, even in international negotiations. Individual civil servants also necessarily cover a much wider range of subjects than their counterparts in larger national bureaucracies. This can sometimes mean that a single official in charge of a dossier in a national ministry may find him- or herself also lobbying the European Commission, acting as the national expert on one or more working groups, attending the relevant meeting of Coreper and even supporting his/her minister in the Council. Officials from such smaller national administrations also need to build closer than usual friendships and working arrangements with their counterparts from other, larger countries.

Luxembourg can plausibly claim another comparative advantage stemming from its very small size; that it has (and importantly is perceived to have) rather few vital national interests of its own to defend, thereby allowing it to appear an honest broker. Such factors – combined with the 'almost obsessive search for consensus' which the presidency shamelessly claimed as 'the dominant national characteristic' – partly explain the traditionally high expectations of Luxembourg's EU presidencies.

I. Problems in Prospect ...

The two most important, and potentially difficult, matters with which the new presidency had been charged were the mid-term review of the Lisbon process and finding agreement on the financial perspective. The Lisbon process, which had been adopted by the European Council in 2000, aims at making the EU 'the world's most dynamic and competitive economy' and the world's largest knowledge-based economy by 2010. The financial perspective was always going to be highly contentious, as it requires agreement on who pays what and who gets what in the enlarged EU of 25. In addition, in his speech to the European Parliament (EP) at the start of the presidency, Juncker also undertook to continue to make progress on the next stage of enlargement, economic and social affairs and the internal market, agriculture and fisheries, food safety and sustainable development, as well as with the external relations and justice and home affairs portfolios.

II. ... and in Retrospect

Somewhat unusually, neither of the two full European Council meetings held during the presidency was in Luxembourg itself, but took place in Brussels. The first, on 22–23 March, focused in particular on the actions to be taken by governments within the context of the various pillars of the Lisbon strategy. The second, on 16–17 June, was dominated by the financial perspective.

The mid-term review of the Lisbon strategy can certainly be seen as a success even though it resulted more in changes in the method of application than in substance. Member States were given more control over the strategy's operation while at the same the presidency tried to introduce a greater sense of urgency into the process by brokering agreement on clearer targets coupled with tighter reporting procedures to improve monitoring. According to a subsequent statement by the Luxembourg government, the revised strategy is supposed *inter alia* to reinforce competitiveness, increase modernization in attitudes and economic policies, as well as making it more innovative and more inclusive (see Howarth in this volume).

The presidency also claimed credit for leading the European Council and the Council of Ministers to adapt the Stability and Growth Pact by bringing to an end a long period of uncertainty giving, it was claimed, a better balance by putting growth and stability on an equal footing (see Verdun in this volume).

There were also a number of foreign policy successes, such as the signing of accession treaties with Bulgaria and Romania, and the opening of negotiations with Croatia and Turkey (see also Lavenex and Schimmelfennig in this volume). A particular highlight was the first ever visit of US President George W. Bush to the European Council in Brussels on 22 February. In the wake of the Iraq war, Juncker claimed that the presidency had helped the Americans and the Europeans to find a common position on this tricky topic. The Luxembourg government also boasted that it had restored good relations between the EU and Russia. The improvement began with a meeting between the Russian and Luxembourg foreign ministers and the EU's External Relations Commissioner in Luxembourg at the beginning of April, followed by another in Moscow devoted to human rights questions and culminated in a summit between Juncker, Commission President Barroso, and Russian President Vladimir Putin on 10 May.

However, in the end three events towards the end of the six-month term blighted what might otherwise have been judged as yet another successful Luxembourg presidency. The first two were the rejections of the proposed

European Constitution by French and Dutch voters (see Taggart, and Sitter and Henderson in this volume). The third was the failure of the June European Council to agree the financial perspective.

The presidency's response to the French and Dutch referendums was to call for the ratification process to continue. Juncker argued that the votes were at least as much due to domestic factors and 'not entirely a judgment on the constitution itself'. Although this defiant, but seemingly doomed, approach can certainly be attributed to his own sincere Europeanism, it would in any event have been impossible for him to do otherwise given that he had effectively pledged his personal political future on a positive outcome in the by then imminent (and ultimately successful) referendum in Luxembourg itself. Nonetheless, the June European Council meeting effectively put the constitution on hold by agreeing to extend the November 2006 deadline for ratification of the Treaty until at least mid-2007.

Despite this, the most difficult dossier which the presidency had to deal with was easily the vexed question of the EU's 'financial perspective'. The European Council had tasked the presidency with finding a political agreement by June. The Luxembourg government proposed tackling this by trying to ensure that differing national positions converged, rather than simply concentrating on the fine details of the package themselves. In the event these efforts were to end in spectacular failure.

The Commission proposed a budget of 1.26 per cent of EU GDP, while the main contributors to the budget, Germany, the Netherlands, the UK, France and Sweden demanded that it be limited to 1.0 per cent, which Barroso rejected as 'very disappointing'. In an attempt to find a workable compromise, the presidency proposed an overall budget of 1.056 per cent of GDP by cutting €50 billion from the Lisbon agenda programme and €40 billion from the regional aid budget. In addition, the UK's famous 'rebate' would be frozen at roughly its current rate of nearly €5 billion per year, thereby allowing what were deemed to be excessive Dutch, German and Swedish contributions to be reduced. The UK, while seeing the overall cuts in the budget as 'a step in the right direction', stressed that the rebate was not up for negotiation. UK Prime Minister Blair attacked the common agricultural policy (CAP) as the basic reason for the 'distortion' in the budget which had justified the rebate in the first place. Britain would veto any cut in the rebate unless farm subsidies were overhauled, something which French President Chirac predictably refused to contemplate 'under any circumstances' (BBC News, 2005).

Faced with this impasse, Juncker took personal charge of the dossier, calling all 24 other heads of government to Luxembourg for intensive one-to-one discussions between 30 May and 12 June. He subsequently told the EP that he had conducted more than 50 hours of such talks and that 'one can do no more and, quite honestly, all those who come after me will do less'. Following these consultations the presidency proposed a new compromise that allowed the British rebate to remain unchanged insofar as the 15 older Member States were concerned, and enabled the UK to co-finance as normal the cohesion policy in the new Member States, but not contribute to the CAP for these same states.

The UK government categorically rejected this proposal, insisting on even deeper cuts in the agricultural budget, and the summit broke up in bitterness and recrimination. Juncker openly blamed the UK for the failure of the EU summit and of Luxembourg's EU presidency itself. He told RTL television that the summit had seen a clash between two competing philosophies, which saw Europe either as a free trade area or a politically integrated union; he was 'disheartened, disappointed and basically sad', but somewhat defiantly then went on to say that 'those who believe in Europe should not just throw in the towel'.

Conclusion

The Luxembourg presidency of 2005 certainly carried the personal stamp of the prime minister who is also his country's finance minister and therefore president of Ecofin, a position he continued to hold for the remainder of 2005 (since the UK, which took over the presidency on 1 July, is not a member of the euro area).

Juncker has acknowledged that the presidency will probably be remembered as a failure as a result of both the budget row and the negative votes in the French and Dutch referendums. What successes there were owed much to both the close working relationship with the European Commission and to the explicit focus the presidency team as a whole brought to conciliation and compromise. These skills proved to be less suited to the more confrontational and 'zero sum' nature of the financial perspective negotiation.

Reference

BBC News (2005) 'EU "in Crisis" over Talks Failure'. 18 June, available at «http:// news.bbc.co.uk/go/pr/fr/-/2/hi/europe/4105970.stm».

JCMS 2006 Volume 44 Annual Review pp. 57–62

The UK Presidency: In the Hot Seat

RICHARD WHITMAN
University of Bath

Introduction

The United Kingdom's presidency of the European Union (EU) commenced on 1 July against the backdrop of 'no' votes in France and the Netherlands on the EU Constitutional Treaty and an acrimonious summit under the Luxembourg presidency in mid-June which failed to reach a deal on the EU budget. Settlement of the EU's financial perspectives for 2007–13, and the attendant question of whether the UK would relinquish any of the British budget rebate, were subsequently to dominate public and Member State discussions of the UK presidency.

The UK government was also in the unusual position of holding the G8 presidency alongside its EU presidency (its sixth EU presidency, and second under the Blair government). There was, however, to be minimal linkage between these two presidencies. The G8 presidency provided an opportunity to focus on the big themes of third-world poverty and climate change, and to work for progress in these key areas with some of the most internationally significant states. The EU presidency required working in a much more circumscribed manner in a more complicated set of institutional arrangements and with more limited objectives.

I. Presidency Agenda

The Blair government's decision to suspend the UK's ratification process of the Constitutional Treaty (and consequently to defer the promised referendum)

Journal compilation © 2006 Blackwell Publishing Ltd, 9600 Garsington Road, Oxford OX4 2DQ, UK and 350 Main Street, Malden, MA 02148, USA and the subsequent agreement of EU governments to defer discussions on the EU Constitutional Treaty with a 'period of reflection' until 2006, removed an agenda item which might have otherwise distracted the UK presidency. However, the UK faced a pressing domestic challenge in the first week of its presidency with the London bombings of 7 July.

As for all EU presidencies the planned work programme for the UK presidency was informed by the multi-annual strategic programme for the period 2004–06 (designed for the Irish, Dutch, Luxembourg, UK, Austrian and Finnish presidencies) and the more detailed operational programme of the Council for 2005, which fleshed out the timetable for implementing this strategy and which had been submitted jointly by Luxembourg and the UK. The UK government set out its own expectations for its presidency to the European Parliament in its White Paper of 23 June 2005, 'Priorities for the UK Presidency of the Council'. This organized the UK's aspirations under three headings: economic reform and social justice, security and stability, and Europe's role in the world. A final paragraph pledged to 'take forward the discussions on future financing'. A second White Paper for the UK Parliament, 'Prospects for the EU in 2005: The UK Presidency of the European Union', published on 30 June 2005, confirmed these priorities.

II. Economic Reform

In conjunction with the Barroso-led European Commission, the UK wanted to place an emphasis on rejuvenating economic reform during its presidency. A key ambition was making progress in the field of better regulation. This included advancing negotiations on the most appropriate way to synthesize chemical regulation (REACH) into one legal structure. The UK put discussion of REACH high on the agenda of both the Competitiveness and Environment Councils during its presidency and significant progress was made with REACH completing its first reading in the European Parliament (EP) on 17 November.

There were also a number of developments relating to the liberalization and integration of service markets. Substantial progress was made towards agreement on the financial services action plan (FSAP). The services directive also passed an important hurdle, when the EP's internal market committee voted it through on 22 November and it moved to its first reading at a plenary session of the EP on 15 February 2006. The operational programme committed the presidency to progress on the working time directive, but no progress was made under a presidency that was unenthusiastic about change.

III. Enlargement

The opening of enlargement negotiations with Turkey on 3 October at the General Affairs and External Relations Council (GAERC) in Luxembourg was a significant achievement for the presidency. The presidency overcame opposition during a long night of negotiations to implement the prior decision that had already been taken to open negotiations. Member State opposition to Turkish accession, including that of German Chancellor-in-waiting, Angela Merkel, who had consistently opposed Turkish membership and espoused an alternative 'privileged partnership', was dissipated by the grand coalition not yet being in place, and the CDU not being represented at the meeting. The Austrian government also threatened the opening accession negotiations. In this case the position of the presidency was assisted by the precipitate reporting of Carla Del Ponte, chief prosecutor at the UN war crimes' tribunal, on 3 October that Croatia had fully co-operated with the tribunal's attempts to bring to justice the fugitive Croatian General Gotovina. This enabled the UK to open simultaneously accession negotiations with Croatia, an Austrian objective. On 7 December, Gotovina was detained in Tenerife. Under the presidency, further progress was made in relationships with prospective Member States in southeastern Europe, with Macedonia being granted candidate country status and stabilization and association agreement negotiations opened with Serbia and Montenegro and Bosnia and Herzegovina.

IV. Justice and Home Affairs

Counter-terrorism assumed an especial importance for the presidency in the aftermath of the London bombings, and the Council adopted a response to the bombings on 13 July. Efforts of the presidency were successfully focused on reaching an agreement on a directive, via qualified majority voting in the Council (and subsequently approved by the EP), to harmonize the retention of telecommunications, email and internet data in all Member States for up to two years. The presidency also advanced policies in allied areas, such as the draft European payment order approved at the Justice and Home Affairs Council on 2 December. The presidency had hoped for agreement on a harmonized counter-terrorism strategy to be reached ahead of the European Council on 15 December, but a large number of ministers were constrained by domestic legislatures from approving the strategy. The 2 December Council also made progress on the European refugee fund to help protect refugees 'at source' by endorsing a Spanish proposal brought forward at the Hampton Court summit to release €400 million from the European neighbourhood policy for financing the initiative.

V. Foreign Policy and External Relations

EU foreign policy remained cohesive during the UK's presidency. This was despite a number of challenges which included the continuing the EU nuclear diplomacy with Iran in the aftermath of the election of populist President Mahmoud Ahmadinejad; maintaining good relations with China, while negotiating voluntary export restraints to limit the impact of Chinese textile and shoe imports; the earthquake in Pakistan; and responding to a growing fear of a 'flu pandemic created by the spread of the bird influenza H5N1 virus. Furthermore, renewed complications in the relationship with the US following allegations of CIA interrogation centres on European soil were effectively handled; a collective EU request to the US government for clarification was a successful exercise in forging a common response.

Elsewhere the EU's international involvement grew at a steady pace in the second half of 2005. There was the launch of the first European security and defence policy (ESDP) operation outside Europe and Africa, the monitoring mission in Aceh (Indonesia). On 15 November the Council adopted a joint action that officially launched an EU police mission in the Palestinian territories (EUPOL–COPPS) from 1 January 2006. However, the EU's involvement in Iraq did not grow at as fast a pace as the UK presidency might have liked. Negotiations on a third-country agreement to increase political and trade co-operation were not initiated during the UK's tenure, nor was a Commission delegation office opened, but a decision was taken to extend EUJUST LEX (the rule of law mission for Baghdad).

The UK led the EU delegation on climate change negotiations at the Montreal Conference from 28 November to 9 December. The conference outcomes included establishing a working group that will determine emission targets for the period 2013–17 – once the Kyoto agreement has expired in 2012. At Montreal the US government also agreed to sign a revised version of a statement calling for co-operation on climate change. The UK government maintains that this outcome would not have been possible without the elevation of the issue of climate change to the top of the agenda during its presidency of the EU and the G8, particularly with the latter including China and India in discussions at the G8 summit at Gleneagles.

The UK presidency had a tangible success with the progress made towards liberalization of the US–EU aviation market. At the end of a week-long conference in Washington at the end of November, the text of the first ever aviation treaty between the US and EU was agreed. The so-called 'open skies' deal awaited a definitive programme on US liberalization at the conclusion of the presidency. Agreement was less forthcoming at the ministerial meeting of the WTO discussing the Doha development agenda in Hong Kong from 13–18

December. Two major stumbling blocks were overcome with the conclusion of an agreement on reform of the EU's sugar regime and agreement to eliminate export subsidies by 2013. The UK presidency, for its part, successfully managed to uphold the mandate of Commissioners Mandelson and Boel to negotiate on behalf of the EU, despite consistent challenges from the French government.

VI. Future Financing

The strategy adopted by the UK government in response to pressure to reach agreement on the financial perspectives during its presidency was to seek to widen the terms of the debate. This was to prove difficult. Prior to the formal commencement of the presidency, and in the aftermath of the failure at the June European Council, Tony Blair gave a widely praised speech to the EP on 23 June calling for the EU to examine how it could engage the interests and enthusiasms of its citizens. Other EU governments waited in anticipation for the UK government to follow up with a plan for a programme of action and, in not doing so, the presidency created disappointment and failed to capitalize on an opportunity to influence the structure of debate on the future of the EU.

The impression gained ground that the UK was just playing for time on future financing, and was reinforced for many Member States by the thin agenda for the informal summit of Heads of State and Government at Hampton Court on 27 October. For many Member States the informal summit was simply an exercise in presidential filibustering rather than tackling the budget issue, which other Member States felt was the most pressing concern. There was, however, an important new initiative at the summit with Prime Minister Blair calling for an EU energy security policy. The successful development of such a policy will fall to future EU presidencies.

The UK failed in its strategy to link reform of the UK rebate to an overhaul of the spending priorities in the financial perspectives, and particularly the expenditure on the common agricultural policy (CAP), as a distorting element of the EU budget. The UK did not present detailed proposals on the budget to EU Member State governments until 5 December, only ten days before the December European Council meeting. The thrust of these initial proposals was an attempt to reduce the burden on the current net contributors to the budget by cutting the €160 million regional aid planned for the central and east European Member States 'by no more than 10 per cent'. This reduction was justified on the basis that these Member States had thus far failed to absorb a substantial amount of aid within the two-year time limit for spending it. The reduction would be linked to an extension of the time limit in which they are allowed to spend aid, as well as a 2009 review of spending, including the CAP. The UK did, importantly, concede that the UK budget rebate could be adjusted and that CAP reform would be decoupled from an alteration to the UK's budget rebate. The UK backed down from this in the absence of significant support from other Member States, most of which did not want to revisit the major reforms to the CAP agreed in 2003, which were not yet fully implemented. The UK then changed tack and sought to present its concessions on changes to the rebate as being driven by the UK's willingness to relinquish a propor-tion of it in order not to disadvantage the new Member States and to make an appropriate contribution to eastern enlargement. The UK proposals were not, however, received warmly and the prospects of a deal on the budget were not auspicious. Commission President Barroso's spokesman likened the approach to that of the Sheriff of Nottingham, robbing the poor to pay the rich.

The stage was set for a tense European Council on 15–16 December. Since the June European Council, however, the UK had conceded that its rebate was negotiable and was willing to make the concessions necessary to secure a budget deal under its presidency. After a very late night negotiation marathon, the UK secured an agreement on the financial perspective. The agreement set total ex-penditure at 1.045 per cent of the EU's gross national income (GNI) (€862.3 billion). Expenditure was reduced by pairing a €10.5 billion reduction to the British rebate over seven years with a €16 billion reduction in aid to eastern Europe. Angela Merkel, in her first appearance at a European Council, finessed the end-game of negotiations by proposing that funds earmarked for regional assistance in Germany be given to Poland. The UK achieved its desired mid-term review of spending in 2008, but with no detail on the intended remit.

The agreement on future financing ensured that, at the conclusion of the presidency, the UK received grudging approval for its achievements. There was notable progress in a number of policy areas, notably enlargement and internal security and market reforms. However, as for all presidencies, policy progress was dependent on other EU institutions, including the EP and the Commission. The UK can claim successes for its presidency but such success was not all of its own making.

JCMS 2006 Volume 44 Annual Review pp. 63–80

Governance and Institutional Developments: In the Shadow of the Constitutional Treaty

DESMOND DINAN
George Mason University

Introduction

The Constitutional Treaty overshadowed EU governance and institutional developments throughout 2005. Although the crucial referendums did not take place until late May and early June, the growing expectation of defeat in France cast a pall over EU affairs for several months beforehand. The decisiveness of the French rejection of the Treaty, together with the equally uncompromising outcome of the Dutch referendum,[1] caused politicians and pundits to proclaim that the EU and the entire process of European integration were in crisis. The nature of the supposed crisis ranged from 'existential', to 'political', to 'profound'; it was a crisis of 'confidence' and of 'identity' that called into question the future of the EU. Two weeks after the referendums, when national leaders failed to reach agreement on a new EU budget at their summit in Brussels, Jean-Claude Juncker, Luxembourg's Prime Minister and President-in-Office of the European Council, went so far as to claim that the EU was not just in crisis, but 'in deep crisis' (*European Report*, 22 June 2005, p. 1). How serious was the situation?

Just as Danish voters' rejection of the Maastricht Treaty in June 1992 and Irish voters' rejection of the Nice Treaty in June 2001 had jeopardized both initiatives, the outcome of the French and Dutch referendums imperilled implementation of the Constitutional Treaty. Whereas the Danish and Irish governments had been able to overcome the embarrassment (as they saw it) of the negative

---

[1] On the domestic politics of the referendums, see Paul Taggart's contribution in this volume.

results by assuaging national sensitivities and holding second referendums, the outcome of the French and Dutch referendums was too consequential and the nature of the Constitutional Treaty too different to justify a similar approach. Seizing the opportunity to avoid a potentially polarizing domestic referendum on the Constitutional Treaty, the British government suggested that the entire ratification process be put in abeyance. The other Member States concurred. Instead of wrapping up EU-wide ratification by the end of 2006, as originally planned, national leaders agreed at their summit in June 2005 to consign the Constitutional Treaty to a potentially limitless 'period of reflection'.

The summit was one of the most disputatious in the history of the EU not because of the Constitutional Treaty but because of the breakdown of the budget negotiations. British Prime Minister Tony Blair and French President Jacques Chirac, already at odds over Iraq and other touchy issues, personified the two opposing camps in the budget debate. Juncker took the unusual step for the Council President of candidly criticizing Blair first at the post-summit press conference and then, several days later, in an address to the European Parliament. Yet Juncker's aggressive chairmanship of the summit itself had done little to bring the two sides together, even had a breakthrough been possible. Nor did the collapse of the budget negotiations represent a crisis, let alone a deep crisis, for the EU. There was time enough to conclude and ratify a budget agreement before the end of the current financial perspective in December 2006. Contrary to prevailing expectations, Blair, then in the Council presidency, secured a budget agreement in December 2005, thanks largely to concessions on his own part and to the constructive contribution of Angela Merkel, Germany's new Chancellor.

With a new budget in the bag, was the EU in crisis because the Constitutional Treaty would not be implemented on schedule, if at all? Regardless of the ratification drama, the EU operated throughout 2005 under the provisions of the existing treaties. Even if ratified in all Member States, the Constitutional Treaty would not have come into effect until November 2006, at the earliest. The existing treaties included the much-maligned Nice Treaty of 2000, which had been implemented in February 2003. According to many of those who claimed that the EU was in crisis following the French and Dutch referendums, the Nice Treaty was inadequate (at best) or unworkable (at worst) for the enlarged EU. Yet national leaders were well aware when they concluded the Nice Treaty that the EU would soon enlarge to at least 25 members. That treaty was far from ideal, but was also far from impracticable. The EU functioned adequately throughout 2005, especially in the area of qualified majority voting, one of the Nice Treaty's least satisfactory aspects.

Beyond operational considerations, talk of an EU crisis seemed far-fetched in 2005. Undoubtedly the EU and the process of European integration were

(and still are) in the doldrums. Yet the results of the French and Dutch referendums were a symptom, not a cause, of the malaise. The underlying problem
was growing public dissatisfaction with the EU or, more accurately, growing
public misunderstanding of what the EU is and what it does, a misunderstanding
compounded by national governments that are apt to exonerate themselves and
blame the Commission, the European Court of Justice and 'Brussels' generally
for everything from the constraints of the Stability and Growth Pact to tough
competition policy rules, regardless of the reasons for those measures. To the
extent that the EU was handicapped operationally in 2005 and might remain
so for the foreseeable future, the underlying cause was political posturing on
the part of national governments rather than intrinsic institutional sclerosis.

I. A Cautious Commission

Such an environment was hardly conducive to activism or entrepreneurship on
the part of the Commission, which remained in eclipse throughout 2005. At the
same time, the Commission struggled – more so than the Council of Ministers
or European Parliament – with the challenge of digesting the ten Member
States that had joined the EU in 2004. Already reeling from a series of internal
reforms that, according to many officials, seriously reduced staff morale, the
Commission had difficulty adjusting organizationally to enlargement. Having to
absorb so many new officials from widely different backgrounds compounded
the sense of bewilderment increasingly prevalent in the Commission.

The recruitment of officials from the new Member States continued
throughout 2005 under the close scrutiny of all the national governments. As
in other areas of EU activity, the Polish government unabashedly advanced its
national interest by pressing for the appointment of Polish citizens at all levels
of the Commission. National governments – new and old – were especially
concerned about the allocation of the most senior posts, those of Director
General and Deputy Director General. Tension grew towards the end of the
year as Commission President José Manuel Barroso prepared to juggle about
50 such posts, in accordance with a decision of the previous Commission
President not to allow people to remain in the same top position for more
than seven years. Brussels-watchers interpreted the Barroso reshuffle with
the same intensity that Kremlinologists interpreted changes in the old Soviet
Union. Their conclusion, echoed in the European media, was that Barroso
deliberately side-tracked French officials and promoted people who shared
his neo-liberal agenda. Barroso may have been emboldened to take a swipe
at France because Chirac was politically damaged by the result of the French
referendum. Regardless of his motivation and the implications for France, the

reshuffle itself was a reminder of the extent of national interest and involvement in the Commission's internal affairs.

The difficulty of operating in 20 official languages became fully apparent in 2005. However, it was the politics rather than the practicality of translation and interpretation that proved most daunting. The Commission estimated that each official language needed about 80 translators. By that reckoning, some of the EU-15 official languages had too many translators, but no national government wanted to see a reduction in 'its' language services. Within the Commission, English, French and German remained the working languages. Only the Italian media, used to the prominence of Italian during the years of Romano Prodi's presidency, complained about this, but to no avail. Also in 2005, national governments agreed that Irish would become an official language as of January 2007, a development that would add to the cost but not necessarily the comprehension of EU business – relatively few Irish people have an adequate grasp of the language but all of them are fluent in English.

Weak Leadership and an Unassuming Agenda

With 25 members (one per Member State) as of November 2004, the college of the Commission is now larger than ever before, apart from an anomalous period of six months immediately after the accession of the new Member States, when it had 30 members. Nevertheless the size of the college was not as disadvantageous as expected, thanks in part to Barroso's decision to organize key parts of the Commission's work around groups of commissioners. Moreover, 2005 was the first full year in which the large Member States were without their second commissioners, having given up that privilege – or right, as they saw it – under the terms of the Nice Treaty. As well as coping with a larger and inherently less manageable college, therefore, Barroso had to deal with a new and so far uncertain dynamic in the relationship between the large Member States and his own institution.

The Barroso Commission contained fewer holdovers from the outgoing Commission than did any previous Commission, although by the beginning of 2005 the neophyte commissioners were finding their feet in Brussels. The few veterans of the Prodi Commission, notably vice-presidents Günter Verheugen and Margot Wallström, were powerful and strong-willed. Not that all of the new arrivals were shrinking violets, by any means. For instance, Charlie McCreevy, the internal market commissioner, who had made no secret of his desire to stay in government in Dublin rather than move to Brussels, liked to speak his mind and act independently. The usual turf wars, ideological differences, and personal animosities complicated the quest for collegiality. This was a difficult team for any president to manage. Indeed, Barroso seemed frustrated early in the year as he tried to stamp his authority on his unruly colleagues. Graham Watson, leader of the Liberal Group in the Parliament, observed in March that Barroso needed to realize 'that being president of the Commission is not the same as being prime minister' and that it required work 'to build a majority all the time' (*Financial Times*, 11 March 2005, p. 8).

The nature of Barroso's appointment compounded the problem. As noted in last year's *Review*, Barroso was a last-minute, compromise candidate in whom Chirac and German Chancellor Gerhard Schröder had reluctantly acquiesced. Neither Chirac nor Schröder overcame their initial lack of enthusiasm for Barroso, which stymied the Commission President, especially in the European Council, the EU's most important decision-making forum. By the middle of the year, Barroso could comfort himself with the thought that Schröder would surely be out of office after the German elections in September – the Commission generally made little secret of its hopes for a Christian Democratic Union victory – and that Chirac was politically wounded as a result of the French referendum.

The shadow of the looming French referendum further weakened the Commission's position, not least by sharpening Chirac's antagonism towards Barroso. The new Commission President had put economic reform at the top of his agenda. In principle, Chirac was committed to economic reform, having signed up to the Lisbon strategy in March 2000. In practice, however, Lisbon was faltering because of the unwillingness of Chirac and other national leaders to take politically painful economic decisions. Fear of globalization, with its connotations of industrial restructuring, job losses and inferior social services, was pervasive in France, where European integration was increasingly caricatured as part of the problem, not the solution. The notorious services directive, an essential building block for the still incomplete internal market, became emblematic in France of all that was wrong with the EU. Chirac did nothing to set the record straight. While pandering to populist antiglobalism, Chirac pressured the Commission to water down the services directive and dismissed Barroso as a misguided neoliberal. In March, Chirac reportedly urged TF2, the French television channel, to drop Barroso from one of its influential current affairs programmes, partly out of spite and partly out of fear that the Commission President would alienate voters in the upcoming referendum (*Le Monde*, 31 March 2005, p. 1).

Barroso's retreat from an avowedly reformist position became painfully apparent in the early months of 2005, and especially in the run-up to the French referendum. The Commission's five-year plan, 'Europe 2010: Partnership for European Renewal', released in January, argued that economic growth and job creation were essential for the well-being of the EU as a whole, and were the most effective means of tackling the alienation of European citizens from the process and institutions of European integration (Commission, 2005a). A Commission paper on breathing new life into the Lisbon strategy, adopted in early February, was more specific about the urgency of reform in order to boost economic growth and employment. Each of these documents nevertheless paid due deference to the goals of social cohesion and sustainable development which, along with economic reform, constitute the three legs of the Lisbon strategy.

Barroso backtracked from his overriding emphasis on economic reform in the face of intense criticism from social democrats, especially in the European Parliament, and from almost all shades of opinion in France. By the time of the European Council in March, which was devoted primarily to a mid-term review of the Lisbon strategy, Barroso was careful to emphasize the importance of the much-vaunted European social model. The outcome of the summit was a setback for Barroso and other champions of economic modernization. National leaders committed themselves to a streamlined but less stringent Lisbon strategy, diluted the Stability and Growth Pact, and agreed that the original proposal for the services directive was iniquitous. Economic nationalists and protectionists were jubilant, reformers were despondent, and Barroso's position was further compromised.[2]

Advocates of a more assertive Commission were disappointed in any case that Barroso had put the Lisbon strategy at the top of his agenda, given that national governments dominated the process. Indeed, the appeal of the Lisbon strategy for national governments was largely that it was an intergovernmental endeavour with only a limited role for the EU's supranational institutions. The nature of the Lisbon strategy, in turn, explains its ineffectualness. Without binding commitments brought about through the so-called 'Community method', including the use (or potential use) of qualified majority voting, national governments are unlikely to enact the measures necessary to achieve the Lisbon goals. By trying to breathe life into the Lisbon strategy, Barroso was making the most of the limited opportunities available to the Commission to boost the EU's economic performance.

Fewer and Better Legislative Proposals

Submitting legislative proposals is a key Commission prerogative. Indeed, it is one of the defining characteristics of the Commission in the EU system. Yet Barroso not only put the non-legislative Lisbon strategy at the top of his agenda, but also pledged to reduce the number (while improving the quality) of legislative proposals emanating from the Commission. A mantra of the lacklustre Santer Commission (1995–99), the idea of reducing the number

[2] For more on these developments, see David Howarth's contribution in this volume.

and improving the quality of legislative proposals became a mainstay of the Barroso Commission in 2005. Rather than legislating for the sake of doing so, the Commission would justify its proposals on the basis of appropriateness (is *any* legislation necessary?) and subsidiarity (is *European-level* legislation necessary?). Apart from those criteria, the Commission strengthened its system for screening proposals based on the legislation's probable impact and conformity with the Charter of Fundamental Rights. While eminently sensible, the idea of scaling back legislative output looked to some supporters of the Community method like a renunciation of the Commission's traditional role and responsibility, and exposed Barroso to criticism of favouring intergovernmentalism over supranationalism.

Improving the quality of legislative proposals would surely be more difficult than reducing their number, which at least is quantifiable. The services directive was already being attacked for favouring business interests over worker concerns. Ironically, the other highly contentious proposal wending its way through the legislative process in 2005 – the regulatory framework for the registration, evaluation and authorization of chemicals (REACH) – was under fire for sacrificing the chemicals industry to environmental and consumer interests. Clearly, the beauty of legislative proposals was in the eye of the beholder. That said, non-business organizations are generally privileged interlocutors when the Commission drafts legislative proposals, whereas business organizations, despite being better funded, are often at a disadvantage. As Barroso acknowledged, there would have to be wider and better consultation in the pre-proposal stage in order to improve the quality of the Commission's draft legislation.

The Commission emphasized the importance of reducing the number of new and existing proposals, as well as culling the corpus of EU legislation, in its work programme for 2005 and in its five-year plan, both of which were adopted early in the year. Yet it was not until September, partly in response to the rejection of the Constitutional Treaty, that the Commission (2005b) came up with a list of 68 proposals to be scrapped. Some of these were redundant or duplicative; others were mired in the decision-making process and seemed unlikely ever to be enacted. In a speech to the European Parliament, Verheugen claimed that the Commission's 'new simplification initiative' was an exercise in reregulation rather than deregulation (an ideologically loaded word), which would help dispel the notion that the EU was a 'bureaucratic monster' (European Parliament, 2005a). Members of the European Parliament (MEPs) were lukewarm. After all, the Parliament thrives on legislative proposals and many of its members saw lurking behind the Commission's initiative the hand of European business, which loudly complains about over-regulation in Brussels. The Council's response to the Commission's initiative was mixed, reflecting

Member States' interest in particular proposals despite their frequent criticism of the Commission's alleged appetite for initiating legislation. 'Legislating less' was therefore more easily said than done, both for political reasons and because of a legal challenge in the Parliament to the Commission's right to withdraw proposals that were already at the second reading stage of the co-decision procedure.

Explaining the EU

Apart from its intrinsic merit, reducing the number and improving the quality of legislative proposals would deny eurosceptics some ammunition to fire at the EU. Yet its public relations value was limited. The challenge of explaining the EU to a jaundiced and unreceptive public was formidable, as the outcome of the French and Dutch referendums showed. The Barroso Commission had made the goal of 'communicating Europe' another one of its priorities, well before the ratification upset. The Commission's (2005c) work programme for 2005, adopted in January, noted optimistically that the debate on the Constitutional Treaty presented 'an opportunity to enhance public understanding of the EU'. Wallström, one of the most experienced members of the Barroso Commission, assumed responsibility for communications strategy in addition to relations with other institutions.

She faced an uphill task. National governments reflexively blame Brussels – usually meaning the Commission – for unpopular actions or decisions involving the EU, while readily taking the credit for any good news. The Brussels press corps, reputedly one of the largest in the world, is organized along national lines and reinforces the governments' approach to explaining EU affairs. The organization and conduct of business in the Parliament defy easy explanation and lend themselves to ridicule in the national media. Coverage of European integration in curricula, especially at the primary and secondary school levels, is generally lamentable throughout the EU.

Wallström first sought to devise a communications strategy for the Commission, then for the EU as a whole. Following a special seminar of the college in April, the Commission decided to draw up an action plan for itself and, based on consultation with the Parliament, Member States and other interested parties, a White Paper on communications for the EU more broadly. The Commission (2005d) eventually approved its own action plan in late July. This included steps such as integrating a communications stratagem into each Commission proposal, inculcating in senior officials a more professional and proactive approach to communications, and improving the communications expertise and effectiveness of Commission offices in the national capitals.

The promised White Paper proved more difficult to draft. Parliament sympathized with the Commission's dilemma and had long acknowledged the challenges of explaining the EU, not least because of the abysmal turnout in direct elections over the years. Indeed, in May 2005 Parliament debated a Commission paper on communications, but a paper presented a year earlier by the Prodi Commission, not the paper then being discussed by the Barroso Commission. The debate demonstrated Parliament's reluctance to co-ordinate communications too closely with the other institutions and preference for its own pet project: the launch of a European Parliament television channel. Despite the obvious need following the referendums in France and the Netherlands to explain the EU, the Commission was unable to complete its promised White Paper before the end of the year.

In the meantime, the Commission received a special mandate at the June 2005 European Council to play a leading part in the public debate on the future of the EU during the period of reflection. The Commission considered how best to proceed at a special seminar of the college at the end of September, shortly after the German general election and a month before the summit called by the British presidency to discuss the challenge of globalization and the survivability of the European social model. Barroso looked forward to the summit as an opportunity to refocus his attention and that of the EU on economic growth and job creation. As for the period of reflection, he had been among the first EU leaders to concede that the Constitutional Treaty was dead in the water and that the EU needed to win public confidence by delivering concrete benefits for its citizens.

Nevertheless Barroso agreed that, as part of the public debate on the EU's future, he and the other commissioners would travel more often to the Member States in order to engage national governments, parliaments and civic groups in discussions about the Constitutional Treaty. This was a key component of 'plan D for democracy, dialogue and debate', the 'road map' intended to guide the EU through the period of reflection, which Wallström drafted and the Commission (2005e) released in October. Other important parts of plan D, none of them new, included calls for greater transparency in Council decision-making and improving the consultation process in EU decision-making. As was the case with the wider communications strategy, plan D reflected the difficulty of explaining and popularizing the EU. At least the Commission was making an effort. By contrast, there was little evidence by the end of 2005 that the Member States – with a few notable exceptions such as Ireland and Spain – were using the period of reflection to promote public understanding of the EU.

II. A Confident Parliament

The confidence of the Parliament seemed unaffected by the fate of the Constitutional Treaty. That was hardly surprising, given that not even the record low turnout in the direct elections of June 2004 had dented the institution's self-assurance. For a directly-elected body – indeed, as it liked to remind the Commission and the Council, the only directly-elected institution at the European level – Parliament appeared to be strikingly out of touch with public opinion. Whereas the Commission and most national governments appreciated the implications of the French and Dutch referendums results, Parliament often gave the impression that nothing much had changed. Reflecting the opinion of a majority of parliamentarians, the leaders of the three biggest political groups advocated pressing ahead with the ratification process regardless of the results in France and the Netherlands, and excoriated Barroso for his supposed defeatism in declaring the Constitutional Treaty moribund.

Relations with the Commission

The confidence of the Parliament, and its assertiveness *vis-à-vis* the Commission, was fully apparent in early 2005 when the two institutions negotiated a framework agreement to govern their relations for the remainder of Barroso's mandate. The investiture of the Barroso Commission by the Parliament in late 2004, discussed in last year's *Review*, provided the backdrop to the negotiations and to a separate parliamentary report on the investiture procedure itself. Having forced Barroso to abandon Rocco Buttiglioni, the commissioner-designate for justice, freedom and security, in November 2004 on the grounds that Buttiglioni was a bigot, Parliament pressed for even greater oversight of the Commission. In the case of Buttiglioni, however, the Socialist Group in Parliament had made the running, and Barroso had been able to drop Buttiglioni only because the Italian prime minister had decided to withdraw support for his appointee to the Commission. Nevertheless Parliament as a whole saw the episode as evidence of its growing power and as justification for gaining additional authority.

The negotiation of the framework agreement and Parliament's internal deliberations on the investiture procedure moved along separate tracks, but overlapped on the question of how to deal with a commissioner-designate who might be appointed to replace an existing commissioner during the mandate of the Barroso Commission. As for the regular investiture procedure, Andrew Duff, a prominent member of the Liberal Group, recommended in a draft report that a single 'grand committee' conduct the hearings, rather than have sepa-rate committees conduct hearings for each commissioner-designate, based on that person's portfolio. That idea never got beyond the Constitutional Affairs Committee, which felt that such a move would marginalize most MEPs and confine the process to a small number of powerful members. Nevertheless the committee supported Duff's efforts to improve co-ordination between the committees in order to boost the quality of the questions and facilitate a comparison of the answers.

Duff also failed to get the support of the Constitutional Affairs Committee for a proposal to bring forward the date of the direct elections from June to May, on the grounds that being seated one month earlier would increase the ability of the newly-elected Parliament to influence the national governments' selection of a Commission President-designate and the other commissioners-designate. While sympathizing with Duff's objective, most of the committee's members thought that national governments would never agree to the proposal if only for the practical reason that the proliferation of public holidays in the month of May precluded the possibility of finding an uninterrupted period (from Thursday to Sunday) for holding the elections. The Constitutional Affairs Committee's final report, which Parliament approved in June 2005, did not change radically the investiture procedure but signalled Parliament's determination to tighten scrutiny of the Commission (European Parliament, 2005b).

The Commission did not object strongly to anything in the Parliament's report on the investiture procedure, but took exception to many of its demands in the proposed new framework agreement. There were a number of controversial issues. One had to do with the appointment of new commissioners during the lifetime of the Barroso Commission. Pressed by the Socialist Group, Parliament wanted the right to hold a hearing and take a vote on such commissioners-designate. The Commission countered that mid-term appointments were entirely the prerogative of the national governments. Nevertheless the Commission agreed that a hearing and vote could take place, and that the outcome would be politically significant. In other words, if the vote of the Committee and of the entire Parliament was negative, the commissioner-designate would have great difficulty functioning in the Commission. But it would be up to the national government in question to withdraw its politically-handicapped new commissioner.

Another contentious item was the censure procedure for the Commission President. Under what circumstances could the Parliament vote to censure Barroso? Would he be forced to resign? The eventual agreement was far from clear-cut, with the Parliament conceding that a vote of censure could be called only for substantive reasons and would have to garner widespread support. The issue was not academic, as a group of 77 parliamentarians introduced a motion to censure Barroso in May 2005, following media reports that the Commission President had taken a vacation the previous August on the yacht of an old friend, a wealthy businessman whose interests were subject to EU regulation (as are the interests of all business people in the EU, wealthy or not). Cognizant of the recent discussions on the framework agreement and aware of the sensitive timing of the censure motion (only days before the French referendum), the leaders of the four main political groups rallied around Barroso, who faced his accusers during a plenary session of the Parliament on 25 May. Barroso easily survived the motion, which won the support of only 35 members, one of whom, a British Conservative, was promptly expelled from the Group of the European People's Party and European Democrats (EPP-ED).

How to handle already identified cases of conflict of interest involving competition commissioner Neelie Kroes also proved divisive during the negotiations for the framework agreement. Kroes had conceded after her investiture hearings that she would disqualify herself from the cases in question. The Greens/European Free Alliance wanted Barroso to inform Parliament before he acted on such cases, either on his own or by assigning them to another commissioner. Barroso countered that this would undermine the independence of the Commission, but agreed to inform Parliament once he had decided how to proceed in each case. Soon after signing the framework agreement, the Commission announced that McCreevy would handle Kroes's conflict-of-interest cases.

As is often the case, Parliament used the opportunity of the framework agreement negotiations to press for greater power on a wide range of issues. One of the most brazen examples of this was Parliament's demand for full representation alongside the Commission in international negotiations covering areas of Community competence. The Commission managed to maintain the *status quo* (the Parliament already has observer status). The Commission succeeded as well in restricting the Parliament's encroachment into the formal consultative process that precedes the drafting of legislative proposals.

Despite these apparent Commission victories, the conduct of the negotiations – and in many cases their outcome – demonstrated Parliament's remorseless push for additional influence in the EU system, especially at the expense of the Commission. The negotiations had been conducted at the highest level – with Barroso and Wallström representing the Commission and Barroso's counterpart (Josep Borrell Fontelles) and the leaders of the political groups representing the Parliament – and had taken up a considerable amount of time. As part of the new framework, concluded on 27 May, Wallström agreed to meet every three months with the leaders of the political groups, thereby tying the Commission's hands a little tighter in its dealings with the Parliament.

Group Politics

The effort to censure Barroso had resulted in a rare case of cross-party support for him – or at least support from the four main political groups. Otherwise, throughout 2005 the Socialist Group frequently and often aggressively opposed

Barroso, whereas the centre-right EPP-ED Group and the Liberals generally supported him. Martin Schulz, leader of the Socialist Group, led the charge against Barroso, calling on him early in the year to be a 'neutral and independent [Commission] President', and citing 'worrying evidence' that Barroso was ideologically biased (*European Report*, 2 February 2005, p. 1). Yet Barroso had made no secret of his centre-right orientation. Indeed, the EPP-ED Group had pressed for the appointment of a like-minded Commission President following its victory in the June 2004 direct elections. It was accepted, therefore, that the Commission President was entitled to have an ideological orientation and to act accordingly. It was also understood, however, that by its nature the Commission is a 'grand coalition', whose members represent the spectrum of opinion corresponding to the ideological positions of the national governments, and that the preferences of the President are constrained accordingly. For instance, Verheugen and Wallström, two of the most influential of Barroso's commissioners, are social democrats.

Schulz's dogged criticism of Barroso succeeded in raising the profile of the Socialist Group (and with it the group's leader) and introducing a sharp political edge into the Parliament's proceedings. It followed on from the reshuffle of commissioners-designate (notably Buttiglione) and portfolios at the end of the investiture hearings, an outcome due largely to Schulz's agitation. Buoyed by that development, Schulz spent much of 2005 confronting Barroso. In February, he attacked the Commission President for participating in a short television spot supporting the Social Democratic Party, which Barroso had led before moving to Brussels, in the forthcoming Portuguese elections. Schulz claimed that this was a violation of the Commission's code of conduct; Barroso argued otherwise. In the event, the Social Democratic Party lost decisively and the issue faded away.

Mostly, Schulz attacked Barroso on ideological grounds. He used the occasion of a debate in the Parliament on January 26, on the Commission's strategy paper, 'Europe 2010', to denounce Barroso's advocacy of economic reform apparently at the expense of social cohesion. Schulz continued the attack in a parliamentary debate on 21 February, on the Commission's 2005 Work Programme, which the Socialist Group voted not to approve (it was carried by 241 to 201 votes on 24 February). The Commission's paper on revising the Lisbon strategy gave Schulz another chance several days later to return to the charge. By that time Barroso was scaling back his reformist rhetoric and agenda. Under intense pressure from Chirac and the entire French government, together with the Socialist Group (whose French members constituted the largest national bloc), the Commission decided in early March to revise the services directive, which had become a battleground not so much between left and right but, as Barroso put it, between 'modernizers and reactionaries' (*Financial Times*, 29 March 2005, p. 7).

The Liberals complained that 'Socialist hostility to President Barroso's Commission shows an excess of zeal over common sense' (*European Report*, 26 February 2005, p. 3). For his part, Hans-Gert Pöttering, leader of the EPP-ED Group, seemed continuously outmanœuvred by Schulz, who set the political pace in Parliament despite the Socialists' inferiority *vis-à-vis* the combined weight of the EPP-ED Group and the Liberals (214 versus 354 seats). With fewer opportunities to criticize Barroso on ideological grounds once the Commission President moderated his position, Schulz instead attacked Barroso for promising to introduce fewer legislative proposals and withdraw some existing ones, and for his alleged abandonment of the Constitutional Treaty after the French and Dutch referendums.

Antonio Vitorino, a member of the Prodi Commission and a shrewd observer of EU affairs, commented at the end of 2005 that, in the year since the appointment of the Barroso Commission, 'party politics have played a key role in the … relationship between the Parliament and the Commission' (Durand, 2006, p. 58). The emergence of a sharp divide between the main political groups in the Parliament, along quasi-government/opposition lines, helped to raise the institution's profile and, arguably, its appeal. Not that many people were aware of what was happening in Brussels and Strasbourg, however. Most media coverage of the Parliament was superficial and misleading, and Parliament itself was partly to blame. Aware of that fact, Parliament attempted in 2005 to improve the conduct of its plenary sessions. Agreement by Parliament and the Council on the statute for Members of the European Parliament, a long-awaited reform of MEPs' pay and expenses, also helped to cast Parliament in a better light.

Parliamentary Reform

Dealing with unruly members who blacken the image of the institution is a problem that all parliaments face. The problem became pressing for the European Parliament in January, during a protest against the Constitutional Treaty. Some eurosceptics dressed up as wolves and bears; others sang the *Internationale*. Their point was that the Constitutional Treaty was predatory and would turn the EU into a communist dictatorship. The effect was to make a laughing stock of the plenary session. An outburst by members of the Northern League during a visit to the Parliament by Italian President Carlo Ciampi in July revived the issue of rowdy behaviour. A majority of members agreed that such conduct was unacceptable, but could not agree on what to do about it. The Constitutional Affairs Committee grappled with the problem throughout 2005 and proposed various disciplinary measures, including a lengthy suspension from the chamber and forfeiture of generous daily allowances. When push came to shove, most members were squeamish about instituting strict sanctions. As a result, the committee's report was carried over into the following year.

The antics of parliamentarians at the national level inevitably attract media attention, but do not necessarily dent the institution's reputation. By contrast, the European Parliament is particularly vulnerable to criticism because of its weak public support and poor media portrayal. The long-standing problem of large discrepancies in MEPs' pay and abuse of allowances, much more insidious than the carry-on of some eurosceptics, was finally resolved in 2005. Because MEPs' salaries are linked to those of national parliamentarians, some MEPs receive a low monthly payment while others receive more than ten times as much. A loose system of reimbursement for travel expenses allows MEPs to top up their salaries, whether those salaries are low or not. In particular, MEPs are allowed to claim the full economy-class air fare for travel between their constituencies and Brussels or Strasbourg, even if they travel by less expensive means.

Over the years, this situation became a major cause of embarrassment for the Parliament in particular and the EU in general. It reached new heights of absurdity after enlargement in May 2004, when the differences in salaries between MEPs became indefensible. For instance, a Lithuanian MEP currently earns as little as €800 a month, whereas an Italian MEP receives more than €12,000 a month. The idea of MEPs holding the Commission to high financial standards while receiving travel reimbursements without having to show receipts was also unsustainable. The solution – standardizing MEPs' salaries and reforming the system of reimbursement – seemed obvious. The challenge was to agree on a common salary and on a taxation regime. Germany and Sweden were adamant that MEPs should not earn more than national parliamentarians and should be subject to national taxation, and the issue even threatened to intrude into the German federal election campaign. In the end, a concerted effort by the Luxembourg presidency, together with the changing dynamics of qualified majority voting (thanks to enlargement, the group of countries that had been holding up an agreement no longer constituted a blocking minority), brought about a resolution, which Parliament approved on 23 June and the Council endorsed on 18 July. In future, MEPs will receive the same salary (€7,000 a month), subject to EU taxation and, depending on the Member State, to national taxation, and will have to show receipts for their travel expenses. Not every MEP or national government was happy with the settlement, which finally removed a persistent sore in Council–Parliament relations and a blot on Parliament's image.

Conclusion

In the shadow of the Constitutional Treaty, EU governance and institutional developments were far from satisfactory in 2005. Relations between the national leaders set a bad tone. Blair and Chirac were at loggerheads, but managed to show some amity at the October summit. Perhaps chastened by the lingering domestic effects of the French referendum and sensitive to Schröder's imminent departure, Chirac thought it best to reconcile with Blair. Schröder made an ill-tempered departure from the European scene at the summit. Merkel, his successor, provided a breath of fresh air at the following summit, in December, where she helped to broker an agreement on the budget and subtly signalled her independence of Chirac. Barroso was conspicuous by his absence from the bargaining on the budget, which, although inherently an intergovernmental process, does not preclude the participation of the Commission President.

The number and significance of the national elections held in 2005 had a bearing on EU governance, given the centrality of national governments in the EU system. Britain's election in May held up the budget negotiations. Germany's elections in September, followed by the delay in forming a new government, impaired the conduct of EU affairs. Poland's elections in October and November not only diminished the effectiveness of the country's EU involvement during the campaign and elections themselves, but also brought to power a government and president highly critical of many EU programmes and policies. In an EU of 25 or more Member States, the frequency of national elections is bound to become problematical for the smooth operation of EU governance.

With the shelving of the Constitutional Treaty, the Council presidency will survive in its current form beyond 2006. The lessons from 2005 suggest that the presidency is not as ineffective as its detractors claim. A small, original Member State (Luxembourg) and a large, later entrant (Britain) produced workmanlike presidencies,[3] Luxembourg's record being marred somewhat by Juncker's overbearing behaviour at the June summit and overwrought performance at the concluding press conference and follow-up speech in the European Parliament.

The activities of the presidency and the European Council receive considerable media attention. Beneath such exalted heights, the humdrum activities of EU governance attract less notice and are little understood. Most citizens appreciate the importance of the EU in their daily lives, but do not comprehend the EU system and are somewhat cynical about EU institutions. The Constitutional Treaty is a step in the right direction, but its implementation, however unlikely in the immediate future, would not necessarily improve the

---

[3] For reports on the Luxembourg and UK presidencies see the contributions by Derek Hearl and Richard Whitman, respectively, in this volume.

EU's popular standing. The problem of the European public's estrangement from the EU, so obvious throughout 2005, seems deep-rooted and endemic.

Key Readings

Durand (2006) contains incisive, up-to-date analysis and commentary on the EU's key decision-making institutions.

Commission (2005c) provides a useful outline of its immediate objectives and approach to inter-institutional relations.

Commission (2005d, e) are a salutary reminder of the difficulty of connecting with European citizens, despite the urgency of doing so.

Commission (2005f) provides an interesting insight into the formal *modus operandi* of a core EU institution.

References

Commission of the European Communities (2005a) 'Strategic Objectives 2005–2009, Europe 2010: A Partnership for European Renewal; Prosperity, Solidarity and Security'. Communication from the President in agreement with Vice-President Wallström, COM(2005)12 final, Brussels, 26 January, available at «http://europa. eu.int/eur-lex/lex/LexUriServ/site/en/com/2005/com2005_0012en01.pdf».

Commission of the European Communities (2005b) 'Outcome of the screening of legislative proposals pending before the Legislator'. Communication from the Commission to the Council and the European Parliament, COM(2005)462 final, Brussels, 27 September, available at «http://www.europa.eu.int/comm/enterprise/ regulation/better_regulation/docs/en_br_final.pdf».

Commission of the European Communities (2005c) 'Commission Work Programme for 2005'. Communication from the President in agreement with Vice-President Wallström, COM(2005)15 final, Brussels, 26 January, available at «http://europa. eu.int/eur-lex/lex/LexUriServ/site/en/com/2005/com2005_0015en01.pdf».

Commission of the European Communities (2005d) 'Action Plan to Improve Communicating Europe by the Commission'. Communication from the President in agreement with Vice-President Wallström, COM (2005),XXX Final, Brussels, July 27, available at http://europa.eu.int/comm/dgs/communication/pdf/communication_ com_en.pdf

Commission of the European Communities (2005e) 'The Commission's contribution to the period of reflection and beyond: Plan-D for Democracy, Dialogue and Debate'. Communication from the Commission to the Council, the European Parliament, the European Economic and Social Committee and the Committee of the Regions, COM(2005)494 final, Brussels, 13 October, available at «http://www.europa.eu.int/ eur-lex/lex/LexUriServ/site/en/com/2005/com2005_0494en01.pdf».

Commission of the European Communities (2005f) 'Commission Decision of 15 November 2005 amending its Rules of Procedure'. Official Journal of the European Union, L 347/83, 30 December 30, available at «http://europa.eu.int/eur-lex/lex/LexUriServ/site/en/oj/2005/l_347/l_34720051230en00830090.pdf».

Durand, G. (ed.) (2006) 'After the Annus Horribilis: A Review of the EU Institutions'. EPC Working Paper No. 22, European Policy Centre, Brussels, January, available at «http://www.theepc.be/TEWN/pdf/119591455_JD%20template%20for%20WPS.pdf».

European Parliament (2005a) Günter Verheugen, Vice-President of the European Commission, 'The New Simplification Initiative'. European Parliament, Strasbourg, 25 October, available at «http://europa.eu.int/rapid/pressReleasesAction.do?reference=SPEECH/05/640&format=HTML&aged=0&language=EN&guiLanguage=en».

European Parliament (2005b) 'Report on guidelines for the approval of the European Commission'. (2005/2024(INI)), Committee on Constitutional Affairs, Rapporteur Andrew Duff, A6-0179/2005 final, 7 June, available at «http://www.europarl.eu.int/omk/sipade3?PUBREF=-//EP//NONSGML+REPORT+A6-2005-0179+0+DOC+PDF+V0//EN&L=EN&LEVEL=0&NAV=S&LSTDOC=Y».

JCMS 2006 Volume 44 Annual Review pp. 81–99

Internal Economic and Social Policy Developments

DAVID HOWARTH
University of Edinburgh

Introduction

Three internal policy agreements attracted considerable attention in 2005: the mid-term review of the Lisbon process; Stability and Growth Pact reform, both agreed at the March European Council; and the financial framework for 2007–13, agreed at the December European Council. The latter two were subject to prolonged, intense and often acrimonious debate between Member State governments. The mid-term review of the Lisbon process sought to address the concerns raised in the 2004 Kok report which criticized the Member States for insufficient progress in meeting the strategy's goals and called for much greater urgency in implementing practical measures. The broad goals and revised measures of the Lisbon process shaped the specific goals, action plans and thematic strategies adopted in each major internal policy area. Another renewed theme in 2005 was 'better lawmaking' – improved governance – considered a main instrument in achieving core goals of the Lisbon process. Commission action plans and strategies in several policy areas incorporated mechanisms to strengthen and simplify the regulatory environment by improving the drafting of legislation and reinforcing implementation and compliance – to address more effectively the concerns of inefficiencies and over-regulation.

I. Economic and Related Policies

The Lisbon Process: Competitiveness, Growth and Employment

The mid-term review of the ten-year Lisbon process launched in 2000 showed mixed results in the goal of transforming the EU into the 'most competitive and dynamic knowledge-based economy in the world' by 2010. On the basis of the Kok report from 2004 and the 2 February Commission communication, 'Working together for growth and jobs – A new start for the Lisbon Process', the March European Council relaunched and refocused the key economic, social and environmental targets of the process. As part of its better law-making strategy, the Commission called for the enhanced 'ownership' of the Lisbon process by all stakeholders and the development of a partnership supported by European Union and national programmes involving firm commitments to advance the process. On 12 July, the Council adopted the first implementation measures for 2005–08 (integrated guidelines, including broad economic policy and employment guidelines) on the basis of recommendations made by the Commission on 12 April. On 20 July, the Commission presented the Lisbon programme to accompany national action programmes on growth and employment. The Commission focused on areas where the EU could provide added value, including: completing the internal market for services; reforming state aid policy; removing obstacles to physical labour and academic mobility; supporting knowledge and innovation throughout the EU; supporting policies that seek to address the social consequences of economic restructuring; developing a common approach to economic migration; improving and simplifying the regulatory framework in which businesses operate; and completing a far-reaching agreement in the Doha round of WTO multilateral trade talks.

Enterprise and the 'Information Society'

A significant part of the Lisbon process is the stimulation of innovation, entrepreneurship and new communication and information technologies. On 6 April, the Commission proposed setting up the first competitiveness and innovation framework programme (CIP) to be implemented over the 2007–13 period. The aim of the CIP is to bring together all the relevant Community support programmes into one of three streams: entrepreneurship and innovation; information and communication technologies; and the promotion of 'intelligent energy'. The CIP proposed financial instruments for small and medium-sized enterprises (SMEs). On 12 October, the Commission set out guidelines on strengthening research and innovation as part of the partnership for growth and employment. Applying its better law-making strategy, the Commission recommended an impact assessment for measures that might affect competitiveness.

The Commission joined with the British Council Presidency to organize a Risk Capital summit in October which emphasized the lack of a single market for venture capital. On 5 October, the Commission – in response to the European Council's invitation from October 2003 – presented its framework for strengthening manufacturing which emphasizes a more integrated approach to industrial policy. The Commission also presented a communication on a modern SME policy for growth and employment which recommends a framework for the more consistent use of enterprise policy instruments and a consideration of the impact upon SMEs of all EU policies ('think small first'). In February, the Commission adopted the fifth annual report on the implementation of the European Charter for Small Enterprises which also recommends the promotion of co-operative societies in Europe.

There were several significant developments in the automobiles and chemicals sectors. The Commission co-ordinated the CARS 21 group ('Competitive automotive regulatory system for the 21st century'), which adopted its final report on 12 December, making specific recommendation to improve the competitiveness of the EU automobile industry. On 21 December, the Commission proposed the introduction of common standards limiting the emission of atmospheric pollutants from motor vehicles ('Euro 5'). In the chemicals sector, there was ongoing debate on the REACH project to set a new legislative framework, on which the Council reached an agreement on 13 December.

Research

The EU continued with its ongoing efforts to create a single European research area (ERA) through the integration of financial and human resources with the scientific and technological capacity of Member States and promoting synergies among various research areas, targeting seven research priority areas and increasing overall spending on research to 3 per cent of gross domestic product (GDP) in 2010 (up from 1.9 per cent in 2005). On 6 April the Commission presented a communication reminding the Member States of the importance of the ERA to the Lisbon objective, calling for several measures including tax incentives, modification of rules on intellectual property rights and state aid, and reinforcing ties between universities and business. On 7 June, the Commission produced its action plan for 2005–09 on improving research in the nanosciences and nanotechnologies and the co-ordination of activities in this area by European industry, research bodies, universities and financial institutions to ensure industrial applications from research. On 29 June, the Commission produced a report on promoting life sciences and the biotechnology sector through, for example, a simplified European patent system and pharmaceutical legislation. The Commission continued its preparation of the seventh research framework programme designed to consolidate the ERA and to run for seven years (2007–13). The new programme sets out guidelines for the joint research centre (JRC) and includes several specific programmes (outlined by the Commission on 21 September) including the 'Co-operation', 'Ideas', 'People', 'Capacities' and Euratom programmes.

A major component of the ERA is to be the European space policy which also embraces a multi-sectoral approach that combines a specific industrial policy, effective investment and management instruments, and co-operation between Member State governments. 'Security and space' is also a theme of the seventh research framework programme. On 23 May, the Commission presented a communication on the European space policy which identified major projects, including GMES ('Global monitoring for environment and security'), the Galileo satellite navigation programme, and research into satellite communications technology under the i2010 initiative.

Economic and Monetary Union (EMU)

On 20 March 2005, the EU ministers of finance reached a formal agreement on a reform to the Stability and Growth Pact (SGP), the formal aspects of which were finalized on 27 June. This agreement followed several months of intense and often acrimonious debate between Member State governments. Under the new Pact, there is considerably greater scope for counterclaim in the event of non-compliance with existing fiscal policy rules, given that Member States can justify their excessive deficits with reference to numerous factors. Furthermore, the increased uncertainty that surrounds the determination of acceptable medium-term balances makes it even more difficult for Ecofin to trigger sanctions against errant Member States (see Amy Verdun's contribution in this volume for further discussion).

On 1 June the Commission published its sixth report on public finances in EMU, which noted progress on deficits, but stressed the need for continued fiscal consolidation to bring down debt levels. On 11 October the Council adopted a new code of conduct to improve the consistent implementation of the SGP and the guidelines for stability and convergence programmes. On 12 December, the Council agreed an amendment on the rules governing the quality of statistical data with regard to the excessive deficit procedure (EDP) which, among various matters, endorses (but does not impose) best national practice for the compilation and transmission of data. Further preparation took place for the enlargement of the euro area, with the Commission producing its second report on 4 November. On 18 January, the Council – problematically – endorsed the Commission's opinion (December 2004) that the EDP launched with regard to France and Germany be dropped as the governments were taking the necessary measures to remedy the situation. On 16 February, the Council noted progress by the Dutch government to reduce its deficit, criticized the Greek and Hungarian governments for the insufficiency of their efforts, recommending their adoption of additional necessary measures, and noted the risk of persistently excessive deficits in the UK, Portugal and Italy.

Internal Market Developments

The further development of the internal market is presented as a major element of the Lisbon process. With regard to the free movement of goods, the Commission continued to monitor mutual recognition (recording 168 new complaints and cases in 2005) and to seek to prevent the creation of new barriers. By 1 December, there were 664 measures (involving all goods) notified to the Commission by Member States. The Commission made 48 reasoned opinions in response to notifications from 2005 and earlier and there were several national legislative readjustments to conform to Community law. The Council and Parliament adopted several directives to further the harmonization of technical regulations (health, safety and environmental protection): six on motor vehicles, and one each on dangerous preparations, noise emissions by machines, medicinal products and on eco-design requirements for energy-using products. To tackle the persistent transposition deficit in the Member States on internal market legislation in a more effective manner, the Commission recommended the reinforcement of administrative co-operation and introduced reforms to improve the operation of the 'Solvit' information network.

With regard to services, intense controversy surrounded the far-reaching liberalization of the proposed services directive – widely referred to as the Bolkestein directive. As a result there was extensive redrafting by the Council. By the end of the year the proposal had cleared scrutiny in the European Parliament's committees. In the area of services of general interest, on 23 March the Commission produced a report on the application of the directive on postal services which confirmed that overall the reform of the postal sector in the EU was well on track.

The Commission engaged in broad consultation on financial services as a follow-up to its 2000–04 action plan in this area. Emphasis has been placed on implementing existing legislation. Adding to the more than three dozen directives already adopted in this area, the Council and Parliament agreed new legislation on motor vehicle insurance and reinsurance. The Parliament adopted the directive on capital adequacy of investment firms and credit institutions, with final Council approval to come. The Commission presented proposals for a directive on payment services and a regulation on information on the payer accompanying transfers of funds. On 1 December, the Commission adopted a

White Paper on financial services policy (2005–10) and it published three Green Papers for public consultation: financial services policy (2005–10) (3 May) which focused on progressing the single financial market; the enhancement of the EU framework for investment funds (12 July); and mortgage credit in the EU (19 July). With regard to capital movements – and specifically ongoing efforts to combat money laundering, crime and terrorism – the Council and Parliament adopted a regulation and a directive: the former on controls on cash entering or leaving the Community requiring travellers carrying more than €10,000 (or the equivalent) to make a declaration on entry to and departure from the EU; the latter on the prevention of the use of the financial system for the purpose of money laundering, incorporating the 40 recommendations of the international financial action task force (FATF) as revised in June 2003.

In the area of company law and corporate governance, the Council and Parliament adopted a directive to facilitate cross-border mergers which was designed to reduce the obstacles caused by differences in national laws. The Parliament approved another directive (yet to be adopted by the Council) which sought to address concerns raised by the Parmalat affair and strengthen the credibility of financial information by improving the statutory auditing of company accounts, with revisions to the fourth and seventh directives on company law with regard to accounting. In the area of intellectual property, the Parliament rejected at second reading the proposed directive on the patentability of computer-implemented inventions, on the grounds that the Council had not incorporated the Parliament's amendments. On 1 December, the Council and Parliament reached an agreement at first reading on the proposal for a regulation allowing EU-based companies to produce copies of patented medicines under licence for export to developing countries without the authorization of the patent holder. By thus aligning EU policy with the WTO General Council decision, the aim was to send a political signal for negotiations at the WTO ministerial conference in Hong Kong. The Commission also presented a report (14 July) on the development of patent law in the field of biotechnology and genetic engineering. With regard to data protection concerns, the Parliament refused its assent to an EC–Canada agreement authorizing airlines running flights from the EU and Canada to transmit certain passenger data to Canadian authorities. The Parliament had already appealed against an earlier agreement on such data between the EU and the United States.

With regard to labour mobility, on 7 September, the Council and Parliament adopted a directive on the recognition of professional qualifications, the outcome of a three-year long legislative process. This first major transformation of the EU system of labour mobility since its conception in the 1960s involved efforts to create a more uniform, transparent and flexible system, incorporating 15 previous directives into one. New reference levels for qualifications were established while national requirements were protected. With regard to regulated professions, the professional and disciplinary rules of the host Member State are to apply (a rule covering the temporary provision of cross-border services). Medical and dental specializations are to be automatically recognized in other Member States under certain conditions. The Commission also proposed a European quality charter for mobility to support trans-national mobility for education and training.

Taxation

Taxation is seen by the Commission and some Member States as another area where further co-operation is necessary to meet the Lisbon objectives. On 27 October, the Commission launched a communication to improve European competitiveness by reducing the negative effects – notably compliance costs and red tape – that coexisting national tax systems can have on market integration. On 1 July, directive 2003/48/EC came into force with a harmonized policy on the taxation of savings income from another Member State. With regard to business taxation, on 17 February, the Council agreed to amend the 1990 directive on deferred taxation for mergers between companies of different Member States, to cover a wider range of companies. On 23 December, the Commission presented a communication to tackle corporation tax obstacles with which SMEs active in more than one Member State are faced, adopting the 'home state taxation approach'. With regard to indirect taxation, on 17 October the Council adopted a regulation to bring about the more uniform application of EU common rules on value added tax (VAT), with the aim of improving transparency and legal certainty. On 12 December, the Council accepted the Commission's proposal to extend the minimum EU 15 per cent VAT rate to the end of 2010, but agreed that reduced rates would be reconsidered in 2006.

Competition and Industrial Policies

The Commission emphasizes the promotion of competition as part of the relaunched Lisbon process and has sought to continue an ongoing modernization of the policy since the May 2004 reform. In 2005, the Commission launched surveys of the gas and electricity markets and banking and insurance in June. The decision to set up an anti-cartel directorate within the directorate general for competition was meant to be a clear signal of the decision to prioritize action against cartels, viewed as particularly distorting for competition.

On 7 June, the Commission set out an action plan seeking an overhaul of state aid policy over a five-year period, focusing on the rationalization of procedures, the acceleration of decision-making and the reduction of the number of aid measures that must be notified to the Commission. The aim of the action plan is to make use of existing rules on state aid in the context of the Lisbon process to improve the competitiveness of industry, create sustainable jobs (with increased aid for research and risk capital targeted at small and medium-sized enterprises), ensure social and regional cohesion and improve public services. Putting into practice the objectives of the action plan, on 15 July the Commission adopted several measures to provide greater legal clarity for the financing of services of general economic interest.

On 21 December, the Commission set out new guidelines on regional aid (for 2007–13) provided by national governments establishing rules to determine the eligibility of regions – the poorest should be targeted – and maximum aid levels. In December, the Commission prolonged the framework for research and development state aid. In September, prior to the adoption of final measures, the Commission began consultation on state aid rules for projects encouraging innovation.

There were several additional reinforcements of competition policy in specific sectors. The start of October saw the abolition of the 'location' clauses created to prevent car dealers from opening vehicle distribution points outside geographical areas established by manufacturers. Towards the end of the year, the Commission published a Green Paper on damages actions for breach of EU anti-trust rules. On 6 September, the Commission published its guidelines on the provision of start-up aid for new routes opened by airlines from regional airports. The Commission seeks to encourage the development of regional airports, but wants to prevent the use of public resources from distorting competition.

There were several noteworthy Commission actions against companies and governments during 2005. There was an increase in the number of mergers notified to the Commission over 2004, 90 per cent of which were approved, with a small number subject to intense investigation. The Commission approved several major mergers (for example, between the German media companies Bertelsmann AG and Axel Springer AG) and take-overs (such as Siemens' takeover of VA Tech group subject to conditions of divestment from certain activities). In the area of abuse of dominant position, the Commission imposed a fine of €60 million on the pharmaceutical firm AstraZeneca for misusing the patent system and the procedures for marketing pharmaceuticals. Making use of new competition policy procedures allowing it to conclude an investigation into abuse of dominant position, the Commission adopted a decision that in effect made legally binding commitments made by Coca-Cola to end certain commercial practices.

There was a significant increase in the number of notifications of state aid (to 650), while the Commission made approximately 600 final decisions, disallowing the aid in 4 per cent of cases. The Commission did grant some explicit exemptions to the application of competition policy rules. Notably in April, it renewed until 2010 a block exemption which allows shipping companies to enter into consortia involving the transport of cargo in and out of the EU.

On 20 April and 9 December, the Commission published updated versions of its state aid scoreboard, noting that the 'downward trend in the overall level of aid had levelled off', with the vast majority of Member States responding '"no" to less aid but "yes" to better aid' to so-called horizontal objectives (including research and development, SMEs, environment and regional economic developments) (Commission, 2005, p. 4). The Commission also concluded that 'the share of horizontal aid has increased largely due to a sharp increase in aid for environmental and energy saving objectives coupled with a reduction in sectoral aid for some Member States, particularly to the coal sector' (Commission, 2005, p. 5). However, this share of total aid varied a great deal among the Member States, as did the progress of total aid levels. In roughly half the Member States, horizontal aid accounts for 90 per cent or more of the total; in France, Spain and Ireland horizontal aid accounts for around 60 per cent; while for others, including several new Member States and Portugal, horizontal aid accounts for 50 per cent or less. The total level of aid provided to the least developed regions increased considerably with enlargement. In some new Member States aid as a percentage of GDP dropped considerably due to the phasing out of pre-accession measures. Aid in relation to GDP increased markedly in France (restructuring of Alstom in 2004), and in Sweden and the UK because of a rise in horizontal aid, especially aid for the environment.

According to figures released in 2005, in 2004 – as in the previous three years – Germany, France and Italy (in that order) provided the most state aids (calculations excluding support for railways) (see Table 1; Commission 2005). As a percentage of GDP, Malta provided by far the most at 3.1 per cent, followed by Finland, the Czech Republic, Poland, Hungary and Portugal. The Greek government provided the least at 0.29 per cent, while another seven Member States – Belgium, Czech Republic, Estonia, Latvia, Luxembourg, the Netherlands and the UK – provided aid equivalent to less than 0.4 per cent of GDP. In 2004, state aid throughout the EU amounted to 0.6 per cent of GDP, 0.57 per cent in the EU-15 – very slightly up from the 0.56 per cent in 2003 – and 1.09 per cent in the ten new Member States. If aid to agriculture and fisheries is eliminated from calculations, state aid reached 0.44 per cent in the EU-25, 0.43 per cent in the EU-15 – again a slight increase from the 0.39 per cent in 2003 – and 0.70 per cent in the ten new Member States. More than €3 billion of aid was allowed by the Commission under block exemptions. Roughly €3.4 billion of unlawful aid has yet to be recovered.

Table 1: State Aid Awarded in the EU-25 Member States, 2004

	Total State Aid Less Railways in €bn	Total State Aid Less Agriculture, Fisheries and Transport in €bn	Total Aid Less Railways as % of GDP	Total Aid Less Agriculture, Fisheries and Transport as % of GDP
EU-25	61.6	45.5	0.60	0.44
EU-15	56.4	42.0	0.57	0.43
Ten new MS	5.2	3.4	1.09	0.70
Belgium	1.0	0.7	0.34	0.24
Czech Republic	0.4	0.2	0.41	0.19
Denmark	1.4	1.0	0.71	0.52
Germany	17.2	15.1	0.78	0.69
Estonia	0.0	0.0	0.39	0.09
Greece	0.5	0.3	0.29	0.20
Spain	4.0	3.1	0.47	0.37
France	8.9	6.3	0.54	0.39
Ireland	1.0	0.4	0.65	0.27
Italy	7.0	5.4	0.52	0.40
Cyprus	0.2	0.1	1.48	1.06
Latvia	0.0	0.0	0.39	0.16
Lithuania	0.1	0.0	0.68	0.13
Luxembourg	0.1	0.0	0.31	0.17
Hungary	1.0	0.7	1.26	0.87
Malta	0.1	0.1	3.10	2.71
Netherlands	1.8	0.9	0.39	0.18
Austria	1.4	0.5	0.61	0.22
Poland	2.9	2.0	1.47	1.01
Portugal	1.5	1.1	1.09	0.83
Slovenia	0.2	0.1	0.96	0.53
Slovakia	0.2	0.2	0.64	0.63
Finland	2.5	0.6	1.66	0.38
Sweden	2.7	2.2	0.99	0.80
UK	5.4	4.2	0.32	0.25

Source: DG Competition.
Notes: (Potentially) distortive state aid as defined under Article 87(1) EC Treaty that has been granted by the 25 EU Member States for all sectors except railways and has been examined by the Commission. Comprehensive data on transport are not yet available for the ten new Member States. All data are quoted at constant prices.

Structural Funds and Regional Policy

In May and July 2005, the Commission proposed a new framework for economic and social cohesion policy for the 2007–13 period, making use of the structural and cohesion funds in the context of the Lisbon process to target three priorities: economic growth and job creation in the least developed Member States and regions; competitiveness and employment; and territorial co-operation with the aim of a harmonious and balanced development of the EU. Applying its better law-making strategy, the Commission also proposed a reform to implementation with more strategic programming, a simplified and more transparent management system, greater decentralization of responsibilities and reinforcement of partnership. In a first reading vote, the Parliament endorsed all of the Commission's proposals.

II. Social Policies

2005 was the final year of the 'social agenda' set up by the December 2000 Nice European Council and the start of a new agenda (for the 2006–10 period) which the Commission presented on 9 February with the slogan that manages to be both unimaginative and unrealistic: 'A social Europe in the global economy: jobs and opportunities for all'. Welcomed by the European Council, the new agenda seeks to facilitate the modernization of national social policy systems and support the harmonious operation of the single market while 'ensuring respect for fundamental rights and common values'. The Commission also outlined necessary instruments to improve implementation of the agenda. With regard to employment policy, in April the Commission adopted a revised version of the guidelines for Member State policies. With regard to social protection and inclusion, the Commission adopted in January the draft of its joint report (adopted by the Council in March). Forming part of the annual assessment of the Lisbon process, this report presents the main conclusions drawn from the application of the open method of co-ordination and progress of national strategies in this area.

Several social policy developments improving the potential for worker mobility can be mentioned. The European health insurance card had met with some success and by June 2005, a year after its introduction it was being carried by more than 30 million people. In April, the Council agreed amendments designed to update and facilitate the application of legislation covering the application of social security schemes to workers and their families moving within the EU. On 20 October, following extensive consultation, the Commission presented a proposal for a directive to improve the 'portability' of supplementary pension rights, with the goal of making it easier for workers to change jobs and move from one country to another and reduce obstacles for acquiring pension rights, preserving 'dormant' pension rights and the transferability of acquired rights. The Commission also proposed the organization of a 'European year of workers' mobility 2006 – towards a European labour market'.

On 1 June, as a follow-up to its 2004 Green Paper on equality and non-discrimination in an enlarged EU, the Commission presented a framework strategy focusing on the provision of effective legal protection against discrimination. The Commission also called for 2007 to be made the 'European year of equal opportunities for all' and, on 28 November, it presented a communication on the difficulties facing people with disabilities in the EU-25 which focused on putting into place the second phase (2006–07) of the EU disability action plan (2004–10). With regard to equality between women and men, the Commission published a report on 14 February, the first covering the enlarged EU. On 7 September, the decision was reached to extend by a year two existing EU action programmes in the field of gender equality whilst awaiting the establishment of a new framework programme for 2007–13. The Commission also proposed (on 8 March) the establishment of a European institute for gender equality, which would be an independent agency responsible for providing technical support for EU institutions and national governments to implement the EU's gender equality policy.

In the area of social dialogue, the Council adopted a directive (on 18 July) to put into effect the agreement between the European Transport Workers' Federation (ETF) and the Community of European Railways (CER) on aspects of the working conditions facing mobile workers engaged in interoperable cross-border services. In April and then October, the Commission launched the first and second consultation phases on the simplification and rationalization of reports on the practical implementation of directives relating to the health and safety of workers. On 29 September in Brussels, Commission President Barroso chaired the tenth social dialogue summit which coincided with the twentieth anniversary of official EU-level social dialogue. The summit provided the opportunity to examine the role of the social partners in the revamped Lisbon process.

On 16 March, the Commission adopted a Green Paper, 'Confronting demographic change: a new solidarity between the generations' which emphasized three priorities in dealing with this major social development: achieving a return to demographic growth; achieving a balance between the generations and building new bridges between the stages of life. The consultation following the publication of the paper had the purpose of identifying EU and national level policies to be strengthened or devised.

Finances

The financial framework for 2007–13 was the subject of intense intergovernmental wrangling throughout most of the year. UK Prime Minister Blair blocked an agreement at the June European Council only to have to take charge of the dossier during the British Council presidency during the second half of the year. The final agreement was reached late in the day at the 15–16 December Brussels European Council, thanks to the British government's willingness to compromise over its rebate and the overall size of the budget. The official objective for the financial agreement was the fair sharing of the costs of enlargement between all the Member States. The agreement reached sets the total budget ceiling at €862.3 billion for the seven-year period, corresponding to 1.045 per cent of the EU gross national income (GNI) (including Romania and Bulgaria) (see Table 2 for a summary of the full financial framework proposed). The annual average payment appropriations for the period 2007–13 was set at 1.00 per cent of the EU GNI (below the average of 1.14 per cent of the EU-25 GNI sought by the Commission), providing a significant margin under the own resources ceiling of 1.24 per cent GNI (as in the Commission's recommendation) varying, depending on the year, between 0.18 and 0.28 per cent of GNI (rather than the Commission's proposed 0.01 to 0.16 per cent).

The UK accepted a reduction in its rebate by €10.5 billion over the period by removing from this rebate most expenditure linked to enlargement. The Blair government, which had previously insisted that its rebate was not up for negotiation without further satisfactory reform of the common agricultural policy, accepted an agreement which – by explicitly excluding calculations based on expenditure linked to agriculture in the new Member States – can be described as political face-saving (see Box 1 for a summary of the UK budget rebate agreement). In exchange for this British compromise, the European Council called on the Commission to undertake an examination of an exhaustive revision of the structure of the EU's budget, including agricultural expenditure and the British rebate and to produce a report in 2008–09. The agreement in the European Council on the financial framework was still subject to an interinstitutional agreement with the European Parliament and the Commission to take place in 2006.

On 15 December, the Parliament adopted the 2006 budget – the last of the 2000–06 spending period – with appropriations for commitments reaching €121.2 billion or 1.09 per cent of GNI and appropriations for payments at €111.9 billion or 1.01 per cent of GNI. The European Council and the Commission presented the budget as an important step towards reform of EU expenditure with increased funds dedicated to the 'knowledge economy' of the twenty-first century, with more and better quality jobs. The appropriations for

Table 2: Overview of the New Financial Perspective 2007–13 (Subject to Inter-institutional Agreement)

Commitment Appropriations	2007	2008	2009	2010	2011	2012	2013	Total 2007–13
1. Sustainable development	51 090	52 148	53 330	54 001	54 945	56 384	57 841	379 739
1a. Competitiveness for growth and employment	8 250	8 860	9 510	10 200	10 950	11 750	12 600	72 120
1b. Cohesion for growth and employment	42 840	43 288	43 820	43 801	43 995	44 634	45 241	307 619
2. Preservation and management of natural resources, of which:	54 972	54 308	53 652	52 021	52 386	51 761	51 145	371 244
market-related expenditure and direct payments	43 120	42 697	42 279	41 864	41 453	41 047	40 645	293 105
3. Citizenship. liberty. security and justice	1 120	1 210	1 310	1 430	1 570	1 720	1 910	10 270
3a. Freedom. security and justice	600	690	790	910	1 050	1 200	1 390	6 630
3b. Citizenship	520	520	520	520	520	520	520	3 640
4. EU as a global player	6 280	6 550	6 830	7 120	7 420	7 740	8 070	50 010
5. Administration	6 720	6 900	7 050	7 180	7 320	7 450	7 680	50 300
6. Compensations	419	191	190					800
Total appropriations for commitments	12 601	121 307	122 362	122 752	123 641	125 055	126 646	862 363
As % of GNI	1.10	1.08	1.06	1.04	1.03	1.02	1.00	1.045
Total appropriations for payments	116 650	119 535	111 830	118 080	115 595	119 070	118 620	819 380
As % of GNI	1.06	1.06	0.97	1.00	0.96	0.97	0.94	0.99
Margin available	0.18	0.18	0.27	0.24	0.28	0.27	0.30	0.25
Own resources ceiling as % of GNI	1.24	1.24	1.24	1.24	1.24	1.24	1.24	1.24

Source: «http://europa.eu.int/comm/financial_perspective/index_en.htm».
Note: All figures are shown in 2004 prices, €bn.

Box 1: Agreement on the UK Budget Rebate Reduction

The UK budgetary correction mechanism (the UK abatement) shall remain in full on all expenditure except in relation to the new Member States as set out below. Starting in 2013 at the latest, the UK shall fully participate in the financing of enlargement costs for countries which have acceded after 30 April 2004 except for CAP market expenditure. To this end the UK budgetary mechanism shall be adjusted by progressively reducing the total allocated expenditure in line with the following modalities:

	% Reduction
2007	0
2008	0
2009	20
2010	70
2011	100
2012	100
2013	100

During the period 2007–13 the additional contribution from the UK shall not be higher than €0.5 billion, in comparison with the application of the current own resources decision. In case of future enlargement (except to Romania and Bulgaria) the additional contribution referred to above will be adjusted accordingly.

Source: Bulletin EU 12-2005.

---

commitments rose by 4.51 per cent over the 2004 budget, while the appropriations for payments rose 5.95 per cent. This should be compared to the rise in commitment appropriations from 2004–05 (by 5.2 per cent) and increase in payment appropriation by 5.4 per cent. Payments as a percentage of EU GNI reached 1.08 per cent, up from 1.01 per cent in 2004 which had been the smallest initial budget since 1990. However, the 2006 payment commitments were much lower than the ceiling agreed in the financial framework for 2005 (at 1.13 per cent of GNI). As in previous years, the total appropriations for commitment and payment in the final budget were somewhat below both the Commission's preliminary draft budget of 27 April and also the budget as amended by the Parliament after its first reading of 27 October (see *Bulletin EU* 12-2005, 1.7.6 for full budget and own resources figures). To take account of the effects of the 2003 CAP reform, which reduces price supports in order to finance rural development policy, on 7 September the Parliament and the Council amended the current financial perspective to modify payments for 2006.

On 3 May the Commission proposed a revision of the financial regulation adopted in 2002 in order to simplify financial procedures; reduce the administrative burden, particularly with regard to the formalities for beneficiaries of

EU subsidies and funding; and improve the effectiveness of EU expenditure. In order to introduce the amendments deemed necessary to simplify further the management of low-value contracts and small grants as quickly as possible, the Commission also approved a draft amendment of the rules for the implementation of the financial regulation on 12 October.

Agriculture

Most of the 2003–04 reform of the CAP came into force in 2005 including: decoupled aid (not linked to production but to compliance with other standards such as environmental and food safety); a 'single farm payment'; decreased payments to bigger farms to finance the new rural development policy; a financial discipline mechanism; and the modification of CAP market policy in several sectors. One of the stated aims of the reform is to encourage farmers to be more market-oriented and assume responsibility for production and dealing with price risks created by, for example, potential agricultural crises such as outbreaks of animal diseases). Nonetheless, several EU mechanisms remained to provide financial assistance to farmers to help them deal with such crises.

Several CAP reforms were also adopted in 2005. On 21 June the Council agreed further reform to CAP financing including the improvement of recovering overpaid EU funds. The Commission also proposed a major reform of rural development policy, creating one funding and programming instrument (the European agricultural fund for rural development: EAFRD); a strategic approach focused on EU priorities; and a reinforced control, evaluation and reporting with an audit system covering all elements of rural development. There was disagreement on the minimum national contribution rates established for each element of the EAFRD. On 20 September, the Council decided that 25 per cent of the national appropriation is to be allocated to the environment and countryside; 10 per cent to agriculture and forestry competitiveness; 10 per cent to improving quality of life in rural areas and diversifying the rural economy; and 5 per cent to the Leader approach. The Commission also drew up the strategic guidelines for rural development policy for the 2007–13 period.

Following lengthy consultation, on 24 November the Council reached a political agreement to reform the common organization of the sugar market (which had remained largely the same for 40 years) including a reduction in the institutional price of sugar by 36 per cent over a four-year period, financial compensation for farmers (decoupled aid) and a fund to provide incentives for the least competitive producers to leave the sector. The Commission outlined an EU action plan for organic food and farming in 2004, including 21 practical measures on improving information, rationalizing public support, reinforcing production standards and contributing to research. Finally, the Council approved a Commission proposal to draw up an action plan for sustainable forest management to improve the co-ordination of EU and national policies in this area and modernize the EU's forestry strategy dating from 1998. As part of the Commission's better law-making strategy, on 19 October the Commission presented proposals for simplifying and making more transparent CAP rules, with the objective of decreasing the bureaucratic burden on farmers and public authorities.

Environmental and Sustainable Development Policies

The sixth Community environment action programme continued to apply in 2005 and the Commission completed – and the Council adopted – four of the seven thematic strategies of the programme during the year: on air pollution, the protection and preservation of the marine environment, the prevention and recycling of waste and the sustainable use of resources. The three thematic strategies which still need to be drawn up include soil preservation, reasonable use of pesticides and urban environment. With regard to sustainable development, on 9 February the Commission presented its assessment of progress in the application of the comprehensive strategy with the aim of drawing up a revised strategy, and it examined general guidelines for future policy. On 28 September, the Commission presented a report to demonstrate how its better law-making agenda applied to the environmental action programme with impact assessments, improved public consultation and the simplification of existing legislation.

On 13 December, the Commission presented a communication on the review of the sustainable development strategy, in which it identified major areas where further progress is necessary (climate change, migration flows, management of natural resources, development challenges, sustainable transport, clean energy and public health) and outlined ways to measure progress and regularly examine priorities. Following a request of the March European Council, the Commission drew up a proposal on the strategy to form the basis of inter-institutional discussions (presented in May and approved by the European Council in June). This proposal outlines a list of general objectives underlying the concept of sustainable development and a list of ten principles to guide EU policies: promotion and protection of fundamental rights; equity between and within generations; open and democratic society; involvement of citizens; involvement of businesses and social partners; consistency of policies at all levels; integration of economic, social and environmental considerations; use of best available knowledge; application of the precautionary principle; application of the polluter-pays principle. In January, the Commission adopted a report on the implementation of the EU's environmental technologies action plan (ETAP), which had been launched in 2004. The report emphasized that further progress was needed in making the most of more environmentally-sound technologies.

With regard to the goal of more sustainable use of natural resources, in December the Commission adopted a thematic strategy on using a life-cycle approach, already applied to waste policy, that takes account of extraction, use and disposal phases. The Commission also sought to modernize waste policy with a new thematic strategy and a proposal for a new waste framework directive with the aim of reducing the environmental damage linked to use of resources and of transforming European society into a recycling economy. The Commission's proposals call for the introduction of national waste-prevention plans and the use of the better law-making approach with regard to waste. With regard to the establishment of the Natura 2000 network, on 13 January, the Commission finalized the list of sites of Community importance for the Boreal bio-geographical region.

In the area of emissions trading and climate change, the Kyoto protocol to the United Nations Convention on Climate Change came into force on 16 February 2005. The Commission presented a paper to the Council summarizing its medium- and long-term examination of the implications – economic, social and political – of the EU's international commitments of reducing its overall emissions of six greenhouse gases by 8 per cent from 1990 levels by 2012. On 27 September, the Commission presented a communication focusing on the need for airline companies to reduce their emissions.

On the subject of air quality, throughout the year the Commission also presented several reports with direct or indirect relevance. Its aim was to adopt a thematic strategy on air pollution – under the sixth framework programme – achieved on 21 September. This strategy focuses on the modernization of existing legislation (combining, updating and streamlining directives), the reduction of emissions of the main pollutants and the integration of environmental policy into other policies and programmes. On 24 October, the Commission also adopted a thematic strategy on the protection and conservation of the marine environment, with the aim of promoting, by 2021, an improvement in the ecological and economic quality of EC territorial seas. Also on 24 October, the Commission proposed a directive recommending the definition of European maritime regions based on geographical and environmental criteria. The ratification of the Aarhus convention at the start of 2005 (signed in 1998) promised improved public access to information and public participation in decision-making on environmental issues and the improved application of environmental law. With regard to energy efficiency, on 22 June the Commission presented a Green Paper to launch a public consultation on the subject.

Further Reading

Commission (2006) is a useful up-to-date overview of all EU internal policies.

Svendsen (2003) is one of the few recent overviews of EU political economy, using an interdisciplinary framework to examine how the design of current EU policies and institutions will determine future economic performance and policy outcomes.

Wallace *et al.* (2005) (eds) contains some of the best and most recent analyses of most aspects of EU internal policies.

References

Commission of the European Communities (2005) *Report: State Aid Scoreboard.* Autumn 2005 update (Luxembourg: OOPEC), COM(2005)624 final.

Commission of the European Communities (2006) *General Report on the Activities of the European Union for 2005* (Luxembourg: OOPEC).

Svendsen, G.T. (2003) *The Political Economy of the European Union: Institutions, Policy and Economic Growth* (Cheltenham: Edward Elgar).

Wallace, H., Wallace, W. and Pollack, M.A. (2005) (eds) *Policy-Making in the European Union.* 5th edn (Oxford: Oxford University Press).

JCMS 2006 Volume 44 Annual Review pp. 101–17

Justice and Home Affairs

JÖRG MONAR
University of Sussex

Introduction

The first full year of the implementation of the 'Hague programme' saw in the asylum policy field the final adoption of the long-delayed procedures directive. As regards migration, 2005 was marked by a major relaunch of the political debate in the EU on comprehensive internal and external action to tackle growing challenges, driven by both an unprecedented range of proposals from the Commission and concerns about migratory pressures from Northern Africa which reached the level of the Heads of State and Government. External border management was taken forward by the establishment of the new border agency, Frontex. While judicial co-operation was further developed through two instruments on the fight against ship-source pollution, the Council was faced with a major problem over the legal basis of criminal law measures as a result of a judgment by the European Court of Justice (ECJ). The internal security agenda was again dominated by the threat of international terrorism with the EU reacting to the London attacks of 7 July by both a speeding-up of legislative action and new strategy documents.

I. Developments in Individual Policy Areas

Asylum

More than five years after the first Commission proposal of September 2000, the Member States were finally able to agree on directive 2005/85/EC on minimum standards on procedures for granting and withdrawing refugee status, which was formally adopted by the Council on 1 December. It establishes a range of common minimum standards for national procedures in granting and withdrawing refugee status which constitute at the same time common minimum interpretations by the Member States of the procedural guarantees for asylum-seekers provided for by the Geneva Convention of 1951. As in the case of the 2004 'qualification directive', the main aim of the 'procedures directive' is to arrive at a common legal platform with a significant enough degree of convergence of national procedures to reduce the potential of 'asylum shopping' of applicants among the Member States, to improve the functioning of the Dublin II regulation of 2003 on determining the Member State responsible for processing an asylum application, and to serve as a Geneva Convention 'proof' basis for further common asylum measures.

In some respects this directive clearly marks a step forward because it establishes for the first time in EU law a number of essential guarantees for asylum-seekers. These include the right of applicants to remain in the Member State pending examination of the application (but not including a residence permit); to be adequately informed of the different stages of the procedure, its time-frame and all necessary evidence they have to provide; to have access to an interpreter for submitting their application; to have a chance to communicate with the UN High Commissioner for Refugees (UNHCR) or an organization working on its behalf; the right (with some exceptions) to a personal interview; the right to be informed of their legal position at decisive moments in the course of the procedure; the right to appropriate notification of a decision and of the reasons for that decision; and a right of access to legal assistance and representation, which shall be provided free in case of a rejection of the asylum application. Member States must also ensure that applications for asylum are neither rejected nor excluded from examination on the sole ground that they have not been made as soon as possible; that applications are examined and decisions are taken 'individually, objectively and impartially'; that sufficient information regarding the situation in the countries of origin is taken into account; and that the personnel in charge of decisions has sufficient knowledge of asylum and refugee law provisions. Asylum-seekers are also not to be held in detention for the sole reason that they are applicants for asylum and, if they are held in detention, Member States have to ensure that there is a possibility of speedy judicial review.

Most of these guarantees had been difficult to agree upon, however, and in its final form the directive ended up providing for such an extended use of the controversial 'safe third country' concept and for so many exceptions that it was adopted only against a barrage of criticisms. In February the UNHCR published another set of highly critical observations which objected, in particular, to the possibility of treating asylum applications as 'manifestly unfounded' if applicants come from third countries which the Council has classified as particularly 'safe' in accordance with a number of specified criteria. These include ratification of the European Convention of Human Rights (often referred to as European 'super safe third countries'), insisting that all applicants should have a right to rebut any presumption of 'safety' in their particular cases. The UNHCR also expressed grave concerns about the extensive possibilities of 'accelerating' the treatment of certain cases, the limitations of the right to a personal interview and the absence of a provision for free legal assistance during the first instance procedure.

Many of the UNHCR concerns were shared by the European Parliament (EP) which was reconsulted by the Council because of extensive amendments to the initial draft presented to Parliament in 2004. On 27 September the Parliament adopted, on the basis of the *Kreissl-Dörfler Report* of its Civil Liberties Committee, a resolution (P6_TA(2005)0349) in which it called for over 100 amendments to the directive including very substantial revisions to the provisions of the 'safe third country' concept aimed at guaranteeing each asylum applicant an individual consideration of his/her claim. The Parliament also asked to be able to participate in the drawing up of the minimum common list of 'safe third countries' on the basis of the co-decision procedure. Yet, as the directive had been introduced under the consultation procedure before the passage to co-decision on 1 January 2005, the Parliament had no opportunity to force the Council substantially to revise the text.

Overall the directive turned out to be another major example of the limitations of the minimum harmonization approach pursued by the EU in the asylum policy domain: while in a few respects – especially as regards judicial review standards and the rights of information of asylum-seekers – it went slightly beyond current guarantees in some Member States, it ended up providing for so many exceptions and limitations that it could even allow many Member States to lower their existing standards. Many of the original procedural guarantees proposed by the Commission were considerably watered down during the negotiations in the Council, and the margin of discretion left to the Member States does not augur well for achieving the objective set by the Hague programme to have all the necessary legal provisions for a common asylum system worth the name in place by 2010. The 'super safe third country' concept now laid down in Article 36 of the directive will also contribute to reinforcing the buffer zone of neighbouring countries of the EU to which asylum applicants can be returned, although serious questions can indeed be raised about the 'safety' of many of them from an asylum rights perspective.

Immigration

Whereas a host of measures have been adopted in the last few years regarding the fight against illegal immigration, only very few decisions have been adopted on the facilitation of legal immigration. Against this background the adoption of a Council directive (2005/71/EC) on 12 October on a specific procedure for admitting third-country nationals for the purposes of scientific research must be regarded as a not insignificant step forward. The directive defines a special procedure for admitting third-country nationals for the purposes of conducting a research project on the basis of a 'hosting agreement' with a research organization in the EU. This must satisfy a number of conditions such as a check on the qualifications of the researcher, the availability of sufficient resources and coverage of sickness insurance. In order to reduce the risk of potential abuse, the research organizations which can conclude 'hosting agreements' must be approved by the Member States. Once this is done, however, national authorities will issue the researcher and his family with a residence permit for the duration of the hosting agreement and he/she will automatically enjoy rights of equal treatment as regards recognition of professional qualifications, working conditions including pay and dismissal, social security rights, tax benefits and access to public goods and services. The researcher also has the right to teach in accordance with national legislation and to travel to other Member States to carry out his research. The directive was completed by a Council recommendation – adopted on the same day – providing, amongst other things, for Member States to refrain from using quotas to restrict the access of those researchers to posts in the EU.

With this directive the EU has come closer to a skill selection approach to legal immigration. It is obviously very much in the Union's interest to facilitate the admission of researchers from third countries as part of its European research area strategy and the Lisbon objectives on international competitiveness. The directive itself refers to the estimate that 700,000 researchers will be needed in order to meet the target set by the Barcelona European Council in March 2002 of 3 per cent of GDP invested in research by 2010. The directive goes a long way to give researchers from third countries similar rights and working conditions to those from within the EU which could indeed contribute to the international attractiveness of the European research area. This of course also has a negative side to it which all skill selective immigration instruments have in common, which is the risk of causing a 'brain drain' from emerging or developing countries. The directive vaguely acknowledges this risk and calls for co-operation with countries of origin in this respect, but does not provide for any concrete measures.

In another field of migration-related co-operation with third countries, however, the EU continued to pursue very concrete objectives and managed to advance two steps: the agreement with Albania on the readmission of persons residing without authorization was signed on 14 April and a similar one with Sri Lanka entered into force on 1 May. Seen by the EU as an essential instrument for the management of illegal immigration, the readmission agreement areas have been heavily criticized by several NGOs as shifting the responsibility for the often precarious fate of irregular migrants to third countries.

Being all too aware of the overall failure of the Union until then to make more progress towards a comprehensive migration policy and under the pressure of a deadline for new proposals until the end of 2006 set by the Hague programme, the European Commission launched several major initiatives during the year to get the policy-making process on migration issues moving again. The first of those was the publication on 11 January of the Green Paper on an EU approach to managing economic migration (Commission, 2005a). With this paper the Commission hoped to re-launch the discussion on common measures regarding economic immigration into the EU which had at least partially reached deadlock after it had become clear in 2002 and 2003 that the directive on legal entry and residence for third-country nationals seeking to work in the EU had no chance of being adopted because of strong resistance in the Member States. To bring a sense of urgency to the debate the Commission warned that between 2010 and 2030, at current immigration flows, the EU's working age population is expected to decline by around 20 million – with corresponding implications for economic growth, the functioning of the internal market and the competitiveness of EU enterprises. It then raised a range of questions about the degree of harmonization needed and different possible courses of action as regards admission principles and procedures for paid employment and self-employment, preferences for the domestic labour market, application for work and residence permits and the rights of third-country nationals.

The public consultation exercise on the basis of the Green Paper, which involved contributions from all national governments, several parliaments, regional and local authorities, a considerable number of trade union and industrial associations, NGOs, academic institutions and even five third-country governments (Australia, Canada, Egypt, Japan and Ukraine), revealed a considerable interest in the issues raised. Yet the 'Contributions on economic migration' (published on the Commission's website) and the public hearing organized in Brussels on 14 June also indicated major differences in national situations, expectations as regards EU action and continuing reservations by national governments about the harmonization of admission principles.

On 1 September the Commission took the next step in its series of migration policy initiatives by issuing a communication on 1 September on a common agenda for the integration of third-country nationals into the EU (Commission, 2005b) based on the set of common basic principles on integration adopted on 19 November 2004. The communication identified a range of measures which Member States should take at the national level to facilitate integration in combination with corresponding measures at EU level. The common denominator of the proposed EU measures was their supporting rather than regulatory nature. They consisted mainly of monitoring measures, such as the monitoring of national labour market integration of immigrants and the application of the two non-discrimination directives of 2000 – the support of good practice identification and transfer – through pilot projects and exchange of personnel, for instance, and the fostering of intercultural and inter-religious dialogue at the European level. This would happen, for instance, through the setting-up of a 'European integration forum' consisting of representatives of stakeholder umbrella organizations. The Commission also used the communication to push further the case for the establishment of a European fund for integration which it had already included in its proposals for the financial perspective 2007–13. Yet the communication was much richer in recommendations for action at the national level than in those at the EU level, a reflection of the fact that Member States continue to be wary about a stronger EU role in a field which remains politically very sensitive in the domestic context.

During the autumn the Commission could certainly feel some political tailwind for its efforts to inject a new dynamic into EU immigration policy. In his invitation letter of 20 October to the informal meeting of the Heads of State and Government at Hampton Court on 27 October, British Prime Minister Tony Blair included illegal migration amongst the primary issues for discussion, and in the press conference after the meeting – which resulted in no formal conclusions – Blair confirmed that there had been 'a great deal of discussion' on both illegal and legal migration. Part of those discussions focused on a Franco-Spanish initiative on 'immigration at a global level' which was presented jointly by French President Jacques Chirac and Spanish Prime Minister José Luis Zapatero and emphasized the need, in particular, to reinforce co-operation with third countries for a better management of Europe's migration problems. Although there was general support for the Franco-Spanish proposals, their impact was slightly weakened by the rather obvious self-interest of the two countries in suggesting an increase in development aid to the sub-Saharan region to €400 million under the next financial perspective as part of a new approach to external action on migration issues. These proposals were also made against the background of the deaths during the assault of hundreds of migrants on the barbed wire fence of the Spanish enclaves of Ceuta in September. The severe rioting by gangs of French youth with a predominantly North African immigration background – which by coincidence started in the suburbs of Paris on the very day of the Hampton Court meeting and led President Chirac on 8 November to declare a state of emergency – added its own sense of urgency to immigration problems in the EU.

Responding to a mandate from the Hampton Court meeting, the Commission issued a communication on 30 November (Commission, 2005c) on priority actions as a first follow-up. Taking into account the concerns of some Member States that there was now a risk of focusing too much attention on the migration challenges in Africa and the western Mediterranean, the Commission made a strong case for approaching migration as a global phenomenon which should also include reinforced co-operation with the EU's eastern neighbours, the western Balkans, as well as Latin American, Caribbean and Asian countries as major countries of origin. The more concrete part of the Communication started, however, with proposals to reinforce operational co-operation between the Member States which were more in line with the EU's traditional focus on restrictive measures at borders. The proposals included an enhanced role for the new border agency Frontex (see below), an improved use of immigration liaison officers (ILOs) by better reporting procedures, the creation of regional ILO networks and the creation, in 2006, of a legal basis for rapid reaction teams to provide technical and operational assistance for Member States facing particular problems. This was followed by a much longer list of proposals to reinforce co-operation with African and other neighbouring countries, including some more innovative elements such as a 'migration routes initiative' on strategic and operational co-operation on specific migration routes and work on facilitating remittances by immigrants to their home countries, as well as more traditional elements such as a focus on migration management capacity-building in the countries of origin. The priority actions suggested by the Commission were discussed by the Justice and Home Affairs Council on 1 and 2 December and then – with a stronger focus again on co-operation with the African and Mediterranean countries – broadly endorsed by the European Council at its meeting in Brussels on 15 and 16 December, which mandated the Commission to report back on progress on implementation until the end of 2006.

It was in a sense characteristic that the Brussels European Council – like the informal Hampton Court meeting earlier – resulted in no substantial statement on legal immigration. As usual the Member States found it much easier to agree on measures aimed at reducing migratory flows into the EU – in this case by enhanced co-operation with third countries and more action on external borders – than on finding common ground on the legal immigration side. Just before the expiry of the deadline set by the Hague programme, on 21 December the Commission adopted a 'policy plan on legal migration' (Commission, 2005d) based on the Green Paper consultation exercise of the first half of the year. If anything the tone of this document was even more alarmist than that of the

Green Paper, the Commission this time pointing – on the basis of Eurostat projections – to an expected fall in the working age population of 52 million by 2050.

Rather than proposing again a comprehensive legislative instrument regulating all entry and residence conditions of economic immigrants (as it had in 2001), the Commission this time proposed, after further extensive consultations and evaluations, using four different directives to address the situation of only selected categories of third-country nationals: a directive on the conditions of entry and residence of highly-skilled workers, one on the conditions of entry and residence of seasonal workers, one on the procedures regulating the entry into, the temporary stay and residence of intra-corporate transferees (ICT); and one on the conditions of entry and residence of remunerated trainees. In all cases admission would be conditional on the existence of a work contract and on an 'economic needs test'. This legislative action should, according to the Commission, be complemented by a horizontal framework directive defining a common framework of rights to all third-country nationals in legal employment already admitted in a Member State, but not yet entitled to the long-term residence status. This horizontal directive would also address the question of the recognition of diplomas and other qualifications and could be based on the idea of a single application for a joint (combined) work and residence permit containing – as the Commission did not fail to emphasize – 'the most advanced biometric identifiers'. The Commission added to this legislative agenda various proposals on enhanced knowledge-building in the domain of migration, as well as the facilitation of integration and the support of circular and return migration (in order to reduce 'brain-drain' risks in third countries). The Commission also drew up a 'road map' according to which the various legislative proposals will be introduced one by one from 2007 to 2009.

At the end of a year of unprecedented activity in the migration field – at least in terms of initiatives and debate – the EU had at least identified some priorities for action over the next few years, as well as sketched out major options for legislative action on the legal immigration side. Yet the time-frame of the Hague programme until 2010 is rather tight, and there remained serious questions at the end of the year on whether there will be enough time for both the further consultations and evaluations and the protracted negotiations which are to be expected because of the continuing unanimity requirement in the field of legal immigration.

Visa Policy

The common (Schengen) visa regime underwent a slight change as a result of an issue which had become more urgent after the 2004 enlargement: even before that the EU was confronted by a number of cases in which citizens of certain Member States had to obtain a visa to travel to certain third countries although these countries appeared on the common list of those whose citizens did not require a visa to travel to the EU. This had been the case of Greek citizens travelling to the US, citizens from Austria, Finland, Greece, Portugal and Iceland travelling to Brunei, Finnish citizens travelling to Venezuela and Icelandic citizens travelling to Guatemala. The 2004 enlargement complicated this situation further with, at the end of the year, 19 third countries exempted by the EU from the visa requirement still requiring visas from citizens of at least one new Member State. The original Council regulation (EC 539/2001) had provided for a quasi-automatic mechanism to react to such a violation of the reciprocity principle under which a simple notification by the Member State concerned would lead to the reintroduction of a visa requirement by the EU as a whole for the respective third country unless the Council decided otherwise. As the Commission had rightly pointed out, however, the considerable implications of using this automatic mechanism had prevented any Member State from actually using it. The result would have been either a major conflict between the EU as a whole and the respective third country, or a major internal conflict in the case of a majority vote against the notification by the respective Member State.

In order to enable the EU to act more effectively on the problem of non-reciprocity in visa requirements, the Council adopted on 2 June a regulation (EC 851/2005) amending the original regulation. This introduced the following: an obligation for Member States to notify Council and Commission within 90 days of any case of non-reciprocity; an obligation for the Commission to take diplomatic steps with the respective third country without delay; and the possibility of the Commission proposing to Council countermeasures at different levels up to the full abolition of visa-free travel of this country within certain time limits if diplomatic steps did not lead to a change in the situation. This problem of the common visa system demonstrates the ongoing tensions arising from the continuing differences in the state of bilateral relations between EU Member States and third countries, and the intra-EU solidarity requirement which comes with a common visa policy.

External Border Management

If the history of EU external border management is ever written, then 2005 will certainly feature in it as the year in which the agency for the management of operational co-operation at the external borders (Frontex) was finally established. After intense negotiations during the previous year and the usual EU haggling over the seat of the agency – which was finally decided only in April by a formal Council decision in favour of Warsaw – Frontex was inaugurated in the Polish capital on 30 June by the Luxembourg Minister of Justice Luc Frieden and Commissioner Franco Frattini. The board of management – consisting of representatives of the Member States – had already met for the first time on 25 May and had appointed Colonel Ilkka Laitinen from the Finnish border guard as director of the new agency. The fact that the Finnish border guard and Finnish border management continue to be seen in many respects as models of efficiency in the EU certainly contributed to his appointment. For its extensive range of tasks as defined in the Council regulation of 26 October 2004 (see the 2005 *Annual Review*), Frontex was granted an initial staffing framework of up to 57 people for 2005–06, consisting of 33 own members of staff (officials and temporary staff) and 24 national experts seconded from the Member States.

With effective external border management considered to be one the most vital elements of the EU's approach to internal security and migration management, the agency started with much potential for its future development. The Commission contributed to that in November by assigning key functions to the agency in the 'priority actions' on the migration management side which it proposed as a follow-up to the Hampton Court meeting (see above) and which were then endorsed by the Council. As a result Frontex was mandated to implement, as a matter of urgency, the border management measures envisaged in its 2006 work programme to combat illegal migration in the Mediterranean region, in particular by pilot projects and joint operations. It was also asked to present a risk analysis report on Africa to the Council by May 2006 and to launch in 2006 a study on the possibility of reinforcing the monitoring and surveillance of the Mediterranean sea with a focus on the feasibility of a Mediterranean coastal patrols' network to ensure permanent contact and co-ordination between Member States' sea border surveillance authorities. In parallel Frontex will have to organize, together with Member States, pilot projects aimed at better patrolling of the EU maritime borders. This range of tasks indicated already that the agency has the potential to outgrow its monitoring and supporting role by initiating the creation of new structures and actively co-ordinating operations of the national border police forces. Colonel Laitinen also seemed to intend the agency not to shy away from sensitive issues with more political implications. In a public speech in Helsinki on 2 November he identified corruption both in neighbouring countries and inside the EU as a key problem for the effective management of external borders (Newsroom Finland, 2 November).

For both the efficiency and the credibility of the EU's (Schengen) external border management, the common set of rules and standards on how controls are to be carried out are of crucial importance. Because of frequent changes, different original documents and a number of obsolete provisions which had not been eliminated, these rules – mainly laid down in the Schengen manual – had become complex and non-transparent. With the aim of consolidating and further developing these rules, the Commission had therefore proposed in April 2004 a regulation establishing a 'code' on the crossing of external borders based on the existing Schengen rules. After intense negotiations both in the Council and between the Council and the EP in the context of the 'co-decision procedure', a compromise text of this code – commonly referred to as the 'Schengen borders code' – was passed by the EP during the first reading on 23 June and was on the way to formal adoption by the Council at the end of the year (provisional text: EP document T6-0247/2005). The code defines the conditions for crossing the external borders and entry into Member States and the principles governing the implementation of external border controls, including surveillance between authorized border crossing-points, co-operation between Member States and the conditions for refusal of entry. It also establishes special rules for border checks for the different kinds of borders (land, air and maritime) and specific procedures for certain categories of persons (such as aircraft pilots, seamen and diplomats).

The adoption of the Schengen borders code on the basis of co-decision by the EP has been seen by some NGOs, concerned about the human rights implication of the EU measures at external borders, as a test case for the emergence of a potentially more liberal EU external border control regime (Peers, 2005). Yet, while the EP made a significant contribution to the strengthening of the procedural rights of third-country nationals as regards checks and potential refusals of entry, it tightened the border regime in other respects, such as the rights of border guards to consult national and EU databases in order to ensure that a person does not represent a danger to internal security (Article 6) and the need for travel documents of third-country nationals to be stamped not only on entry (as proposed by the Commission) but also on exit (Article 9). This suggests that the involvement of the Parliament as a co-legislator will not lead to any fundamental change in the strong security rationale of the EU approach towards external border management.

Judicial Co-operation

In the field of judicial co-operation a breakthrough was achieved as regards the strengthening of the legal framework in the fight against ship-source pollution which had become a major item on the EU's JHA agenda priority since the environmental disaster caused by the oil tanker *Prestige* off Cape Finisterre in Spain in November 2002. Although declared an EU priority, the negotiations had been slowed down by concerns by some Member States – in particular Cyprus, Greece and Malta – that a much tougher penal law framework could have negative implications for their shipping interests. On 12 July the Council finally adopted a framework decision (2005/667/JHA) on strengthening the criminal law framework of the enforcement of the law against ship-source pollution which was complemented on 7 September by an EC directive (2005/35/ EC). Disagreements over the levels of penalties led to a complex compromise package distinguishing between different degrees of gravity of the offences and leaving wide margins of discretion to the Member States as regards minimum/maximum penalties. The transparency of the measure was not increased by the fact that – because of the 'pillar' division in the JHA domain – the actual infringements were defined in the directive and penalty levels in the framework decision. However, in the end the Member States were able at least to agree on the principle that all discharges of polluting substances are considered infringements if they are committed with intent, recklessly or through serious negligence. They also agreed a minimum maximum level of penalty between five and ten years' imprisonment for the most serious pollution offences, the possibility of imposing professional disqualifications and minimum maximum financial penalties for legal persons of between €750,000 and €1,500,000. While the financial penalties may still appear a trifle in comparison with the damage maritime pollution can cause, they are up to ten times higher than current penalty levels in some Member States. It must be noted, however, that the effect of these measures will be limited by the fact that the United Nations Convention on the Law of the Seas makes this legislation enforceable only on ships which enter an EU port and prohibits the imposition of prison sentences on offences committed by 'foreign ships' outside territorial waters. Unanimity could not be reached in the Council on excluding EU vessels from the 'foreign ships' category, thereby making them subject to the tougher EU rules because of the concerns of Cyprus, Greece and Malta that this would lead owners of EU-registered ships to switch their flags to third countries.

The Council's strategy of using 'third-pillar' legal instruments for criminal law measures in the environmental sphere was thrown into disarray by a judgment by the Court of Justice on 13 September (Case C-176/03 *Commission* v. *Council)* which resulted in the annulment of the Council framework decision on the protection of the environment through criminal law of 27 January 2003. While confirming that, as a general rule, neither criminal law nor the rules of criminal procedure fall within EC ('first-pillar') competence, the Court accepted the Commission's argument that an EC legal basis – rather than a 'third-pillar' basis – can be justified if the application of effective, proportionate and dissuasive criminal penalties by the competent national authorities is essential for the protection of the environment which is an EC competence. This came as a major vindication of the Commission's long-standing objections against the use of third-pillar instruments with their corresponding decision-making rules for EC objectives, not only in the field of environmental protection, but also in areas such as counterfeiting of the euro, money-laundering and corruption in the private sector. The Commission almost immediately made the most of its victory by deciding in November to appeal to the Court to annul on the same ground the framework decision on ship-source pollution (see above) and proposing to the Council on 24 November a simplified procedure to amend no fewer than eight previously adopted legislative acts in line with the Court's affirmation of Community competence (Commission, 2005e). This was combined with a thinly veiled threat that, if the Council did not accept this approach, the Commission would use its right of initiative to propose more wide-ranging substantive changes to all of these legislative acts. The Commission would have a good chance of getting such changes at least partially through because of co-decision by the EP and the qualified majority requirement in the 'first-pillar' domain. The Court's decision will obviously also have major implications for all pending and future proposals involving criminal measures if these are linked to EC objectives.

While this legal storm was unfolding over the Council the negotiations on a framework decision on the European evidence warrant (EEW) for obtaining objects, documents and data for use in proceedings in criminal matters made only slow progress. At the end of the year major issues, such as the grounds for refusal based on the principle of territoriality, definitions of offences and legal remedies, and the question of which authorities should be competent for issuing, postponing and refusing EEWs, still remained unresolved.

In the civil law field, more progress was achieved in the negotiations on the draft regulation on a European order for payment procedure which is aimed at simplifying and reducing the costs of litigation in cross-border cases concerning uncontested claims. On 2 December the Council reached, on the basis of a compromise package of the British presidency, a common approach on the text of the regulation which – allowing for the free circulation of payment orders in the EU – is of considerable importance to the functioning of the internal market.

The Fight against Terrorism and Serious Crime

Coming only 16 months after the Madrid terrorist attacks, the four bombs in London on 7 July, which killed 56 people and injured 700, caught the EU in the middle of the implementation of its revised action plan against terrorism. With this action plan already providing over 200 measures, most of which had not yet been fully implemented, it made little sense just to add others to the list. At an extraordinary meeting of the JHA Council in Brussels on 13 July, the ministers therefore decided instead to prioritize certain measures for speedy implementation and bring deadlines forward accordingly (Council document 11116/05). These included legal instruments on the retention of telecommunications data (see below), on the European evidence warrant (see above), and on the exchange of information between law enforcement authorities and a decision on the exchange of information concerning terrorist offences. In addition the Member States agreed to speed up the negotiations of several instruments to combat terrorist financing including a regulation on wire transfers, the third money laundering directive and a regulation on cash control as well as the adoption of a code of conduct to prevent the misuse of charities by terrorists. Member States were also urged to intensify the exchange of police and judicial information, in particular through Europol (and its counter-terrorist task force) and Eurojust, and improve support from Member States' security and intelligence services to the EU situation centre – which had been rather sluggish – as well to improve information-sharing on lost and stolen explosives. Although progress was achieved on some of these instruments, most of the deadlines set for legislation to be adopted by the end of the year were – not for the first time – missed.

Amongst the most notable elements of progress was the first reading agreement reached between Council and Parliament in December on a directive on the retention of traffic and location (but not content) data processed by telecommunications companies which is aimed at making it easier for national law enforcement authorities to investigate terrorist and other serious criminal activities by granting them access to a list of all telephone calls, SMS or internet connections made by suspects. Hotly contested not only because of its data protection implications, but also the costs it is likely to entail for telecommunication companies, the compromise reached in the end provided for data to be retained by the telecommunications companies for a minimum of six months and a maximum of 24 (EP document P6_TA-PROV(2005)0512). Only authorities specifically identified by Member States will get access to retained data, and Member States will have to ensure independent monitoring of the use of those data. Parliament insisted on the limitation of access to the data on a case-by-case basis (the so-called 'push system'), so that authorities will have to request data on each individual suspect rather than getting access to the complete databases. In an interesting twist of internal negotiations in the EP, Spanish MEPs played a key role in constructing a majority within the EP for the Council position on extending the retention to location data on calls also to unsuccessful calls, a particularly expensive measure for companies as these currently do not register unsuccessful calls. The reason for that was that the investigation of lost calls had played a major role in the successful prosecution in Spain of the terrorist offenders of the Madrid attacks of March 2004. It is most unlikely that the first reading agreement with the EP would have been possible without the additional pressure generated by the London bombs.

The London attacks provided clear evidence of the dangers of 'home grown' terrorism emerging from marginalization and radicalization inside the EU. Against this background the Member States agreed on 2 December on a European Union strategy for combating radicalization and recruitment to terrorism which focused on three key lines of action (Council, 2005a): the disruption of the activities of networks and individuals who draw people into terrorism (addressing 'facilitational' factors which provide for recruitment); efforts to ensure that voices of mainstream opinion prevail over those of extremism (addressing 'motivational' factors which can lead individuals to become radicalized); and the promotion of security, justice, democracy and opportunity for all (addressing 'structural' factors creating the socio-economic environment in which the radical message becomes appealing).

At the same JHA Council, agreement was also reached on a 'new' EU counter-terrorism strategy (Council, 2005b). Based on the measures already provided for by the action plan, this strategy in fact contained little new substance, but what it did do was to bring the enormous range of measures taken or planned within a structured conceptual framework with strategic objectives under the following headings:

> *Prevent:* to prevent people turning to terrorism by tackling the factors or root causes which can lead to radicalization and recruitment, in Europe and internationally;

> *Protect:* to protect citizens and infrastructure and reduce the EU's vulnerability to attack, including through improved security of borders, transport and critical infrastructure;

> *Pursue:* to pursue and investigate terrorists across our borders and globally; to impede their planning, travel and communications; to disrupt support networks; to cut off funding and access to attack materials, and bring terrorists to justice;

> *Respond:* to prepare, in a spirit of solidarity, for managing and minimizing the consequences of a terrorist attack, by improving the capability of dealing with the aftermath, the co-ordination of the response and the needs of victims.

One declared aim of the strategy was to make the EU's action against terrorism more comprehensible and transparent for the general public, and for this reason it was published in the highly innovative form of a series of PowerPoint slides with an accompanying narrative. While one might feel that Member States should rather focus on a more rapid and effective implementation of their decisions rather than on producing visual slides, the 'area of freedom, security and justice' can certainly also benefit from a greater transparency towards the EU citizens as its legitimizing beneficiaries.

Key readings

Commission (2005b) is the first response to the Council's invitation to establish a coherent framework for the integration of third-country nationals living and working in the EU.

Commission (2005d) lists legislative initiatives intended to lead to a coherent policy on legal economic migration into the EU.

Commission (2005e) provides its assessment of the implications of the ECJ judgment on the distribution of powers between the first and third pillars with regard to provisions of criminal law.

Council (2005a) sets out a strategy for combating radicalization and the recruitment to terrorism.

Council (2005b) presents the EU's counter-terrorism strategy.

Lavenex and Wallace (2005) reviews the evolution and characteristics of co-operation in this field, and discusses recent policy developments and reform proposals.

References

Commission of the European Communities (2005a) 'Green Paper on an EU approach to managing economic migration'. COM(2004)811, 11 January.

Commission of the European Communities (2005b) 'Communication ... a common agenda for integration framework for the integration of third-country nationals in the European Union'. COM(2005)389, 1 September.

Commission of the European Communities (2005c) 'Communication ... priority actions for responding to the challenges of migration: first follow-up to Hampton Court'. COM(2005)621, 30 November.

Commission of the European Communities (2005d) 'Communication ... policy plan on legal migration'. COM(2005)669, 21 December.

Commission of the European Communities (2005e) 'Communication ... on the implications of the Court's judgment of 13 September 2005 (Case C-176/03 Commission v. Council), COM(2005)583, 24 November.

Council (2005a) 'The European Union Strategy for Combating Radicalisation and Recruitment to Terrorism'. Council document 14781/1/05, 24 November.

Council (2005b) 'The European Union Counter-Terrorism Strategy'. Council document 14469, 30 November.

Lavenex, S. and Wallace, W. (2005) 'Justice and Home Affairs: Towards a "European Public Order?". In Wallace, H., Wallace, W. and Pollack, M. (eds) *Policy-Making in the European Union*, 5th edn (Oxford: Oxford University Press).

Peers, S. (2005) 'Revising EU Border Control Rules: A Missed Opportunity?'. *Statewatch News,* July, available at «http://www.statewatch.org/news/2005/jul/eu-border-code-final.pdf».

UNHCR (2005) 'UNHCR Provisional Comments on the Proposal for a Council Directive on Minimum Standards on Procedures in Member States for Granting and Withdrawing Refugee Status'. Geneva, 10 February, available at «http://www.unhcr.ch/cgi-bin/texis/vtx/home/opendoc.pdf?tbl=RSDLEGAL&id=42492b302».

JCMS 2006 Volume 44 Annual Review pp. 119–35

Legal Developments

MICHAEL DOUGAN
Liverpool Law School, University of Liverpool

Introduction

The Community courts, during the course of 2005, delivered several judgments which received significant media attention: for example, the *Feta Cheese* case on the protection of designations of origin for foodstuffs;[1] the *Marks & Spencer* ruling on the compatibility with the freedom of establishment of national rules on corporate tax relief;[2] the *Alliance for Natural Health* judgment affirming the validity of the controversial food supplements directive;[3] and the *Yusuf* case dealing with the legality of restrictive measures adopted by the Community against the Taliban and Al-Qaeda in implementation of various United Nations Security Council resolutions.[4] These were, of course, only the tip of the iceberg of important cases decided by the Community courts across a broad field of Union activity: ranging from compatibility with the rules on the free movement of goods of Austrian legislation intended to protect the environment from pollution caused by heavy goods vehicles;[5] to the scope of the Council's discretion to reserve implementing powers to itself, pursuant to Article 202 EC, in the area of freedom, security and justice;[6] and from the legal effects of the partnership and co-operation agreement signed between the Community and

---

[1] Joined Cases C-465-466/02 *Germany* v. *Commission* (25 October 2005).
[2] Case C-446/03 *Marks & Spencer* (13 December 2005).
[3] Joined Cases C-154-155/04 *Alliance for Natural Health* (12 July 2005).
[4] Case T-306/01 *Yusuf* (21 September 2005).
[5] Case C-320/03 *Commission* v. *Austria* (15 November 2005).
[6] Case C-257/01 *Commission* v. *Council* (18 January 2005).

the Russian Federation;[7] to the conditions under which Community institutions may incur non-contractual liability even in respect of lawful acts.[8] As usual, this chapter offers a more detailed analysis of just several of the rulings which should prove to be of most interest to EU lawyers.

I. Equal Treatment and Educational Mobility

In its famous *Gravier* judgment of 1985, the European Court of Justice (ECJ) found that access to vocational training falls within the scope of the Treaty for the purposes of the principle of non-discrimination on grounds of nationality contained in Article 12 EC;[9] but in subsequent rulings such as *Lair* and *Brown* dating from 1988, it was decided that, having regard to the Community's marginal role in the field of educational policy, the Treaty did not entitle migrant Community nationals to claim equal treatment with own nationals as regards assistance with maintenance costs.[10] Those principles were codified in the 'students residency' Directive 93/96.[11] However, the expansion of Community competence in the field of education agreed under the Treaty on European Union (TEU), coupled with the introduction of Union citizenship and its increasingly dynamic interpretation by the ECJ, led commentators to speculate that the *Lair* and *Brown* caselaw – and perhaps even their legislative codification in Directive 93/96 – might be ripe for overruling.

The dispute in *Bidar* gave the Court its first opportunity to consider access to maintenance assistance by migrant EU students in their capacity as Union citizens.[12] The claimant, a French national, entered the UK in 1998 with his sick mother, then lived with his grandmother as her dependent. After completing his secondary schooling, Bidar commenced his university education in 2001 at University College London. For these purposes, he received public assistance with his tuition fees, but was refused access to a state-subsidized student loan: although Bidar had been resident in the UK for three years prior to commencing his degree, as required under domestic rules, he could not furthermore be considered 'settled' in the UK; indeed, thanks to the drafting of the national legislation, it was difficult to see how any migrant EU student

---

[7] Case C-265/03 *Simutenkov* (12 April 2005).
[8] Joined Cases T-69/00, T-151/00, T-301/00, T-320/00, T-383/00 & T-135/01 *FIAMM* (14 December 2005).
[9] Case 293/83 *Gravier* [1985] ECR 593. As to which, see Case C-147/03 *Commission* v. *Austria* (7 July 2005).
[10] Case 39/86 *Lair* [1988] ECR 3161; Case 197/86 *Brown* [1988] ECR 3205.
[11] Directive 93/96, OJ 1993 L 317, p. 59.
[12] Case C-209/03 *Bidar* (15 March 2005). Other judgments had already addressed access by migrant EU students to social security benefits, e.g. Case C-184/99 *Grzelczyk* [2001] ECR I-6193.

could ever fulfil the latter condition. Bidar challenged this refusal on the grounds that, despite *Lair* and *Brown*, it should now be considered incompatible with Article 12 EC.

The principal thrust of the Court's ruling is to give with one hand, but take back with the other. It is indeed true that, in the light of the TEU's expansion of Community competence in the field of education, and the introduction of more extensive rights to residence and equal treatment linked to the status of Union citizenship, the judgments in *Lair* and *Brown* can no longer be considered good law insofar as they suggest that maintenance assistance to migrant students falls altogether outside the scope of the Treaty for the purposes of Article 12 EC. Nevertheless, the Court continued to observe that Union citizens who go to another Member State to start or pursue higher education and enjoy for that purpose a right to residence under Directive 93/96 are expressly precluded by that measure from enjoying any right to maintenance assistance. In other words: the caselaw may have evolved, but the legislation remains the same, and the latter continues to act as an effective bar to the enjoyment of equal treatment as regards grants or loans for migrant EU students.

But that was not the end of the line for Bidar himself. The Court observed that, on the facts of this particular dispute, the claimant's right to residence was not based on Directive 93/96, but rather derived from the 'general residency' Directive 90/364,[13] since he was *already* lawfully resident in the UK when he decided to commence his higher education. In such circumstances, the express prohibition on equal treatment as regards maintenance assistance contained in Directive 93/96 did not apply, and Bidar was indeed entitled to rely on Article 12 EC in order to challenge the UK's discriminatory qualifying criteria for student loans. In this regard, the ECJ accepted that it is perfectly legitimate for a Member State to wish to reserve maintenance assistance to those who can demonstrate a 'certain degree of integration' into the host society. For these purposes, the UK was entitled to expect three years' prior residency in the national territory before considering applications for student loans; but the additional requirement that the claimant must be 'settled' in the UK, which it was technically impossible for migrant EU students to satisfy, regardless of their actual degree of integration into the host society, was disproportionate.

Bidar is entirely representative of the Court's caselaw on Union citizenship: in most cases, financial responsibility for the upkeep of economically inactive individuals continues to lie with their country of origin, rather than the Member State where they would actually like to reside; but in difficult situations, where that general principle might cause undue hardship, the Court usually manages to find a way of ensuring that the host state demonstrates some degree of welfare

[13] Directive 90/364, OJ 1990 L 180, p. 26.

solidarity towards the deserving claimant.[14] As regards maintenance assistance for migrant EU students, the Court's finding that, in most cases, the exclusion of equal treatment contained in Directive 93/96 remains enforceable and, even in the exceptional cases, the host state retains a relatively generous margin of discretion to exclude those who are not genuinely integrated into its society, should ensure that Union citizenship has only limited financial consequences for the national systems of maintenance assistance. Indeed, following the adoption of the new Citizenship Directive 2004/38, even claimants such as that in *Bidar* might find themselves excluded from the right to equal treatment: this measure draws no distinction between migrant Community nationals who entered the territory for the purposes of study, and those who only subsequently decide to take up higher education; *all* economically inactive migrant students are expressly excluded from equal treatment as regards maintenance assistance (unless they are entitled to be treated as permanent residents by virtue of having lived continuously for five years within the host state).[15]

II. Legal Effects of Unimplemented Directives

Readers of the 'Legal Developments' section in last year's *Annual Review* may recall the judgment in *Pfeiffer* and its relevance for the long-rumbling debate about the capacity of directives to affect the legal obligations incumbent upon individuals even in the absence of correct and timely transposition into national law.[16] In particular, *Pfeiffer* cast serious doubt on the distinction favoured by certain commentators between the (clearly prohibited) substitutionary and (supposedly permissible) exclusionary effects of unimplemented directives.[17] That distinction has generally been mooted within the context of horizontal actions: one individual attempts to rely on an unimplemented directive during the course of a dispute with another private party. The *Berlusconi* case illustrates how the same important issues of principle can arise even as regards vertical disputes, *in casu*, where the Member State itself seeks to rely on the unimplemented directive against a private individual.[18]

Among the cases joined in the *Berlusconi* litigation was a criminal prosecution for false corporate accounting, commenced in 1999, relating to the defendant's business activities during the period 1986–89, in accordance with the Italian legislation applicable at that time. Luckily for the defendant, he had

[14] Cf. rulings such as Case C-184/99 *Grzelczyk* [2001] ECR I-6193; Case C-413/99 *Baumbast* [2002] ECR I-7091.
[15] Directive 2004/38, OJ 2004 L 158, p. 77.
[16] Joined Cases C-397/01 to C-403/01 *Pfeiffer* [2004] ECR I-8835.
[17] See the 'Legal Developments' chapter in the 2004/2005 edition of this *Annual Review*.
[18] Joined Cases C-387/02, C-391/02 & C-403/02 *Berlusconi* (3 May 2005).

since become the prime minister of Italy and, in 2002, the Italian legislature found itself minded to pass new and significantly more lenient false accounting laws. Under the Italian criminal code, the courts must always apply the legislation which is most favourable to the defendant, even if that legislation was adopted subsequent to the allegedly criminal behaviour. On that basis, Berlusconi argued that his prosecution for false accounting should be halted. However, Community law threw an inconvenient spanner into the smooth running of the defendant's works. Italian legislation on false accounting fell within a regulatory field occupied by various EC company law directives: whereas the original Italian rules were assumed adequately to have implemented those directives, it was argued that the new rules adopted in 2002 breached the Member State's obligation to impose effective and dissuasive sanctions upon those who infringe their Community law responsibilities. The question arose, were the national courts obliged to set aside the (non-compliant) 2002 legislation, and permit the defendant's criminal prosecution to proceed in accordance with the original (compliant) Italian rules?

The substitution–exclusion analysis suggested one solution to this problem: there was, in principle, no bar to the public authorities seeking to rely on a misimplemented Community directive against Berlusconi. This was not a case of substituting new rules derived from that directive which did not already exist under Italian law (something which would indeed not be permissible, under well-established caselaw, if enforced against a private party). It was rather a case of excluding certain provisions of national law which did not comply with the Community directive (something which was merely a consequence of the principle of supremacy, not an illegitimate manifestation of the doctrine of direct effect). Indeed, there is more than a hint of this analysis in the opinion delivered by Advocate General Kokott.[19] However, as in *Pfeiffer*, the ECJ in *Berlusconi* rejected this line of analysis (and implicitly, the entire conceptual understanding of the Community legal order it represents).

The Court accepted that the principle of the retroactive application of a more lenient criminal penalty represents a general principle of Community law which national courts must respect when applying national legislation adopted for the purpose of implementing Community law. Difficulties arise in a situation (such as the present dispute) where the more lenient penalty is itself alleged to be incompatible with Community law. However, the Court did not consider it necessary to address this difficulty as a matter of principle; the obligation to impose effective and dissuasive sanctions for false accounting derives from the First Companies Directive,[20] yet directives cannot of themselves

---

[19] Opinion of 14 October 2004.
[20] Directive 68/151, OJ 1968 English Special Edition (I), p. 41.

impose obligations on an individual and cannot as such be relied on against private parties. More specifically, a directive cannot of itself have the effect of determining or aggravating the criminal liability of persons who act in contravention of that directive. Here, reliance on the First Companies Directive so as to set aside the incompatible provisions of the 2002 Italian legislation would have the effect of rendering applicable to the defendant the original and manifestly more severe regime contained in the original national legislation – and that would be contrary to the limits which flow from the essential nature of any directive.

From one perspective, the judgment in *Berlusconi* is a welcome affirmation of the Court's understanding in *Pfeiffer* about the proper scope of the direct effect of unimplemented directives and (more fundamentally) the interrelationship between the principles of direct effect and supremacy. But by these means, the Court did avoid addressing the important question of principle: how to resolve a conflict between the general principle of Community law requiring the retroactive application of more lenient criminal penalties (on the one hand), and the direct effect and supremacy of a provision of Community law – other than a directive – requiring Member States to impose effective and dissuasive penalties on those who infringe their treaty obligations (on the other hand). Moreover, the Court only avoided addressing this issue by something of a sleight of hand. The duty to impose effective and dissuasive sanctions for false accounting was held to derive from the First Companies Directive, *not* from the general duty of loyal co-operation found in Article 10 EC and which in turn reflects another general principle of Community law whereby Member States must effectively penalize infringements of the Treaty. But the Court could, and arguably should, have held that the First Companies Directive merely embodies or reflects the underlying (and indeed identical) obligations imposed by the Treaty itself and the general principles of Community law. On that analysis, there would have been no technical issue concerning the direct effect of an unimplemented directive *vis-à-vis* a private party to relieve the Court from tackling the important question of principle.

Yet the idea concealed through sleight of hand in *Berlusconi* – that the obligations imposed by a given directive merely reflect a more fundamental principle of the Community legal order, and the latter principle can indeed be enforced as against private individuals, even if the relevant directive has not been properly implemented into national law – was confidently and marvellously applied by the Court in its subsequent judgment in *Mangold*.[21]

Directive 2000/78 was adopted under Article 13 EC, and lays down a general framework for combating discrimination, *inter alia*, on grounds of age in the

---

[21] Case C-144/04 *Mangold* (22 November 2005).

field of employment and occupation.[22] Article 2 of the directive contains the basic prohibition on age discrimination; but Article 6 permits Member States to provide that differences in treatment shall not constitute age discrimination if they are objectively and reasonably justified by a legitimate aim, and are appropriate and necessary to achieving that aim. Germany was given until 2 December 2006 to transpose into its national law the age discrimination provisions contained in Directive 2000/78. *Mangold* concerned the German legislation for protecting workers employed under fixed-term contracts of employment. As a general rule, such contracts may be concluded only if there are 'objective grounds' for doing so, but thanks to a derogation taking effect on 1 January 2003 and running until 31 December 2006, fixed-term contracts could (in certain circumstances) be concluded without showing any 'objective grounds' where the worker was aged 52 or above. As regards the compatibility between this derogation and Community law, the Court observed that the German rules amounted to *prima facie* discrimination under Article 2 Directive 2000/78 which could not be justified under Article 6 of that measure; although the German rules pursued a legitimate aim (promoting the vocational integration of older workers who might otherwise encounter serious difficulties in finding work), those rules could not, however, be considered appropriate and necessary to achieving that aim.

Having established that the German rules on fixed-term contracts were, in principle, incompatible with Directive 2000/78, two issues remained to be addressed, both relating to the potential effects of the unimplemented directive within the national legal system. First, the deadline for transposition of the directive into German law had not yet expired; according to well-established caselaw, directives cannot have direct effect until such deadlines have elapsed. Secondly, the actual dispute in *Mangold* was horizontal: a private employer had hired a worker aged 56 on a fixed-term contract, relying on the German rules; the legality of that fixed-term contract was challenged by the worker, relying on Directive 2000/78 – yet directives cannot of themselves be relied upon in litigation between two individuals. To overcome these twin obstacles, the Court played its trump card: the principle of non-discrimination on grounds of age must in fact be regarded as a general principle of Community law. Directive 2000/78 does not in itself lay down the principle of equal treatment as regards employment and occupation. As such, observance of the general principle of equal treatment on grounds of age cannot be made conditional on expiry of the implementation period in respect of Directive 2000/78; it is the responsibility of national courts to provide the legal protection which individuals derive from

[22] Directive 2000/78, OJ 2000 L 303, p. 16.

Community law, if necessary, by setting aside any incompatible provision of domestic law.

Some commentators will no doubt interpret the ruling in *Mangold* as a piece of judicial mischief. After all, it has been widely noted that Article 13 EC, as introduced by the Treaty of Amsterdam, was consciously drafted by the Member States so as to exclude any possibility that the principle of non-discrimination contained therein might have direct effect independently of its Community implementing legislation. But whatever its constitutional cheekiness, *Mangold* is an exciting development, since it suggests that the Court is actively exploring a new avenue for avoiding the (heavily criticized) strictures of its own caselaw on the legal effects of unimplemented directives: 'we are not enforcing this directive against an individual, only the general principle of Community law which the directive embodies'. To be fair, *Mangold* is not entirely without precedent. After all, the Court has long held that the Equal Pay Directive[23] merely elaborates on the provisions of Article 141 EC and, as such, can be relied upon even in horizontal disputes against national rules which do not fully comply with the requirements imposed by Community law.[24] Admittedly, that concerned a treaty provision, not a general principle of Community law, and cases like *Berlusconi* hardly suggested that the Court was minded to extend any such approach further. By contrast, *Mangold* throws open the door to intensive academic speculation about just how far the Court will now be prepared to go.

On the one hand, such speculation will surely focus on which other directives should be considered merely to embody some general principle of Community law which is enforceable on its own terms. The Court in *Mangold* clearly anticipated that its ruling should apply not only to equal treatment as regards age, but also the other forms of discrimination referred to in Directive 2000/78 (such as religion, disability and sexual orientation). Moving beyond Directive 2000/78: surely (say) the principle of equal treatment on grounds of sex is recognized as a general principle of Community law which gives rise to enforceable rights, and should be capable of doing so *à la Mangold* even in horizontal disputes where the Equal Treatment Directive[25] has not been correctly implemented into national law. Whereas (for example) even if a principle such as consumer protection were to be treated as one of the general principles of Community law, it is surely too nebulous to be capable of creating justiciable individual rights and obligations independently of the various directives adopted by the Community legislature to deal with specific categories of consumer disputes.

[23] Directive 75/117, OJ 1975 L 45, p. 19.
[24] E.g. Case C-381/99 *Brunnhofer* [2001] ECR I-4961.
[25] Directive 76/207, OJ 1976 L 39, p. 40.

On the other hand, we should not let our speculation run away with itself altogether, by seeing in *Mangold* a virtual replacement-in-waiting for the lop-sided direct effect of whole swathes of directives. After all, national law must respect the general principles of Community law *not* in the abstract *but only* where it falls within the scope of the Treaty, in particular, by either derogating from or implementing one of the Member State's obligations. In *Mangold* itself, this requirement was satisfied because the German rules on fixed-term employment contracts were intended to implement the provisions of the framework agreement on fixed-term work as put into effect by Directive 1999/70.[26] In the absence of such Community secondary legislation, one assumes that the German rules on fixed-term contracts would not have fallen within the scope of Community law at all, and the general principle of equal treatment on grounds of age would have been inapplicable. Thus, the latter cannot act as a substitute for Directive 2000/78 in every case; it can only do so as regards those situations which are otherwise regulated by Community law. Similarly, the principle of equal treatment on grounds of sex could not act as a substitute for the Equal Treatment Directive across the entire field of employment law. It could only do so as regards those aspects of the employment relationship which, because they are already subject to regulation at the supranational level, are capable of bringing the relevant national legislation within the scope of Community law so as to become subject to its general principles.

III. Cross-Currents Between the First and Third Pillars

The Court delivered two major judgments exploring the legal interplay between the first and third pillars: *Pupino* shows how the third pillar can usefully borrow certain important legal concepts about effective judicial protection from the Community legal order;[27] *Commission* v. *Council* illustrates how the Community itself enjoys certain legislative competences in the field of criminal law without the need to have recourse to Title VI TEU (see also Monar, in this volume).[28]

One of the main legal instruments used under the third pillar – the framework decision – is very similar to the directive as employed under the first pillar, save for this major difference: Article 34(2) TEU expressly states that framework decisions 'shall not entail direct effect'. The question which has vexed academic lawyers for years is whether framework decisions might nevertheless be capable of producing independent effects within the national

---

[26] Directive 1999/70, OJ 1999 L 175, p. 43.
[27] Case C-105/03 *Pupino* (16 June 2005).
[28] Case C-176/03 *Commission* v. *Council* (13 September 2005).

legal systems by means other than direct effect – the most likely candidate being the duty of consistent interpretation developed by the ECJ under the first pillar in cases such as *von Colson* and *Marleasing*.[29] Indeed, given the importance of the subject matter falling within the third pillar for individual rights and fundamental freedoms, it was felt imperative that the Court find ways and means of enhancing the legal protection of those subject to Union intervention in the field of criminal law. The dispute in *Pupino* furnished the Court with an opportunity to address this crucial issue.

Italian criminal procedure comprises two stages: a preliminary enquiry, investigating whether to proceed further or dismiss the matter; then the adversarial stage, which is the trial proper. Evidence gathered during the preliminary enquiry can generally only be treated as admissible during the adversarial stage if it is subject to cross-examination; by way of exception, the evidence of young victims of sexual offences may be taken at the preliminary enquiry by means of a 'special inquiry', and in specially designed facilities, then treated as admissible *per se* at the adversarial stage. However, this exception does not apply to the young victims of non-sexual offences (even though the latter may involve the same evidential problems as sexual offences). *Pupino* concerned an Italian nursery school teacher charged with physically maltreating pupils under the age of five. The defendant objected to the use of the special inquiry or the specially designated facilities in her case, on the grounds that this would be contrary to the Italian criminal procedure rules as described above. The national court asked the ECJ whether it was nevertheless obliged to construe the Italian legislation in conformity with Framework Decision 2001/220 on the standing of victims in criminal proceedings (according to which Member States must ensure, *inter alia*, that particularly vulnerable victims benefit from specific treatment best suited to their circumstances).[30]

The Court decided that the duty of consistent interpretation is indeed binding in relation to framework decisions adopted under the third pillar; national courts are thus obliged to construe domestic law, so far as possible, in the light of the wording and purpose of the framework decision in order to attain its objectives. That finding was justified by several considerations. First, the duty of consistent interpretation derives from the binding character of framework decisions *vis-à-vis* all national authorities, including the national courts. Secondly, the Court's (albeit limited) jurisdiction to give preliminary rulings in the context of the third pillar under Article 35 TEU would be deprived of most of its useful effect if individuals were not entitled to invoke framework decisions before the national courts in order to obtain a consistent interpretation of domestic law. Thirdly, it would be difficult for the EU effectively to carry

[29] Case 14/83 *Von Colson* [1984] ECR 1891; Case C-106/89 *Marleasing* [1990] ECR I-4135.
[30] Framework Decision 2001/220, OJ 2001 L 82, p. 1.

out its task of creating an ever closer union among the peoples of Europe if the principle of loyal co-operation – requiring Member States to take all appropriate measures to ensure fulfilment of their obligations under Union law – were not also binding as regards the third pillar. This was true even though Title VI TEU lacked any express provision equivalent to Article 10 EC, the legal basis on which most of the first pillar caselaw on the principle of loyal co-operation has been developed.

The Court went on, however, to make clear that the limitations to the duty of consistent interpretation as developed under Community law also apply within the context of the third pillar: it is a duty to construe only 'so far as possible', not to interpret domestic rules *contra legem*. Moreover, the duty to interpret national law in the light of a framework decision cannot lead to an individual's criminal liability being determined or aggravated (a parallel to the principle affirmed in the *Berlusconi* case). Finally, the Court pointed out that the framework decision itself must be interpreted so as to respect fundamental rights as general principles of Union law, as derived from the European Convention on Human Rights and the common constitutional traditions of the Member States. Taking all of those considerations into account, the ECJ found that the Italian court must construe its criminal procedure rules, so far as possible, in conformity with Framework Decision 2001/220, to offer young children who claim to be the victims of physical maltreatment an appropriate level of protection, provided this would not make the criminal proceedings against Pupino incompatible with Article 6 of the European Convention on Human Rights on the right to a fair trial.

Pupino is a very welcome development. The system of legal protection applicable to the third pillar is clearly unsatisfactory for a variety of reasons: for example, the Court's limited jurisdiction to entertain direct actions challenging the validity of third-pillar measures; the voluntary nature of the Court's jurisdiction to respond to preliminary references from the national courts of the Member States; as well as the express exclusion of any possibility of direct effect for unimplemented framework decisions. The Court in *Pupino* could not overcome these inherent, structural deficiencies; but it identified two useful legal devices for bolstering the rule of law within the context of the Union's third-pillar activities. In the first place, the duty of consistent interpretation helps ensure that, even in the absence of direct effect for the relevant framework decision, national law will conform so far as possible to the regime of criminal law adopted by the Union. In the second place – and perhaps even more important – the obligation of national courts to construe the framework decision *itself* so far as possible in conformity with the general principles of EU law helps to ensure that the regime of criminal law adopted by the Union will *in its turn* respect human rights and fundamental freedoms.

Many issues will require further clarification, of course. For example, will these twin duties apply not only to the national courts of Member States (such as Italy) which have accepted the jurisdiction of the ECJ to deliver preliminary rulings, but also to the national courts of Member States (such as the UK) which have refused to recognize the Court's jurisdiction at all? On the one hand, the *effet utile* of the preliminary reference system under Article 35 TEU certainly played a role in the Court's justification for recognizing that the duty of consistent interpretation should apply in the third pillar. On the other hand, the other considerations relied upon by the Court – such as the binding effect of framework decisions, and the need for Member State co-operation in attaining closer European integration – remain persuasive in respect of both referring and non-referring states alike.

Union action under the third pillar is problematic not only thanks to the ECJ's limited jurisdiction, or the exclusion of direct effect for framework decisions, but also because of the prevailing system of inter-institutional relations; in particular, offering the European Parliament a lesser role in the legislative process than it usually enjoys under the first pillar, and forcing the Commission to share its prerogative of legislative initiative with the Member States. Viewed in that broader context, the Court's achievements in *Pupino* might appear even more modest. But the judgment in *Commission* v. *Council* illustrates how the Court can sometimes address this whole bundle of problems quite effectively by other means, i.e. by expanding the criminal law competences available to the Community, so as to minimize the fields of activity left to the unsatisfactory third pillar.

In 2001, the Commission made a proposal to the Council, on the basis of Article 175 EC, for a directive on the protection of the environment through criminal law, defining the conduct which Member States should establish as criminal offences under domestic law, including a list of the Community environmental measures which should become subject to those criminal offences. In the end, however, the Council, acting on a Danish proposal under Title VI TEU, adopted Framework Decision 2003/80 on the protection of the environment through criminal law (which nevertheless incorporated certain aspects of the Commission's draft directive).[31] The Commission sought annulment of the framework decision on the grounds that the Community enjoys competence to require Member States to prescribe criminal penalties for infringement of first-pillar legislation where this is necessary to ensure that that legislation is effective; as such, the framework decision infringed Article 47 TEU, according to which nothing in the Treaty on European Union is to affect the EC Treaty,

---

[31] Framework Decision 2003/80, OJ 2003 L 29, p. 55.

and whose purpose is thus to prevent third-pillar measures encroaching on the powers properly conferred upon the Community.

The ECJ began by ascertaining whether the relevant provisions of the framework decision could indeed have been adopted under Article 175 EC. It noted that protection of the environment constitutes one of the Community's fundamental objectives and must be incorporated into the full range of Community policies and activities, though Articles 174–176 EC provide the framework and legal basis for conducting the Community's environmental policy (generally through the co-decision procedure contained in Article 251 EC). Although, as a general rule, criminal law and criminal procedure fall outside the Community's competence, this does not prevent the Community legislature from adopting measures relating to national criminal law, which it considers necessary to ensure that the rules it lays down on environmental protection are fully effective, in particular, where the application of effective and dissuasive criminal penalties by the competent domestic authorities is essential for combating serious environmental offences. Having regard to the aim and content of Framework Decision 2003/80, the contested provisions had as their main purpose the protection of the environment and could properly have been adopted on the basis of Article 175 EC. By thus encroaching upon the powers reserved to the Community under the EC Treaty, the framework decision infringed Article 47 TEU and was annulled in its entirety.

Commission v. *Council* is the first case in which the Court has confirmed unequivocally that the Community does enjoy certain legislative competences of its own in the field of criminal law. Those competences are, to be sure, of a derivative nature: they presuppose the existence of a substantive Community policy initiative, and seek merely to reinforce the latter's effectiveness by harmonizing the criminal sanctions to be applied by national authorities for the enforcement of the relevant Community norms. There can be no question of the Community harmonizing national criminal rules for their own sake, independently of its other regulatory activities. Moreover, the judgment describes the threshold for exercising the Community's derivative criminal competences in quite stringent terms: criminal sanctions must be 'essential' in the case of 'serious' offences, and their use 'necessary' to ensure that Community rules are 'fully effective'. Still, the ruling remains a legal breakthrough, and opens up a whole host of questions, not least in defining exactly what should be considered a 'serious' offence, and when criminal (as opposed to civil or administrative) sanctions should be deemed 'essential'. In particular, there seems no reason to restrict the judgment to the field of environmental policy: why should the Community not be able to insist that Member States enact harmonized criminal sanctions also in fields such as the internal market, non-discrimination, consumer protection or agricultural policy (assuming that the same threshold for engaging the Community's derivative criminal competences is traversed)? This is certainly the view taken by the Commission, which has furthermore identified other third-pillar framework decisions deemed (in hindsight) to have infringed the Community's own criminal competences.[32]

But *Commission* v. *Council* is also a victory for the Community method over the third pillar. Just because a measure deals with 'criminal law' does not mean that it properly belongs to the field of judicial co-operation in criminal matters in the sense of Title VI TEU. It would have been most unsatisfactory if (say) a directive dealing with the substantive rules on environmental, consumer or employment protection were to be adopted under the EC Treaty (with full judicial scrutiny of their legality by the Community courts, extensive legal protection for individuals before the national courts, and the full involvement of the Commission and European Parliament in the legislative procedure); but a derivative framework decision prescribing criminal sanctions in respect of those substantive rules had to be adopted under Title VI TEU (with only limited judicial review by the Union judiciary, more limited legal protection for individuals before the national courts, even despite *Pupino*, and only a marginal decision-making role for the Commission and European Parliament). The scope of judicial co-operation in criminal matters under the third pillar thus seems limited to issues such as jurisdiction over and extradition of persons who have committed criminal offences, together with the approximation of national criminal rules insofar as this facilitates the mutual recognition and enforcement by Member States of judgments in criminal cases.

Of course, many of the problems raised in cases like *Pupino* and *Commission* v. *Council* would have been resolved by the Treaty establishing a Constitution for Europe 2004. Indeed, the process of de-pillarization would have seen the field of police and judicial co-operation in criminal matters more-or-less fully assimilated to the 'Community method' as regards its legal instruments, legislative procedures, judicial review and other aspects of effective legal protection.[33] But unless and until that Constitutional Treaty enters into force, cases like *Pupino* and *Commission* v. *Council* suggest that the ECJ will try to make the best of a decidedly bad job.

IV. The WTO Agreements and the Community Legal Order

Readers of this *Annual Review* may recall the ECJ's jurisprudence that the World Trade Organization (WTO) agreements are not capable of providing the basis for reviewing the legality of Community measures: first, the global trading

---

[32] COM(2005) 583 Final.
[33] Published at OJ 2004 C 310.

rules place considerable emphasis on political negotiation as a means of resolving disputes between contracting parties; secondly, some of the Community's most important trading partners do not treat the WTO agreements as direct grounds for invalidating their own internal acts. The Court concedes that the situation would be different only where the Community institutions intended to implement a particular obligation assumed in the context of the WTO, or where the relevant Community act expressly refers to precise provisions of the WTO agreements.[34] That well-established caselaw dealt with the situation existing *before* binding decisions are adopted by the WTO's Dispute Settlement Body (DSB). The *Biret* litigation in 2003 raised the question whether the legal framework should differ *after* the DSB has found the Community in breach of its WTO obligations and obliged to remedy the situation – but thanks to the particular factual characteristics of the *Biret* case, the ECJ was able to postpone expressing any firm opinion on this legally complex and politically controversial issue.[35] The problem soon arose again in the *Van Parys* case, and this time, the Court took the bull firmly by its horns.[36]

Van Parys forms part of the interminable wrangling over the regulations establishing a common organization of the market in bananas. The Community's original regime was adopted in 1993, but declared by the DSB to be incompatible with certain provisions of the General Agreement on Tariffs and Trade (GATT) in 1997. Having declared its intention to comply with its obligations towards the WTO, the Community's revised regime was adopted in 1998, but the DSB decided in 1999 that this had failed to remove the Community's infringement of the GATT. The Community enacted further amendments to the common organization of the market in bananas in 2001. During the same year, agreements were negotiated with the United States and Ecuador with a view to bringing the Community legislation into line with WTO rules. Van Parys was a Belgian company whose applications during 1998–99 for licences to import bananas into the Community from Ecuador were not fully granted by the national authorities. Van Parys then brought an action before the domestic courts arguing that the Community legislation upon which the national authorities had based their decisions was itself unlawful under the WTO agreements.

The ECJ rejected the idea that, by undertaking after the 1997 decision of the DSB to comply with the GATT, the Community intended to assume a particular obligation in the context of the WTO capable of enabling the Community courts to carry out a judicial review of the relevant Community legislation in the light of the WTO rules (and nor did the disputed regulations

---

[34] E.g. Case C-149/96 *Portugal* v. *Council* [1999] ECR I-8395.
[35] Case C-94/02 *Biret* [2003] ECR I-10565. See the 'Legal Developments' chapter in the 2003/2004 edition of this *Annual Review*.
[36] Case C-377/02 *Van Parys* (1 March 2005).

expressly refer to specific provisions of the WTO agreements). In particular, the ECJ observed that, even where there is a decision of the DSB holding that a given measure is incompatible with the WTO rules, the dispute settlement system still accords considerable importance to negotiation between the parties; and indeed, even expiry of the time limit granted by the DSB within which to implement its decisions does not exhaust the possibilities provided under the WTO rules for finding a negotiated solution between the parties. Against that background, to enable the Community courts, merely on the basis that the DSB's time limit has expired, to review the legality of Community legislation in the light of the WTO rules could undermine the Community's attempts to reach a mutually acceptable solution to the relevant dispute in conformity with the WTO's own rules (as demonstrated in this case by the Community's further reforms to the common organization of the market in bananas during 2001, as well as the international agreements reached with the United States and Ecuador that same year). And of course, just because the DSB had found Community legislation to be incompatible with the WTO rules did not change the fact that some of the Community's most important trading partners did not treat the WTO agreements as a direct grounds for invalidating their own internal acts. In such circumstances, the ECJ had no reason to deprive the Community's legislative and executive institutions of a discretion enjoyed by its major commercial rivals.

Thus, Van Parys was not entitled to plead before the Belgian courts that the relevant Community legislation was incompatible with the GATT, even though the DSB had already stated that that legislation is indeed in breach of the WTO rules. This is not to say that the door to more extensive judicial review on the basis of the WTO agreements has been shut totally: the Court might yet adopt a different approach in future cases similar to *Biret*, where the deadline for compliance by the Community with the decision of the DSB expired and the Community institutions had taken no action to bring their legislation into conformity with the WTO rules (whereas in the case of the banana regulations, serious efforts were at least made within the applicable deadlines to address the inadequacies identified by the DSB). But for now, it seems that individuals wishing to challenge the validity of Community action in the light of the WTO agreements will continue to find an unsympathetic ear in Luxembourg.

Key Reading

For further analysis of some of the issues discussed in this chapter, readers may find the following academic papers useful.

Dougan, M. (2005) 'Fees, Grants, Loans and Dole Cheques: Who Covers the Costs of Migrant Education within the EU?'. *Common Market Law Review,* Vol. 42, No. 4, pp. 943–86.

Editorial (2006) 'Horizontal Direct Effect: A Law of Diminishing Coherence?'. *Common Market Law Review,* Vol. 43, No. 1, pp. 1–8.

Kuijper, P.J. and Bronckers, M. (2005) 'WTO Law in the European Court of Justice'. *Common Market Law Review,* Vol. 42, No. 5, pp. 1313–55.

Prechal, S. (2005) *Directives in EC Law,* 2nd edn (Oxford: Oxford University Press).

Relations with the Wider Europe

SANDRA LAVENEX
University of Lucerne
FRANK SCHIMMELFENNIG
ETH Zürich

Introduction

In 2005, one year after the biggest round of enlargement ever, the European Union (EU) had to take difficult decisions on how to proceed with the remaining candidates and those countries which, for the foreseeable future, would not be granted a membership perspective. Whereas, contrary to some expectations, enlargement policy has stuck to established paths, the s (ENP) provides an opening for new and differentiated forms of association below the threshold of accession. The EU's relations with its neighbours, including Switzerland, have deepened, contributing to the consolidation of varied patterns of deep association and flexible horizontal integration in Europe.

I. Enlargement: The Balkans and Turkey

2005 might simply have been 'the year after' the EU's biggest enlargement round ever. Yet, in many ways, it turned out to be a defining – and surprising – year for the future of EU enlargement. It was a defining year because it set the stage for how the EU will proceed with enlargement in the future, and it was surprising because, while the EU's enlargement policy seemed to be in deep crisis in mid-2005, it appeared intact by its end.

After the 2004 enlargement, which increased EU membership from 15 to 25, the prevailing mood was 'enlargement fatigue'. The widespread impression was that the EU had expanded too far too fast. It was agreed that the EU needed time to digest the admission of ten new members and to adapt its institutions, procedures and budget before it could undertake further expansion. The Constitutional Treaty and the agreement on a new financial perspective for 2007–13 were seen as keys to this, yet both the budget negotiations and the ratification of the new Treaty failed in the first half of 2005.

At the same time, the EU was faced with path-breaking and difficult decisions on enlargement. First, it had to deal with two 'leftovers' of the 2004 enlargement round: Bulgaria and Romania. Would they be ready to join in 2007 as planned? Second, the EU had promised to decide on opening accession negotiations with Croatia and Turkey provided that they each solved some remaining problems. These decisions would determine whether the EU was serious about the membership perspective for the Balkans and Turkey.

However, these candidates lagged behind the recently admitted central and east European states in democratic consolidation and economic and state transformation. The legacies of the 'wars of Yugoslav succession' loomed large. The region is still rife with ethnic tensions; co-operation with the war crimes tribunal at the Hague is contested; in the case of Serbia, Montenegro and Kosovo, it is not even clear with which political entities the EU would negotiate and how many countries might eventually join. Finally, while Turkey might become the biggest Member State, it is also poorer than the EU's present membership, struggling with the illiberal legacies of 'Kemalism', geographically located in Asia for the most part, and with a Muslim population.

These conditions cast doubts on the EU's appetite for further expansion, particularly when its internal reforms were frozen. They also raised questions about the future effectiveness of the EU's accession conditionality, which had been highly successful in locking in democratic transformation and ensuring the adoption of the *acquis communautaire* in the new Member States. Would conditionality work when membership was distant and uncertain or when state consolidation and capacity were low? In addition, it was unclear whether the EU would be willing (or forced) to lower its standards to keep enlargement alive or whether it would create even higher hurdles for the remaining enlargement candidates in order to prepare them for membership and make sure that they would not renege on their commitments.

Bulgaria and Romania

When Bulgaria and Romania signed their accession treaties on 25 April 2005, the EU for the first time inserted a safeguard clause, which may postpone accession for one year should they be manifestly unprepared to meet the requirements of membership by January 2007. For Romania, the EU even listed 11 specific commitments (in the areas of justice and home affairs, as well as competition) to be met ahead of accession. Under these circumstances, the 'Comprehensive Monitoring Report on Bulgaria and Romania' of 25 October

2005 had special significance (Commission, 2005a). In Bulgaria, in particular, the election campaign and weeks of post-election deadlock had delayed reforms over the summer.

In general, the report confirmed that both countries met the political and economic accession criteria and that they should be able to adopt the *acquis* by 2007 provided that they step up their efforts. Yet administrative capacity, judicial reform, corruption and organized crime remained areas of major concern. So did, more specifically, food safety and structures and mechanisms for participation in the structural funds.

In December 2005, the European Parliament (EP) broadly supported the Commission's conclusions, but assessed Bulgaria's prospects for joining in January 2007 more positively than those of Romania, and made explicit that each country would be assessed on its own merits. In the case of Bulgaria, MEPs put specific emphasis on the partial closure of the Kozludoy nuclear power plant. In the case of Romania, however, they noted 'persistent delays' and called for 'immediate steps to make good these shortcomings'.[1]

Turkey

The December 2004 European Council noted the reforms Turkey had introduced, agreed that Turkey fulfilled the political conditions for opening accession negotiations, and fixed 3 October 2005 as the date to start accession negotiations. Two further main conditions had remained to be fulfilled: enactment of the revised penal code, which had been adopted shortly before the Commission's decisive report in October 2004, and signature of an additional protocol, which would extend the 1964 Ankara agreement of association and the customs union with the EU to the ten new Member States, which raised the issue of recognition of the (Greek) Republic of Cyprus. On 1 June 2005, the revised penal code entered into force. On 29 July 2005, Turkey also signed the additional protocol, although it issued a political declaration that the protocol did not entail recognition of the Republic of Cyprus.

On 29 June 2005, the Commission released its negotiating framework for the accession negotiations with Turkey, which contained a number of novel elements (Commission, 2005e, f). First, whereas the objective of the talks will be accession, the negotiations are declared to be 'open-ended'. That is, accession is not guaranteed. Should Turkey fail to qualify in full for all obligations of EU membership, the EU would ensure that the country is 'fully anchored in the European structures through the strongest possible bond'. Second, the Commission may include long transition periods, derogations,

[1] See «http://www.europarl.eu.int/news/expert/infopress_page/027-3555-349-12-50-903-20051208IPR03372-15-12-2005-2005--false/default_en.htm».

specific arrangements or permanent safeguard clauses in its proposals, and accession negotiations will not be concluded before 2014, the scheduled date for the EU's next financial perspective. Third, negotiations can be suspended in case of a 'serious and persistent breach … of the principles of democracy, respect for human rights and fundamental freedoms and the rule of law'. Suspension would require a Commission initiative or a request to that effect by one-third of the Member States. The final decision would be made by the Council by qualified majority, and the EP would be informed. These terms of negotiation reflected the persistent political conflict among Member States on the desirability of Turkish membership as well as persistent concern about the viability of reform in Turkey and about the consequences of membership for the EU market and budget.

These qualifications did not, however, prevent last-minute bargaining among the Member States on the start of accession negotiations. Most prominently, whereas the UK and Germany (under the Schröder government) strongly advocated the membership perspective for Turkey, Austria and France threatened to hold referendums on Turkey's accession. In addition, the Austrian government was not content with the open-endedness of accession negotiations, insisting that the negotiating framework explicitly identify 'privileged partnership' as a possible alternative negotiating goal. The unresolved Cyprus conflict also continued to haunt the EU. After weeks of debate, the EU on 21 September agreed to require Turkey to normalize relations with the Republic of Cyprus 'as soon as possible' in the course of accession negotiations (rather than before their end, as the EU had demanded before). Moreover, the centre-right majority in the EP refused to ratify the additional protocol because Cypriot ships are still barred from Turkish ports. On the other hand, the Greek-Cypriot government did not achieve its goal of making recognition (and the full implementation of the additional protocol) a precondition of opening accession talks. At the last minute, on 3 October, the Council approved the negotiating framework proposed by the Commission without explicit reference to 'privileged partnership' and opened negotiations symbolically just after midnight.

After the so-called screening process, accession talks proper are set to start in the first half of 2006. The Turkish government, however, still refuses to implement the additional protocol and demands that restrictions on the Turkish Republic of Northern Cyprus be ended reciprocally. By contrast, the Republic of Cyprus rejects reciprocity or recognition of the Turkish Republic. Rather, the Greek-Cypriot government continued to use its status as an EU member (and its concomitant veto power over Turkish accession) as a bargaining chip in order to achieve reunification of the island on its own terms.

Despite major reforms introduced by the Erdogan government, the 'Europeanization' of Turkey continues to meet opposition, and the Commission

(2005b) detected a slowdown in the pace of change in 2005. Repressive laws, such as that prohibiting the insulting of Turkish identity, remain in force and are used by a conservative and nationalist judiciary. The trial of novelist Orhan Pamuk was the most prominent case in 2005. Moreover, the government seemed under pressure to appease nationalist opinion – for instance, when Minister of Justice Cemil Cicek in May 2005 called off a conference organized by a group of academics and intellectuals on the mass killing of Ottoman Armenians in 1915. Yet the fact that the Pamuk trial was called off in February 2006 and the conference took place later in 2005 also demonstrates the impact of EU conditionality.

Croatia

Croatia is the most advanced country of the 'western Balkans'. After the end of the Tudjman regime in 2000, it has moved quickly in the direction of EU membership. The stabilization and association agreement (SAA) entered into force on 1 February 2005, and the December 2004 European Council decided to open accession negotiations on 17 March 2005. The only remaining obstacle was full co-operation with the International Criminal Tribunal for the former Yugoslavia (ICTY). In particular, the EU expected the Croatian government to assist the ICTY in arresting suspected war criminal General Ante Gotovina. In March 2005, the EU followed ICTY Chief Prosecutor Carla Del Ponte in concluding that Croatia was not fully co-operating. However, it also adopted a negotiating framework so that accessions talks could begin as soon as full co-operation was established.

In October 2005, Gotovina was still at large, and so it came as a surprise – including at the Hague – that Chief Prosecutor Del Ponte testified that Croatia was now in full co-operation with the ICTY and that the EU decided to open accession negotiations with Croatia at the same time as with Turkey. Many observers initially suspected that the EU had exercised political pressure on Del Ponte and that the positive decision for Croatia was a concession to Austria in return for its acquiescence toward opening accession negotiations with Turkey. However, after Gotovina was arrested in Tenerife in December 2005, it became clear that Del Ponte's positive assessment resulted from the fact that Gotovina had already been located in October and that the tribunal had received crucial information from the Croatian government. What had seemed to be evidence of the EU's political bargaining and double standards in the enlargement process now appeared as another success of its credible political conditionality.

The Rest of the Western Balkans

The EU had confirmed the membership perspective for the remaining countries of the western Balkans – Albania, Bosnia-Herzegovina and Macedonia, as well as Serbia and Montenegro – at the 2003 Thessaloniki European Council, but progress has been slow. Macedonia's SAA entered into force in April 2004, shortly after it had filed its application for EU membership. Negotiations with Albania, however, had been dragging since the beginning of 2003, and Bosnia-Herzegovina and Serbia-Montenegro had not even started negotiations.

2005 saw fresh emphasis on the western Balkans. The Directorate General for Enlargement is now responsible for managing all relations with this region, including political relations and the development and management of the Community assistance for reconstruction, development and stabilization (Cards) programme. On 26 January, the Commission made active preparation for future enlargements and bringing the western Balkans closer to the membership perspective priorities for EU action in 2005–09 (Commission, 2005c).

Moreover, in its November enlargement strategy paper, the Commission found that reforms in Albania had advanced far enough to sign the SAA in 2006. Negotiations concluded in February 2006. There was also progress in Bosnia-Herzegovina. In 2005, the focus was on police reform, which was supposed to centralize police competences and assure recruitment according to professional rather than ethnic criteria. Although it was the last hurdle set by the EU before the start of SAA negotiations, it continued to be blocked by the Serbian Republic. On 5 October, however, two days after the EU had decided to open SAA negotiations with Serbia-Montenegro and threatened to leave Bosnia-Herzegovina as the only country in the region without EU association, the parliament of the Serbian Republic suddenly agreed. On 21 October, the Commission duly recommended that the Council open SAA talks, which started officially on 25 November 2005.

In February 2005, the Macedonian government submitted a 14,000-page response to the Commission's questionnaire, which informed its opinion on Macedonia's membership application. In November 2005, the Commission recommended that Macedonia be granted the status of a candidate country for membership – a halfway solution similar to that used in EU relations with Turkey from 1999 to 2005. Whereas the Commission found that the country had made considerable progress in implementing the 2001 Ohrid framework agreement and in co-operating under the SAA, it questioned whether it met the conditions for opening accession negotiations. France, together with the Netherlands and Denmark, was reluctant to put another country on the track towards membership and proposed waiting until the EU had come to terms with its budget and the Constitution and conducted a general discussion on further enlargement in 2006. The Member States' foreign ministers therefore deferred the decision to the Brussels European Council in December which, in the end, followed the proposal of the Commission. A date for the start of membership talks has not been set yet; it will depend on the level of reforms and compliance.

Finally, Serbia-Montenegro also started SAA negotiations in 2005. On 25 April, the Council approved the Commission's feasibility report and, on 3 October, it authorized the Commission to open negotiations. These negotiations, however, are being sidelined by three issues. First, both the Serbian government and the EU have come under pressure from ICTY Chief Prosecutor Del Ponte to make the continuation (and not the conclusion) of talks dependent on the delivery of General Ratko Mladic, who is sought in connection with the 1995 Srebrenica massacre. Second, Montenegro is holding a referendum on independence in May 2006, which was part of the deal brokered by the EU in 2003 to keep Montenegro from seceding. Third, the international process to determine the future status of Kosovo started in October 2005. The parallel SAA negotiations with Serbia and a membership perspective in the EU are thought to provide a carrot to Serbia for agreeing to the independence of its former province. On 20 April 2005, the Commission explicitly extended the membership perspective of the Thessaloniki declaration to Kosovo.

II. European Neighbourhood Policy

While EU enlargement politics did not change fundamentally, the experience of enlargement has shaped the EU's association relations with neighbouring countries in various ways. This became very salient in 2005, the first year of implementation of the ENP (Commission, 2005d). The ENP emulates key concepts and routines developed in the context of enlargement – ranging from the general conception of negotiated bilateralism to the emphasis on positive conditionality – and borrows concrete instruments, such as action plans, enhanced monitoring through regular reports, and twinning of public administrations. At least from a sectoral perspective, one can argue that the ENP does indeed promote enlargement – albeit only at the level of selected policy areas and without access to the core decision-making bodies of the EU.

The ENP has brought new priorities into existing association relationships and has intensified webs of integration, not only in the traditional field of trade, but also formerly domestic domains such as justice and home affairs (JHA), energy, the environment, transport and, with some countries, also foreign and security policy. Sectoral integration notwithstanding, developments in 2005 also called into question whether intensified functional co-operation can be a long-term alternative to accession for aspiring countries, such as Ukraine or

Moldova. Doubts also emerged as to the ENP's potential to meet its proclaimed ambitions with regard to conflict resolution (e.g. in the Caucasus and Middle East) or political change in autocratic regimes. The absence of incentives comparable to EU accession, budgetary constraints, competing priorities within the ENP and its oscillation between normative and strategic priorities may hamper its transformative potential.

During 2005, a number of inconsistencies resulting from such competing priorities became salient. For example, Tunisia's action plan entered into force before that of other Mediterranean countries despite its inferior political record. In addition, the EU sought to promote internal security co-operation with Belarus and Libya, even though neither meets the political conditions for participation in the ENP. It seems that the EP realized this ambiguity when it emphasized in its December 2005 report on the ENP that it should not be an instrument of 'settling for the status quo but of committing the European Union to support the aspirations of the peoples of our neighbouring countries to full political freedom, with democracy and justice … ' including the stricter use of political conditionality (EP, 2005).

The ENP is built on top of established partnership and co-operation agreements (PCAs) and association agreements, as well as the Barcelona process. Its main instrument is the action plan, a bilateral partnership for reform, which is agreed jointly between the EU and the partner country and which identifies priorities for action across a broad range of areas. During 2005 ENP action plans were negotiated and formally adopted with seven countries – Israel, Jordan, Moldova, Morocco, the Palestinian Authority, Tunisia and Ukraine – and are being prepared with five others: Armenia, Azerbaijan, Egypt, Georgia and Lebanon. Four other countries qualify in principle for the ENP: Algeria, Belarus, Libya and Syria.

Each action plan should run for at least three years and can be renewed by common agreement. The action plans' implementation will be monitored in the framework of the institutions provided for in the relevant association or co-operation agreement. Financial support for ENP partner countries (and Russia) will be provided through a single European neighbourhood and partnership instrument (ENPI) from 2007. Its funding was set at €14.9 billion for 2007–13, compared to approximately €8.5 billion for 2000–06 under the old instruments, Meda and Tacis.

Eastern Europe

Ukraine. The first action plans to enter into force were with Ukraine and Moldova in February 2005. After the presidential election in November 2004, the new Ukrainian President Victor Yushchenko immediately raised the issue of a membership perspective, going beyond the scope of the ENP action plan, agreed by the previous government of Viktor Yanukovich. The EU's response was a ten-point programme that goes beyond what had been agreed with the outgoing regime, but remains silent on the question of membership. It includes, *inter alia*, consultations on an enhanced agreement to succeed the PCA; closer co-operation in foreign and security and defence policies; acceleration of the preparations for a free trade area; continued support for Ukraine's accession to the World Trade Organization, including its acquisition of 'market economy status' (formally granted on 23 December), and intensified negotiations regarding visa facilitation.

Sectoral co-operation has also steadily intensified. Probably the most prominent example is in the energy sector, with Russia's ambitions to align gas import prices in Ukraine to world market standards culminating in a regional energy crisis at the end of 2005. Even before Russia announced its intention to raise prices, the EU's General Affairs and External Relations Council called for strengthened energy co-operation on the launch of the action plan in February 2005. At the December 2005 EU–Ukrainian summit, a memorandum of understanding on energy was signed that foresees increased co-operation in all energy fields, with the long-term prospect of integrated energy markets. Another important energy-related development was the decision of the Ukrainian government to switch the flow of the Odessa–Brody pipeline, thereby contributing to the EU's policy of diversifying its oil supplies.

With regard to JHA, the action plan was scheduled for joint revision by the end of 2005. In an attempt to speed up talks with the EU on facilitating visas, Ukraine decided in May 2005 to suspend the requirement of entry visas for EU citizens on a short-term visit to Ukraine. In return, the EU agreed to negotiate on visa facilitation, but only in parallel with negotiations on a readmission agreement, which had started in 2002.

Important steps were also taken in the field of transport. In July 2005, an air services agreement was adopted and negotiations opened for a second, more specific, aviation agreement that should lead to a common EU–Ukraine aviation area. Moreover, both sides agreed on Ukraine's participation in Europe's satellite navigation system Galileo. Finally, the EU and Ukraine have been intensifying their dialogue and co-operation on foreign and security policy issues, including on crisis management. Ukraine has been participating in the EU's police mission (EUPM) in Bosnia and Herzegovina, and will also participate in the EUPM in Macedonia.

Moldova. The focus of foreign policy co-operation between the EU, Ukraine and Moldova has been the 'frozen' conflict in the Transdniestria region of Moldova. In 2005, Ukraine and Moldova jointly asked the EU for assistance in establishing effective border controls between them, including the Transdniestrian segment. As a first step, the Council appointed an EU special representative to Moldova. A border control mission was launched on 20 November, under which 50 EU experts monitor border crossings.

2005 saw parliamentary elections in Moldova, which the OSCE's Office for Democratic Institutions and Human Rights mission considered met most of the requirements of the Council of Europe/OSCE, but failed to meet some of the requirements of a genuinely competitive election. The day it was installed, the Moldovan parliament endorsed a non-partisan declaration aimed at achieving the objective of European integration. Moldova aspires to SAA negotiations, which would include the prospect of EU membership. Like Ukraine, Moldova wants to see an improvement in the visa regime the EU applies to its citizens. The prospect of Romania's accession in 2007 and the fact that up to 40 per cent of Moldova's citizens might then obtain 'EU passports' by claiming Romanian citizenship, gives a sense of urgency to these aspirations.

South Caucasus. Although originally not included in the ENP, Georgia, Armenia and Azerbaijan joined in 2004. In March 2005, the Commission published country reports that form the basis for the adoption of ENP action plans. Initial hopes that these would be concluded during 2005 did not materialize. Officially, the EU argued that it wanted to wait for the outcome of the parliamentary elections in Azerbaijan in November; unofficially, negotiations were stalled due to a row between EU Member State Cyprus and Turkey-friendly Azerbaijan over the latter permitting commercial flights to Northern Cyprus.

It is important to recognize that the countries of the Caucasus have very different expectations of the ENP. For Georgia and Azerbaijan the ENP is a means of preserving their close links to Ukraine and establishing a counterweight to Russia. Armenia, by contrast, sees the ENP as a vehicle to gain EU support in resolving outstanding regional conflicts. In particular, it hopes to put pressure on Turkey to reopen its borders and railway connections with Armenia. The EU, however, may concur with Azerbaijan that the Armenian–Turkish border is one of the very few levers the international community can bring to bear on Armenia to resolve the conflict in Nagorno-Karabakh.

From the EU's perspective, there is much room for improvement. The EU's report on Georgia (March 2005) was the least critical. Yet, several developments in the second half of the year tarnished Georgia's liberal-democratic image. Among these were the staffing of election commissions with people loyal to the ruling elite and excluding national minorities and, in October, the dismissal of Foreign Minister Salome Zourabichvili, following pressure from neo-communist and pro-Russian forces in the country. The main concerns in the reports on Armenia and Azerbaijan relate to deficient legislation, widespread

Russian influence on decision-making, breaches of fundamental freedoms and a general lack of willingness to reform. The parliamentary elections in Azerbaijan revealed shortcomings, especially in vote counting and tabulation. A 2005 referendum in Armenia approved a set of constitutional amendments, supported by the EU, the OSCE and the Council of Europe, focusing on president–parliamentary relations and strengthening the independence of the judiciary. Notwithstanding vocal resistance by leading opposition groups and confirmation by international observers that the referendum featured instances of abuse, the government stopped short of declaring the result invalid. Despite different geopolitical standpoints, both Georgia and Armenia have declared that EU membership is their long-term goal.

Mediterranean Countries

The launch of the first ENP action plans with Mediterranean countries in 2005 coincided with the celebration of the tenth anniversary of the Barcelona process and provided an opportunity to recalibrate the focus and tools of Euro–Mediterranean co-operation. The negotiated bilateralism of the ENP and the possibility for individual countries to deepen their relations with the EU were welcomed by the Mediterranean countries.

In substantive terms, the ENP puts new emphasis on security issues, such as preventing terrorism and the proliferation of weapons of mass destruction, as well as the management of migration flows. The ENP also seeks to provide more stringent policies to promote better governance and the respect of human rights. Its economic leverage towards the Mediterranean countries stems less from market access for industrial goods which, in contrast to its eastern neighbours, is already quite open, than from other economic areas, such as trade in agricultural goods and services, as well as technical assistance for adapting to EU standards.

These issues were also at the centre of the November 2005 Euro–Mediterranean summit, which marked the tenth anniversary of the Barcelona declaration and agreed a five-year work programme for the further development of the partnership and a code of conduct for countering terrorism. By adopting the work programme, the partners have agreed on several issues, including the governance facility to support and accompany political reform; the liberalization of trade in services and agriculture; migration-related issues and the fight against illegal migration, increasing resources for education; reinforcing the role of civil society and improving its engagement with governments and parliaments.

The summit was anticipated by a number of prominent plurilateral activities. In March, the first plenary session of the Euro–Mediterranean parliamentary assembly was held in Cairo to discuss the progress made under the Euro–

Mediterranean partnership. As a step to strengthening civil society in these countries, the Anna Lindh Foundation for the Dialogue of Cultures was created in Alexandria by the EU Member States and their ten Mediterranean partners with the general objective of developing partnership in social, cultural and human affairs. Similar goals are also at the centre of the Euro–Mediterranean non-governmental platform. Finally, in the area of security policy, the June European Council approved the implementation of the strategic partnership between the EU and the Mediterranean region and the Middle East.

Sectoral developments focused on trade, energy, internal security/migration, and transport. In November, it was decided to open negotiations on trade in agricultural and fisheries products and liberalization of services and investment, services making up to 60 per cent of GDP in the Mediterranean countries. Guidelines for a Euro–Mediterranean free trade area in energy were adopted in February. A first step in this direction is a project signed in December between the European Commission, Algeria, Morocco and Tunisia reforming Maghreb electricity markets in the light of their future integration into the EU internal electricity market. In December the Euro–Mediterranean ministers of transport met for the first time in Marrakech to discuss a Blue Paper aimed at creating an 'integrated Euro–Mediterranean transport system'.

At the bilateral level, a first wave of ENP action plans entered into force with the countries having EU association agreements or interim agreements: Israel, Jordan, Morocco, the Palestinian Authority and Tunisia. Negotiations began with Egypt and Lebanon during the final trimester of 2005. For Algeria, the Euro–Mediterranean association agreement signed in 2002 could finally enter into force after its ratification. While association agreements with all other Mediterranean partner countries have entered into force, negotiations with Syria were particularly slow and finalized only at the end of 2004. The Council has not signed the agreement pending Syria's response to the independent UN investigation commission investigating the assassination of former Lebanese Prime Minister Rafik Hariri and associated UN Security Council resolutions.

The action plans with most partners in the region reflect a delicate balance between the EU's desire to promote human rights and fundamental freedoms and its concern to maintain stability, including issues such as terrorism and weapons of mass destruction. Commitments in the political field are thus limited and reflect each government's own intentions with respect to political reform.

Israel and the Palestinian Authority. In Israel, the ENP was welcomed as an opportunity to develop bilateral relations with the EU at a pace that reflects Israel's own capacities and aspirations. A particular attraction is participation in EU programmes and agencies, such as the research framework programme and the Galileo satellite navigation system (agreed in June 2004). Some Israeli representatives look to an arrangement similar to the European economic area (EEA) as an ultimate goal short of membership.

2005 saw the expiration of the deadline set by the Quartet roadmap on a comprehensive settlement to the Israel–Palestine conflict. The beginning of the year was marked by cautious optimism following the election of Mahmoud Abbas as President of the Palestinian Authority and the formation of a new Israeli government under Ariel Sharon, which was committed to withdrawal from Gaza and certain parts of the West Bank. In addition to the action plan, which entered into force in February, the Commission reacted with a new initiative entitled 'EU–Palestinian co-operation beyond disengagement – towards a two state solution' in October that identifies priorities for EU engagement following the Israeli disengagement, including support for the reform and institution-building efforts of the Palestinian Authority. The Commission also proposed preparing a country strategy paper for the West Bank and Gaza Strip to be completed by mid-2006. To facilitate an agreement between Israel and the Palestinian Authority on 'movement and access' in November, the Council agreed on an EU police mission in the Palestinian territories under the European security and defence policy (EUPOL-COPPS), which supports the Palestinian Authority in establishing sustainable and effective police arrangements. By the end of the year, however, cautious optimism had given way to new disillusionment. Prime Minister Ariel Sharon's decision to leave the Likud Party with many of its senior figures to form the centrist Kadima Party in November profoundly changed the political landscape, which was shaken again by his suffering of a severe stroke in late December. In the Palestinian territories, the decision to allow radical groups, such as Hamas, to participate in the legislative elections in January 2006 heralded a weakening of moderate forces.

Jordan, Morocco and Tunisia. The three other Mediterranean partners to have concluded action plans with the EU are Jordan, Morocco and Tunisia. The fact that the first action plan to enter into force was Tunisia's on 4 July shows that commitment to common values does not necessarily guide the pace of the ENP, as was underlined by a EP resolution in September expressing concern with the lack of progress on projects related to human rights, women's issues, health and justice. Alluding implicitly to the progress made with Morocco, the EP requested the accelerated establishment of a fully operational sub-committee on human rights, as foreseen under the EU–Tunisia association agreement. Such a sub-committee was agreed with Morocco, to begin operating in 2006. Co-operation with Morocco also deepened at the sectoral level. The Council gave a mandate to negotiate a fisheries partnership agreement, which contains all the provisions for the activities of the EU fleet in Moroccan waters. In transport, a comprehensive air transport agreement was initialled, which will be the first of its kind with a third country, paving the way for the future development of a Euro–Mediterranean common air space.

These countries were also the first to sign twinning contracts with the EU, thereby importing instruments first developed in eastern enlargement. These contracts, supported by EU funds, open a new chapter in the EU–Mediterranean co-operation by linking public administrations with their European counterparts and promoting the transfer of legislation, know-how, and organizational concepts between civil servants.

Egypt and Lebanon. The next Mediterranean countries to start negotiations on ENP action plans (in September) were Egypt and Lebanon. The year 2005 saw the first ever multi-candidate presidential election in Egypt, with President Hosni Mubarak being re-elected for a fifth term. Restrictions on the full enjoyment of human rights and fundamental freedoms, however, persist. In Lebanon, the assassination of former Prime Minister Hariri in February and the following destabilization of the Lebanese government did not prevent ratification of the 2002 association agreement, which is expected to enter into force in early 2006. The assassination triggered a profound political crisis, backed by the findings of the international independent investigation commission of the UN that pointed to the involvement of Lebanese and Syrian intelligence services in the murder. The EU deployed an election observation mission for the subsequent parliamentary elections in May and June which saw the victory of an anti-Syrian tripartite alliance.

Libya. Libya is an observer to the Euro–Mediterranean partnership and has neither started association negotiations nor benefited from financial co-operation under the Meda programme. Participation remains dependent on Libya's readiness to accept the declaration and the Barcelona *acquis* in full and unconditionally. Nonetheless, political and technical contacts have intensified. Consultations have been particularly intense on immigration with a view to stipulating an agreement on rescue at sea and in the desert and adopting a joint action plan.

III. The European Economic Area and EFTA

For the countries of the European Economic Area (EEA) and Switzerland, the recent widening and ongoing deepening of the EU has given new impetus to the discussions on the long-term viability of their respective forms of association.

Switzerland

In Switzerland, two themes dominated the agenda in 2005: the ratification of the second round of bilateral agreements and the extension of free movement of persons to the new Member States. The new bilateral agreements cover nine sectors: taxation of savings, participation in the Schengen agreement and Dublin convention, judicial and administrative co-operation against fraud, trade in processed agricultural products, participation in the European environment agency, statistical co-operation, participation in the Media programme, preparations for participation in future programmes in the fields of education, youth and training, and avoidance of double taxation of retired EU officials. In line with the rules of direct democracy, a referendum was successfully requested with regard to association with Schengen agreements and the Dublin convention. The vote took place on 5 June 2005, just a few days after the overwhelming rejection of the EU Constitutional Treaty in France and the Netherlands. In this context, the clear approval by 54.6 per cent of the Swiss electorate was welcomed as a rather untypical pro-European vote from this non-Member State. Three of the 'bilaterals 2' agreements – on processed agricultural products, avoidance of double taxation of former EU officials, and taxation of savings – entered into force in 2005.

A second EU-related referendum in September 2005 concerned the adaptation of the existing agreement on free movement of persons to allow for the accession of the new Member States. Two elements in particular assured the vote's positive outcome (56 per cent in favour): transition periods comparable to those granted to the old Member States and the invocation of the so-called 'guillotine clause', which allows for suspension of the whole first package of bilateral agreements should one party quit one of them unilaterally.

A third, unexpectedly controversial issue in 2005 was Switzerland's financial contribution to EU social and economic cohesion. EU internal divisions on the distribution of this money obstructed ratification of the second bilateral agreement and the extension of freedom of movement on the part of the EU until December. Following the example of Norway, which will pay about €220 million, Switzerland agreed to contribute €130 million per year over five years. Its wish to earmark this money to selected projects in the new Member States raised concerns on the part of the 'old' beneficiaries of EU structural funds (Greece, Portugal and Spain) and Malta that this could amount to a precedent on the distribution of EU aid.

The steady intensification of relations with the EU has prompted an intensive debate in Switzerland on the viability of the 'sectoral' model of association and the status of the membership application originally deposited in 1992. In the summer, the Swiss government decided to downgrade accession from a 'strategic goal' as formulated in 1993 to merely a 'long-term option'. At the same time, it commissioned a study to look into the feasibility of various alternative options, including accession to the EEA, a continuation of the bilateral sectoral approach and a framework agreement to merge existing agreements under one joint committee, which would be empowered to update agreements regularly in line with the EU's evolving *acquis*. 'Membership lite', with opt-outs, which was also floated in this context, is not likely to be sympathetically received in the EU, although various Member States have expressed similar ideas towards other, contested candidates for membership.

Norway

Current debates in Norway may also temper Switzerland's interest in EEA accession. Although the new Stoltenberg government declared that it would not apply for membership, discussions on the adaptation of the EEA agreement, the scope of which remains limited to the internal market, remained high on the agenda. Following its earlier association with JHA co-operation (Schengen 1999, Dublin and Europol 2001, and mutual assistance in criminal matters 2003), Norway signed a co-operation agreement with Eurojust in 2005 and sought closer co-operation with the EU common foreign, security and defence policy. Norway also sought an informal link with the Lisbon process as it incorporates relevant EU legislation through the EEA agreement.

The European Economic Area

For the EEA as a whole, 2005 saw new impetus for active participation in the new EU agencies, which play an increasing role in the implementation and preparation of EU regulatory policies. After joining the European aviation safety agency in 2004, the EEA states adopted a decision to participate in the European centre for disease prevention and control in February 2005, and the European railway agency in June 2005. Work is also ongoing regarding the European food safety authority and the European network and information security agency.

Conclusions

Developments in 2005 suggest that, in spite of widespread expectations, EU enlargement policy has not changed fundamentally. The EU has stuck to its enlargement promises, criteria and routines; and it took incremental decisions in line with established policy and according to schedule. The attempts by some Member States to freeze the enlargement process, link it to progress in the deepening of the EU, or introduce alternative forms of membership have failed thus far. In addition, developments – such as Croatian co-operation with the ICTY, constitutional and judicial reforms in almost all target countries, the peaceful management of ethnic conflict in Macedonia, and the liberalization of political debate in Turkey – suggest that political accession conditionality continues to work. By contrast, ENP has been particularly dynamic at the sectoral level – as has co-operation within the EEA and with Switzerland – ranging from trade to justice and home affairs, energy or transport links. This cannot, however, hide the strong heterogeneity prevailing among ENP countries, and the uneven effects of the new policy. Finally, it is not clear how, in the absence of the lure of accession, the ENP will succeed in promoting democracy and human rights.

Key Readings

Commission (2005f) contains a number of novel elements concerning the EU's framework for negotiations with Turkey and may set a precedent for accession negotiations with other candidate countries.

Commission (2005b) presents the Commission's overall enlargement policy for all candidate countries, stressing the need to consider the EU's absorption capacity and declaring three fundamental principles: consolidation, conditionality and communication.

Sedelmeier (2005) examines the EU's general enlargement decision and the uneven pattern of accommodation of the central and east European countries' preferences in concrete policies (trade liberalization, regulatory alignment, and foreign policy consultations) and shows the impact of the EU's discursively constructed role identity *vis-à-vis* the CEECs and of sectoral policy paradigms.

Vachudova (2005) analyses how the EU has facilitated a convergence toward liberal democracy among credible future members of the EU, revealing how the EU's membership conditionality influenced domestic politics, particularly in illiberal democracies.

The collection of case studies in Schimmelfennig and Sedelmeier (2005) cover the impact of the EU accession process in a wide variety of accession countries and policy areas. They demonstrate the explanatory power of an external incentives model of Europeanization, emphasizing the size and credibility of EU membership incentives and the domestic costs of the target governments.

Kelley (2006) analyses the institutional set-up of the ENP and discusses critically its potential in terms of encouraging democratization. She underlines the path dependencies of enlargement politics and thereby illuminates the organizational idiosyncrasies within the Commission and in the new policy.

References

Commission of the European Communities (2005a) 'Comprehensive monitoring report on the state of preparedness for EU membership of Bulgaria and Romania'. COM (2005)534, 25 October.

Commission of the European Communities (2005b) '2005 enlargement strategy paper'. COM (2005)561 final, 9 November.

Commission of the European Communities (2005c) 'Strategic objectives 2005–09'. COM (2005)15 final.

Commission of the European Communities (2005d) 'Communication on implementing and promoting the European neighbourhood policy'. Brussels, 22 November, SEC (2005)1521.

Commission of the European Communities (2005e) 'Commission presents a rigorous draft framework for accession negotiations with Turkey'. IP/05/807, 29 June 2005.

Commission of the European Communities (2005f) 'Negotiating Framework [with Turkey]', 3 October.

European Parliament (2005) 'Report on European Neighbourhood Policy'. Foreign Affairs Committee, Rapporteur Charles Tannock, Document A6-0399/2005 final of 7 December.

Kelley, J. (2006) 'New Wine in Old Wineskins: Promoting Political Reforms through the New European Neighbourhood Policy'. *Journal of Common Market Studies* Vol. 44, No. 1, pp. 29–55.

Schimmelfennig, F. and Sedelmeier, U. (eds) (2005) *The Europeanization of Central and Eastern Europe* (Ithaca: Cornell University Press).

Sedelmeier, U. (2005) *Constructing the Path to Eastern Enlargement. The Uneven Policy Impact of EU Identity* (Manchester: Manchester University Press).

Vachudova, M. (2005) *Europe Undivided. Democracy, Leverage, and Integration After Communism* (Oxford: Oxford University Press).

JCMS 2006 Volume 44 Annual Review pp. 155–70

Relations with the Rest of the World*

DAVID ALLEN AND MICHAEL SMITH
Loughborough University

I. General Themes

Foreign, Security and Defence Policy

At the start of 2005 a leading commentator on EU external policy identified ten priorities for the EU (Cameron, 2005a): the EU needed to improve its relations with the US; stand up to Russia; support Ukraine; stabilize the Balkans; promote Middle East peace; meet the millennium development goals; establish a strategic partnership with China; promote global multilateralism; deal with Iran; and prepare an EU diplomatic service. All these issues are referred to in the following pages.

The EU-25 reached agreement on some 25 joint actions, mainly in relation to European security and defence policy (ESDP) actions or the appointment and reappointment of special representatives. Thus in the Balkans the mandates of the European Union police mission (EUPM), which replaced the international police task force (despite claims that it had failed as crime figures increased and war criminals were not apprehended), and the European Union monitoring mission (EUMM) in Bosnia were extended, along with the mandate of the EU special representative (Christian Schwarz-Schilling). In Macedonia the mandate of the EU police mission (EUPOL Proxima) was extended, an EU

---

* This year's entry is organized differently to previous years to exclude material on the Western Balkans, the Mediterranean and the Middle East and parts of the former Soviet Union now covered by the European Neighbourhood Policy . This material is now covered in the chapter by Sandra Lavenex and Frank Schimmelfennig.

police advisory team was established and a new special representative (Erwan Fouere) appointed. In the southern Caucasus the mandate of the EU special representative (Peter Semneby) was amended and extended. In Asia an EU monitoring mission (consisting of 219 observers) was established in Aceh, Indonesia (AMM). The mandate of the EU special representative in Afghanistan (Francesc Vendrill) was extended, and a new EU special representative (Jan Kubis) to Central Asia appointed. In Africa the EU police mission in Kinshasa, Democratic Republic of Congo (DRC) (EUPOL 'Kinshasa'), was extended, and a mission on security sector reform in the DRC established (EUSEC GRD Congo); an EU special representative to the Sudan (Pekko Haavisto) was appointed; an EU civilian support mission to the African Union mission in Darfur (AMIS11) was established; and the mandate of the EU special representative to the African Great Lakes region (Aldo Ajello) was extended once more. In the Middle East an EU border assistance mission (involving 80 officials led by an Italian Major-General Pietro Pistolesi) to the Rafah crossing point (EUBAM Rafah) was established; a police mission in the Palestinian Territories (EUPOL COPPS) was launched with 20 EU policemen; the mandate of the EU special representative (Marc Otte) extended; and a rule of law mission for Iraq (Eujust LEX) adopted. In eastern Europe, an EU special representative for Moldova was appointed (Adriaan Jacobovits). As well as progress with these ongoing missions, three EU operations were concluded in 2005: Concordia in Macedonia, Artemis in the DRC (both military missions) and the 'rule of law' mission in Georgia (EujustThemis).

Under the ESDP, the EU continued to develop its 'battle group' concept, agreeing to create an additional five battle groups, making a total of 18, with the aim of being able to conduct two operations simultaneously and within five days of a Council decision to launch an operation. The European Defence Agency (EDA), with an initial budget of €20 million and just 80 staff working towards the objectives agreed at its establishment in 2004 (Solana, 2005), focused on command and control, communications and interoperability, research on a unmanned long endurance aircraft, co-operation in the armoured vehicles sector and other procurement initiatives.

In 2005 France called for further ESDP development with an enhanced planning centre, a European gendarmerie force drawn from Spain, Italy, the Netherlands, France and Portugal and an EU defence college, as well as further work by the EDA to develop the A400M transport aircraft, the FREM frigate and the NH90 helicopter (Alliot-Marie, 2005). France also called for an EDA-backed procurement code to try to exploit better the EU's €30 billion equipment market. For instance, there is a proven need for up to 10,000 new armoured fighting vehicles, but there are currently in the EU some 23 different programmes to develop these.

The 'no' votes in France and the Netherlands on the Constitutional Treaty will have significant consequences for the common foreign and security policy (CFSP) and ESDP. It now seems unlikely that the High Representative (HR) Javier Solana will be able to take up his appointment as the EU's first foreign minister. Immediately after the 'no' votes it was clearly Solana's preference (supported by Elmar Brok in the European Parliament) to carry on with preparations for the creation of an European external action service (EEAS), but this produced a negative response in a number of EU Member States (Beatty, 2005c). Prior to the 'no' votes, Solana and Commission President Barroso had produced a joint paper proposing that the EEAS be answerable to Solana, but be created independently of both the Commission and the Council. There were those who argued that more could be done to enhance the EU's external performance despite the loss of the Constitutional Treaty (Cameron, 2005b), including relieving the HR of his responsibilities as Secretary-General of the Council, allowing the HR to participate in Commission meetings that discuss external affairs, organizing regular meetings between Council and Commission planning staffs to facilitate joint six-monthly reports on external priorities, increasing the number of national policy officials seconded to EU institutions and increasing the budget for the CFSP. To make the EU more visible on the global stage it was argued that the HR should speak for the EU at the United Nations (UN), that the EU should establish a diplomatic academy and, to make it more capable, that the EU should maintain its growing list of military and civilian external ESDP missions, improve its political reporting, involve the European Parliament and national parliaments more in EU foreign policy deliberations and allow the HR and the Commissioner for External Relations to engage more freely with both the media and the chairs of the foreign affairs committees of the EU national parliaments.

At the Brussels European Council in December Solana presented four short papers on matters related to the 'EU's rapid expansion in crisis management and its increasingly important role in the world' (Council of the European Union, 2005). These papers covered proposals to increase levels of defence research spending and research collaboration; enhance ESDP capabilities; enhance crisis management structures, following the experience of the Asian tsunami; increase CFSP funding in particular for civilian operations; ensure that the EU was ready to assume a greater role in Kosovo; and improve its co-ordination in the Balkans in general with regard to organized crime.

On Iran's perceived nuclear ambitions, the 3+1 (UK, France and Germany + Solana) talks broke down in the summer when the EU's plan for Iran to give up its nuclear activity in return for EU trade concessions was rejected along with a Russian plan to provide the necessary enriched uranium under international controls. In Darfur, the EU sought to work through the African Union, but got entangled in an argument with the North Atlantic Treaty Organization (Nato) about who would do what in terms of military support. In Iraq the EU provided reconstruction finance totalling €80 million, including €31.5 million in support of the presidential elections; established its rule of law mission; and prepared to establish a Commission delegation in Baghdad, despite the enormous security risk that this presented. Over China the EU was divided in the face of US opposition over the lifting or not of the arms embargo. (France and Britain are responsible for over 95 per cent of the 202 separate arms deals, worth €340 million, concluded with China by eight EU Member States (Cronin, 2005).)

At the UN Security Council, where the EU has two permanent and three non-permanent members, proposals for reform of that membership – including a suggestion that, instead of three non-permanent members (two from 'western' Europe and one from 'eastern' Europe, the EU have just two representatives – faltered (Guerot and Missiroli, 2005).

External Trade Policy

EU external trade policy was dominated in 2005 by the ongoing negotiations in the World Trade Organization with the aim of concluding the 'Doha development round' (DDA). The challenge of trade in agricultural products is especially demanding, and intersects with the EU's efforts to reform the common agricultural policy more generally. The entire negotiating context has also been changed with the consolidation of a relatively coherent group of emerging economies, often described as the group of 20 (G20) and led by Brazil, China, India and South Africa among others. Thus in 2005, despite the apparent 'win' of seeing Pascal Lamy (an ex-EU Trade Commissioner) confirmed as Director-General of the WTO, it was apparent that the EU faced in negotiations an almost Herculean task.

For the EU, the intersection of the agriculture negotiations with discussions on reform in the Union itself (and also later in the year with discussions on the EU budget) was only one of a number of potential 'double-binds'. The negotiations on trade in services coexisted worryingly with internal negotiations on the services directive, whilst the focus of the DDA on developing countries and their needs cut across the EU's efforts to reshape its relations with the African, Caribbean and Pacific (ACP) countries and others subject to its development assistance regime. The fact that there was a new Trade Commissioner in the shape of Peter Mandelson served only to accentuate this set of tensions.

By the spring of 2005, it was widely perceived that the DDA negotiations were in crisis, and that the EU was one of the key causes of the apparent deadlock. During the summer, there was an inexorable focus not only on agriculture, but more specifically on the EU's position, which led to some very small progress.

This had the effect only of raising the stakes for negotiations in the autumn, when Mandelson came under steadily escalating pressure from both the United States and the G20. At the same time, the Commissioner was under attack in the General Affairs Council from the French, who accused him of exceeding his mandate. His efforts to widen the basis for the negotiations in the WTO, so that he could be seen to be dealing with a broad package rather than simply with agriculture, met opposition on both fronts, but the fact that he was supported by the vast majority of EU Member States meant that he was able slowly and grudgingly to make further concessions. These related especially to export subsidies, and ultimately meant that, at the WTO ministerial meeting in Hong Kong during early December, Mandelson could promise a complete phasing out of these troublesome measures by 2013. The Hong Kong meeting in many respects set only a revised negotiation timetable for the WTO members, which means that by summer 2006 the confrontation will be resumed (for a detailed review of the Hong Kong ministerial, see *European Voice*, 2005).

Alongside the global DDA negotiations – and inevitably linked with them at some stages – went two significant disputes in agricultural trade. The first related to the EU's sugar regime, which was found in April 2005 to be contrary to WTO rules. Sugar is a distinctive area of the EU's agricultural trade, since it is an area in which the EU is both a major importer of cane sugar, especially from the Caribbean, and also a major producer itself of beet sugar. The enlargement of 2004 had also brought new producers of beet sugar into the Union, the largest of which is Poland. The EU Agricultural Commissioner, Marianne Fischer Boel, put forward proposals for a price cut to EU producers combined with 'adjustment payments' for those external producers who would lose tariff-free access to the EU market. This was a situation in which there were lots of potential losers both inside and outside the EU: on the one hand, Caribbean producers felt they might be driven out of business, and on the other the beet sugar producers in the EU predicted 95,000 job losses. Eventually the proposed price cut was reduced in the agreement reached at the end of November, but this has not disposed of the problem.

The second persistent dispute was over the EU's banana regime, which had been reformed in response to a WTO judgment in the late 1990s, but which still raised problems because of the EU's proposal to set the tariff level at €230 per tonne – a level that Central American producers claimed would exclude them from the market whilst privileging those countries that would retain tariff-free quota access. During 2005, after the proposals had been rejected by the WTO during July, the dispute saw successive EU concessions on the level of the proposed tariff, and by the end of the year it had come down to €176 per tonne – still without fully disposing of the complaints by the Central American producers.

In other areas of trade policy, the pressures are rather less and policy can be made in what might be termed the traditional 'technocratic' style. Thus during 2005, progress continued with the reform of the EU's customs regime, with the investigation of anti-dumping cases and with reform of the generalized system of preferences. This is not to say that these areas cannot become politically sensitive, and indeed during 2005 the investigation of alleged dumping of shoes from China and Vietnam aroused fierce tensions between EU shoe retailers, shoe producers and a third category of interested party – shoe producers from the EU who had shifted their production facilities to Asia. There were also strongly politicized disputes (see below) between the EU and the US over civil aircraft and between the EU and China over textiles.

Development Co-operation Policy and Humanitarian Aid

In 2005 the EU focused on the millennium development goals in anticipation of the UN world summit which was held in September. The British presidency of the Council, which coincided with the British presidency of the G8, was determined to prioritize development issues in general and Africa in particular. In 2005 the EU delivered a total of €7.5 billion in overall development aid but this, combined with the unilateral aid programmes of the EU Member States, still added up to only 0.35 per cent of EU gross national income (GNI). This figure does not raise expectations that the EU will meet its stated development aid target of 0.7 per cent of EU GNI by 2015. In 2005 the EU decided to increase its overall effort by €20 billion a year (50 per cent of which is to go to Africa) and this is designed to increase the EU's development aid to 0.56 per cent of EU GNI by 2010. Of the 25 EU Member States only four (Netherlands, Sweden, Denmark and Luxembourg) currently contribute over the target 0.7 per cent of GNI, whilst the larger states like the UK, Germany, France and Italy struggle to reach half that figure.

The EU also managed to complete most of the negotiations for the renewal of its partnership agreement (Cotonou) with the ACP countries, although agreement has still not been reached on the second five-year tranche of funding (all that is agreed to date is that the funding will at least match that of the first five-year period). The new agreement is broadly similar to its predecessor, although there is a greater emphasis on political dialogue and, in particular, on good governance and action against terrorism and the proliferation of weapons of mass destruction. In addition, considerable emphasis is placed on the role of the agreement in moving towards the millennium goals, on increasing the role of the European Investment Bank and on the new devolved policy implementation procedures. The EU has also continued to develop its focus on enhancing the cohesiveness and coherence of its many development-related programmes, as well as targeting regional integration processes between the recipients of EU aid. Measures to improve access to EU markets by developing countries include a new scheme of generalized tariff preferences due to enter into force at the start of 2006, and the amendment of the preferential rules of origin also due to take effect from 2006.

In 2005 the EU's humanitarian effort was dominated by the assistance offered to those countries affected by the Asian tsunami. This assistance was co-ordinated by the Commission's Directorate General for Humanitarian Aid (Echo) and totalled some €1.5 billion in funds for short-term emergency assistance and medium-term reconstruction aid. Elsewhere, the EU offered over €600 million in humanitarian aid, just under half of which went to the ACP countries.

During 2005 there were complaints about the lack of new funding for the EU satellite centre in Torrejon at a time when satellite image analysis is required to play a greater role in crisis identification and monitoring. For instance, the EU has just 20 image analysts and even its unfunded target of 50–60 analysts over the next five years compares unfavourably with the 1,200 employed in the United States or the much greater numbers employed but not co-ordinated in the EU Member States.

II. Regional Themes

Russia

The EU's relationship with Russia in 2005 proved as difficult as in previous years, with Russia still expressing general unhappiness about the EU's 2004 enlargement and specific concerns about the EU's role in the events that led up to the overturning of the 2004 Ukrainian presidential election result and the subsequent election of Victor Yushchenko, whose stated objective is to take the Ukraine into both Nato and the EU. Russia's position *vis-à-vis* the EU is strengthened by the EU's growing dependence on Russian supplies of oil (35 per cent of EU oil imports) and gas (50 per cent of EU imports) at a time when world oil and gas prices are rising as a reflection of greater demand and growing insecurity of supply. This energy dependence undoubtedly serves to restrain the EU in its response to its perception of a growing Russian authoritarianism so that the EU tends to rationalize its acceptance of Russian heavy handedness in Chechnya and elsewhere in terms of the need for Russia to get to grips with terrorism.

At the first of the two EU–Russia summits, which was held in Moscow in May, both parties agreed 'road maps', meant to lead to the establishment of the four common spaces (trade, external security, internal security, and research and education). However this exercise served mainly to point out the many areas of disagreement between the two sides, with the EU seemingly determined to move from the bland and general to the more focused and specific at the second summit held in London in October. Having identified some 400 actions that needed to be taken, the EU identified 15 priorities for the trade and economic space, and four to five priorities for each of the other spaces. Little was achieved, however, beyond agreement on some areas for future co-operation (commercial policy, space policy, satellite navigation, telecommunications and transport) and an EU reaffirmation of its support for Russia's membership of the WTO. The EU continued to worry about Chechnya, but preferred support for constructive engagement with Chechnyans to outright confrontation with Russia (Steele, 2005). The EU's problem is a geo-strategic one (Beatty, 2005e) in that Russia, despite the energy cards that it holds, is anxious for a 'realist' partnership with the EU in the face of a worsening relationship with the US and growing rivalry with China in the Far East. The EU, internally divided between both Member States and institutions, has been feeble (Patten, 2005; Stephens, 2005a, b) in its response to date, but will come under renewed pressure from Russia as the need to replace the present partnership and co-operation agreement approaches in 2007. The development of the EU's neighbourhood policy is a further complication with much of 2005 being taken up with a semantic argument between Russia, which regards its immediate neighbours as the 'near abroad', and the EU which regards them as the 'neighbourhood'. It was only at the end of 2005 that the two parties began to discuss the possibility of joint crisis management in the area they now both agree to call 'regions adjacent'. In 2006 they will get down to the much more difficult task of resolving who might lead joint missions in these 'regions adjacent'.

Africa

The EU, aware that the UN was due to take stock in the autumn of the millennium development goals, always planned for 2005 to be a special year for its approach towards sub-Saharan Africa and, in December, the European Council did indeed adopt an EU strategy for Africa (Council of the European Union, 2006). The document entitled 'Towards a Strategic Partnership for Africa' was based on two papers – one produced by Javier Solana (on peace and security) and one produced by the Commission (on the acceleration of development assistance). The main emphasis of the strategy was on the more urgent development of a political dialogue to build on the first EU–Africa summit, held in Cairo in 2000. To this end the EU committed itself to holding a second summit with Africa in Lisbon 'as soon as possible'. The EU has committed itself to four basic priorities in its future dealings with Africa: improving governance and enhancing peace and security in Africa; creating regional infrastructure along EU lines particularly for energy and water; strengthening EU–African trade co-operation; and promoting environmental sustainability and equitability, in particular with regard to access to health and education services. To facilitate this the EU also agreed to increase its total aid to Africa by €10 billion (50 per cent of its increased aid programme designed to meet the millennium goal targets), with the extra money to be spent on trans-African networks, fighting disease, creating an African Erasmus network, making greater use of satellites and establishing a peace facility.

Whilst the EU concluded its limited military mission (Artemis) in the Great Lakes Region of Africa, the great political-military challenge of 2005 was the conflict in the Darfur region of the Sudan, which had led to the harassment and displacement of large numbers of refugees. The EU's attempts to work with and in support of the African Union (Operation AMIS) were frustrated for much of the year by an unfortunate inter-European institutional squabble with Nato, which was eventually resolved by Nato agreeing to provide strategic airlift assistance and the EU providing planning assistance and advice on the civilian policing of the refugee camps. This solution pleased the British, but is unpopular in France, as the French would prefer the EU (once its battle groups are operational) and not Nato to provide the military assistance. Elsewhere in Africa the EU used the conditionality clauses of the Cotonou agreement to take restrictive measures (not for the first time) against Côte d'Ivoire, the Democratic Republic of the Congo, Sudan and Zimbabwe. In Guinea the EU might even claim some success arising from the use of European development fund conditionality to force electoral reform.

Asia

For the past ten years the EU has pursued various initiatives designed to enhance its profile in Asia at the same time as managing its relations with the world's most dynamic economies. Both China and India have been proclaimed as 'strategic partners,' this being a term intended to convey real substance not only in economic relations but also in terms of the stability of Asia more generally, and Tony Blair's visits as holder of the EU presidency to both New Delhi and Beijing during the second half of the year were intended to bolster this new state of relations. At the same time, the EU has pursued an active inter-regional strategy towards the Asia-Pacific, and has endeavoured to use multilateral institutions such as the WTO as key instruments in managing its relationships with the region. This has not prevented the EU from being attacked in various media for its lack of any recognizable strategy towards the 'Asian superpowers' or Asia as a whole, although during 2005 there were also the first stirrings of a possible strategic approach to Asia co-ordinated with the USA and Japan (Beatty 2005a, b).

Very large areas of EU external activity during 2005 were defined in terms of the challenge posed by China, the need to manage it and the need to handle the links between commercial and political interests in the country. The issue most symbolic of these linkages is that of the embargo on arms sales, imposed in the aftermath of the Tiananmen Square events in 1989. During the past two years there has been incessant pressure from France and Germany within the EU to lift the embargo and to replace it with a strengthened version of the existing EU code of conduct on arms sales. The embargo itself is not comprehensive, and has in fact been accompanied by an increase in sales of certain types of weaponry and spare parts to China, but it has come to be a symbolic as well as a substantive commitment by the EU – a commitment which is also seen as important by the USA. Thus during the early part of 2005, the message from Washington could not have been clearer: do not lift the embargo, and be prepared for various types of sanctions if you do. The EU was in a quandary, disinclined to move in any direction lest it offend one or more powerful interest. Luckily the Chinese themselves came to the EU's assistance, passing legislation in March designed to counter any possibility of secession by Taiwan and thus giving a clear basis on which to suspend any thoughts of ending the embargo.

The Chinese also posed a second major dilemma for the EU during 2005, this time in trade. China is poised to become the biggest importer into the EU, and is the trade partner with which the EU's has the largest trade deficit. By late 2004, it had been clear that the removal of remaining quotas and restrictions on textile trade on 1 January 2005 would lead to only one result – a further and rapid intensification of the EU's deficit with China. This duly appeared in the first half of 2005, concentrated in certain parts of the clothing market such as blouses, T-shirts and trousers. The Commission launched an investigation in April, and by the end of that month the 'surge' in Chinese exports to the EU was fully revealed. Warnings to the Chinese were to no avail, and although some marginal adjustments were made to export tariffs in the key areas, the surge continued.

As a result, Commissioner Mandelson set about negotiating a quota deal with the Chinese in the most sensitive areas, basing his position on the provision in agreements for Chinese entry into the WTO that 'special safeguards' could be imposed if there were destabilizing surges in Chinese exports. All the time, he had to contend with the fact that within the EU there was an almost equal division between those Member States that saw such measures as creeping protectionism and a threat to the interests of EU consumers, and those that saw it as a necessary defence of EU producers. This division, incidentally, could also be observed in relations with India: during March, 11 Member States blocked reform of the generalized system of preferences because of fears about a potential surge in Indian exports to the EU. The quota agreement with China had been made hastily, without taking full account of the fact that garments ordered months previously were still on their way to Europe; thus the threat of a 'trouser mountain' and other mountains was imminent. In addition, retailers all over the EU mobilized to put pressure on the Commission. It took two months to reach a compromise, with the Chinese not inclined to do much to help their European 'hostages', and by the time this compromise was reached another problem was looming, that of a 'shoe mountain'. Perhaps not surprisingly (and because shoes were not part of the general problem with textiles), the Commission chose to deal with this through the more traditional anti-dumping route. When the sums were done at the end of the year, it appeared that overall clothing exports to the EU were around the same as previous years, despite the concern over China; the real losers, it appeared, were other Asian producers whose sales had been ruined by the Chinese, and to a lesser extent by the Indians.

Although the EU's links with the rest of Asia suffered by comparison with the 'China problem', there were significant developments in a number of areas during 2005. The EU sent its first monitoring mission to an Asian location – Aceh in Indonesia – during the year, and continued to play an active role in relations with such bodies as the ASEAN (Association of South East Asian Nations) Regional Forum. Its relations with ASEAN itself survived the threat posed by Myanmar's assumption of the rotating chair in that organization, by simple dint of the fact that Myanmar 'chose' to relinquish its turn. Negotiations continued with a number of countries in pursuit of bilateral agreements under the Trans-Regional EU–ASEAN Trade Initiative (TREATI). Major relief efforts were made by the EU (as well as by individual Member States) following the tsunami that hit many countries during December 2004, and the earthquake that shook Kashmir later in 2005.

Finally, in the former Soviet part of Asia, events in Uzbekistan were of concern to the EU following the excessive use of force and allegations of torture that characterized the Uzbek government's response to demonstrations in Andijan in May. Although the EU failed in its call for an independent inquiry, the Council decided against suspending the partnership and co-operation agreement, but did place a travel ban on 12 members of the Uzbek government. This travel ban was then ignored by the German government which, in November, allowed one of the 12 (Zakirjon Almolov) to visit Germany to receive medical treatment. Germany has a military base at Termez in Uzbekistan.

Latin America

The EU's relations with Latin America, compared to those with Asia, have remained untroubled in recent years – possibly because they are simply less dynamic and there are fewer threats to the EU's 'domestic' interests. In December the Commission adopted a new Communication on EU–Latin American relations (Commission, 2005a). This reiterated the EU's commitment to a bi-regional approach, focusing on four key areas: political dialogue, trade and investment, stability and prosperity within the region, and enhancing the process of co-operation and mutual understanding. At the same time as pursuing this broad agenda, the EU brought into force a bilateral association agreement with Chile, and continued to work towards an agreement with Mercosur (the organization including Argentina, Brazil, Paraguay and Uruguay), which it hopes to conclude in 2006. This did not prevent commentators from describing Latin America as the 'forgotten region' in EU external relations or from criticizing the 'bi-regional' approach as imposing a single model on a very diverse continent (Beatty, 2005d).

The most important bilateral developments in EU–Latin American relations during 2005 concerned Cuba, which has been a focus of tensions both within the EU and between the EU and the US for several years. Formal contacts had been suspended in 2003 after the Castro regime had imprisoned a large number of dissidents. Pressure from Spain especially for a resumption of high-level contacts paid off in the first half of 2005, with the temporary suspension of sanctions and a visit from Development Commissioner Louis Michel, and political dialogue was subsequently restored – without any suggestion that more formal agreements might follow.

Transatlantic Relations

EU–US relations in 2005 had a generally more positive feel than in preceding years when the 'transatlantic crisis' over Iraq in particular had prevailed. President George W. Bush had been re-elected decisively in November 2004, and it was clear by the beginning of 2005 that the administration had decided on a 'charm offensive' in relation to western Europe, leading up to the President's visit in February. At the same time, the Commission was working on an evaluation of ten years of the New Transatlantic Agenda, and on a new communication designed to express the new state of relations (Peterson *et al.*, 2005; Pollack, 2005; Commission, 2005b). This did not, however, mean that everything was positive. The continuing decline of the US dollar, allied to a massive US trade deficit, created economic turbulence, whilst the continuing conflict in Iraq was a constant reminder of the reasons for the previous crisis. Thus, although the EU–US summit in Washington in June reached agreement on a number of issues, including consultations on conflict prevention and 'states of concern', and it might be argued that the EU and the US were 'friends again' (Zabarowski, 2006), this label came with a question mark rather than an exclamation mark.

Evidence to support this mixed verdict came from the ways in which the EU and the US interacted over two major common problems. The first was that of Iran, and its suspected desire to acquire nuclear weapons whilst attempting to conceal any moves towards that condition. The 'EU3' (Britain, France and Germany) had been pursuing dogged diplomacy for several years. The Iranians continued to be evasive in the first half of 2005, professing their willingness to submit to inspection and oversight whilst never quite agreeing to what the EU3 were proposing. Even the Americans were tempted to offer some incentives, in the form of concessions over the Iranian application for WTO membership, possibly as the result of co-ordinated policy with the EU3. But in June 2005 everything changed. The election of a hard-line Iranian president with a record of intransigence on issues such as nuclear capability, made this an almost impossible issue to resolve in the short term, hard as the EU3 tried. The net result was that EU3 positions increasingly resembled that of the US, with the threat of reference from the International Atomic Energy Agency to the UN Security Council becoming the most prominent feature.

The second common problem that confronted the EU and the US was how to deal with China. In terms of trade, the EU had a major dilemma over how to address the surge in Chinese textile exports during the first half of the year (see above). There is no doubt, however, that the problems faced by both the EU and the US in this area intersect: the Americans did eventually reach their own agreement with Beijing, but along with the EU they have to face conflicting domestic demands as well as international challenges and obligations. The other area in which the EU and the US experienced a 'China problem' during 2005 was that of the arms embargo (see above), and here again the difficulties of managing an international problem in the face of conflicting domestic demands were apparent. By the end of 2005, the EU's position was roughly where the US had wanted it to be, but this did not guarantee that it would stay there or that the French in particular would not be back with the demand to lift the embargo.

Apart from the 'China problem', the EU and the US continued to experience their established diet of disputes and 'competitive co-operation'. Nowhere was this more apparent than in the dispute over the European Airbus, which became particularly acrimonious in 2005. One reason for this was the cycle of new product launches by both Airbus and Boeing, the US manufacturer, which saw the A380 'super jumbo' and the A350 launched by Airbus and the B787 'dreamliner' launched by Boeing. Another reason for the dispute's escalation seems to have been more personal, and to have reflected the fact that Robert Zoellick, the US Trade Representative (who left the job to become Assistant Secretary of State in the new administration, but retained an interest) and Peter Mandelson did not get on. As a result of this combination of factors, together with the usual cocktail of domestic pressures from Boeing and Airbus and local or regional interests, the dispute led in July 2005 to formal complaints by both sides to the WTO. If pursued to a final judgement this would be the most costly dispute ever handled by the WTO, and thus there is a significant incentive to agree as well as a set of reasons to pursue brinkmanship on both sides.

There were other, more positive experiences in EU–US negotiations during 2005. From a position in early 2005 where they had appeared dead in the water, negotiations on an 'open skies' agreement covering transatlantic air transport produced a first-phase agreement in December. The EU continued to make efforts to soften the US position on matters of climate change, and had mixed success: in July, the US established a new grouping, the Asia-Pacific partnership on clean development and climate with China, India, South Korea, Japan and Australia, with the apparent aim of undermining the multilateral Kyoto convention, but in December, at the Conference of Parties (COP) 11 conference in Montreal, the US appeared to yield to EU-led pressure to further negotiations to establish a regime for global emissions after the expiry of Kyoto. In the latter case, both India and China supported the EU position, so it is apparent that alignments on this issue are complex to say the least. Finally, in 2005 there was what is surely only the beginning of a battle for multilateral control of the internet, focused on the fact that an American body effectively controls the allocation of domain names. The struggle reached its peak at the world summit on the information society held in November 2005, where the Commission argued for a multilateral solution, but the US was able on this occasion to repel the assault.

EU–US relations during 2005 continued to experience the fall-out from the 'war on terror', and indeed at the end of the year there was an intensification of the frictions. Two established issues were prominent in the early part of the year. First, the long-running problems over European conformity with US requirements to introduce biometric passports continued, with every possibility that at least half of all EU Member States would fail to meet the (US-imposed) deadline at the end of the year. Eventually – and not least because it appeared that the US itself would fail to meet the deadline – the problem was postponed by a year. There continued to be friction over the issue of air passenger data transfer, following on a complaint by the European Parliament in 2004 that this had been agreed and implemented illegally by the Commission. In November 2005 an Advocate-General of the European Court of Justice (ECJ) issued an opinion holding that the agreement was illegal, but full ECJ consideration was not due until 2006. The most dramatic and potentially explosive development came late in the year, with the claims that the US had been involved (with several EU Member States or prospective Member States) in the process of 'extraordinary rendition', whereby prisoners taken in the course of the 'war on terror' were transferred by the Central Intelligence Agency to countries where they were allegedly subjected to torture in order to gain information. The Commission was able to threaten any Member States where such events were found to have occurred with sanctions, using the human rights provisions of the treaties, and the EP set up a temporary committee to investigate, in face of denials by countries such as Poland and Romania (as well as the US administration) that they had had anything to do with it. If evidence of such dealings were to be uncovered, this would clearly be a very damaging development for EU–US relations in general.

Key Readings

The European Commission's General Report for 2005 (Commission of the European Communities, 2006, pp. 137–76) provides a good review of the external activities of the EU along with footnoted links to all the relevant Commission documents.

Chaillot Paper No. 87 (Institute for Security Studies 2006) brings together all the key Council documents on the EU's ESDP for 2005.

Ojanen (2006) gives a useful overview and commentary on recent ESDP activities.

For a more academic consideration of the meaning of EU external activities, the special issue of the *Journal of European Public Policy* edited by Sjursen (2006) is excellent, as is the report by Peterson *et al.* (2005) for the European Commission on the state of relations between the EU and the US.

For a thoughtful account of his experiences as the Commissioner for External Relations, see Chris Patten's (2005) memoirs.

References

Alliot-Marie, M. (2005) 'Security could be Europe's Great Rallying Point'. *Financial Times*, 5 December.

Beatty, A. (2005a) 'Europe Plots China Talks with America and Japan'.*European Voice*, 21–27 April, p. 2.

Beatty, A. (2005b) 'Steering China in the Right Direction'. *European Voice*, 28 April–3 May, pp. 16–17.

Beatty, A (2005c), 'Diplomat Corps Joins Treaty in Cold Storage'. *European Voice*, 9–15 June, p. 1.

Beatty, A. (2005d) 'Latin America – Forgotten by the EU?'. *European Voice*, 14–20 July, p. 7.

Beatty, A (2005e) 'Russia's European Overture'. *European Voice*, 20–26 October, p. 15.

Cameron, F. (2005a) 'All the World's a Stage for the EU in 2005'. *European Voice*, 13–19 January, p. 13.

Cameron. F. (2005b) 'Making the EU a Global Actor'. *European Voice*, 1–7 September, p. 14.

Commission of the European Communities (2005a) 'A Stronger Partnership between the European Union and Latin America'. COM(2005) 636, Brussels, 8 December.

Commission of the European Communities (2005b) 'A Stronger EU–US Partnership and a More Open Market for the 21st Century'. COM (2005) 196, Brussels, 18 May.

Commission of the European Communities (2006) *General Report on the Activities of the European Union 2005*, pp. 137–76.

Council of the European Union (2005) Letter from the Secretary-General/High Representative to Tony Blair, Council S416/05, Brussels 14 December.

Council of the European Union (2006) *Presidency Conclusions*, Brussels European Council, 15–16 December 2005, 15914/1/05 REV1, Part 111,7, Brussels, 30 January.

Cronin, D. (2005) 'EU Military Exports to China Continue Despite Arms Embargo'. *European Voice*, 8–14 December, p. 4.

European Voice (2005) 'WTO Negotiations'. Special report, 8–14 December, pp. 22–9.

Guerot,U. and Missiroli, A. (2005) 'Fewer Europeans, More Europe: The Recipe for a UN Coup'. *European Voice*, 24–30 November, p. 11.

Institute for Security Studies (2006) 'EU Security and Defence: Core Documents 2005'. Vol. VI, Chaillot Paper No. 87, Paris.

Ojanen, H. (2006) 'Two Competing Models for a Common Defence Policy'. *Journal of Common Market Studies,* Vol. 44, No. 1, pp. 77–112.

Patten, C. (2005), *Not Quite the Diplomat: Home Truths about World Affairs* (London: Allen Lane)

Peterson, J. *et al.* (2005) *Review of the Framework for Relations Between the European Union and the United States: An Independent Study* (Brussels: CEC).

Pollack, M. (2005) 'The New Transatlantic Agenda at Ten: Reflections on an Experiment in International Governance'. *Journal of Common Market Studies* Vol. 43, No. 5, pp. 899–920.

Sjursen, H. (ed.) (2006) 'What Kind of Power? European Foreign Policy in Perspective'. *Journal of European Public Policy,* Vol. 13, No. 2, Special Issue.

Solana, J. (2005) 'Europe should Pool its Defence Resources'. *Financial Times*, 23 May.

Steele, J. (2005) 'Europe is Risking Silence to End its Longest War'. *The Guardian*, 25 March.

Stephens, P. (2005a) 'Europe cannot Afford to Retreat from the World'. *Financial Times*, 10 June.

Stephens, P. (2005b) 'The West Pays a Heavy Price for Foreign Policy Realism'. *Financial Times*, 14 October.

Zabarowski, M. (ed.) (2006) *Friends Again? EU–US Relations after the Crisis* (Paris: European Union Institute for Security Studies).

JCMS 2006 Volume 44 Annual Review pp. 171–98

Political Developments in the EU Member States

NICK SITTER
Norwegian School of Management BI

KAREN HENDERSON
University of Leicester

Introduction

2005 was the first full year of membership for the ten new Member States, and the first full year the European Union (EU) operated as a 25-member organization. For the new Member States EU membership was more than the much discussed 'return to Europe'. As it turned out, 2005 was a less eventful year than the preceding years, and political developments in the new and old Member States are broadly comparable in terms of elections, changes of government, party system change and the domestic politics of European integration. In other words, 2005 indicated that there had been a certain degree of political stabilization in the new Member States. This is not to say that the political dynamics are the same as in the old Member States: the 'European question' still includes debates about Schengen and economic and monetary union (EMU), whereas ratification of the Constitutional Treaty has been more controversial in some of the old Member States. The present article therefore maintains the distinction between the old and new Member States and, although the same themes are covered in the two sections, the emphasis inevitably differs somewhat. In what follows, in the first section, the major political developments in the old Member States are chronicled in a review that takes a roughly counter-clockwise sweep through western Europe. The second section turns to developments in the new Member States, including the Polish elections and the European question in domestic politics.

Public opinion across the EU shifted somewhat against European integration during the summer of 2005 according to the *Eurobarometer* survey question

Table 1: % of Voters who See EU Membership as 'a Good Thing'

	Autumn 2005	Spring 2005	Autumn 2004	Spring 2004
Luxembourg	82	80	85	75
Ireland	73	75	77	71
Netherlands	70	77	75	64
Spain	66	66	72	64
Belgium	59	67	73	57
Lithuania	**57**	**59**	**69**	**52**
Denmark	56	59	61	54
Portugal	54	61	59	55
Greece	54	56	61	71
Poland	**54**	**53**	**50**	**42**
Germany	53	58	60	45
Italy	50	56	57	54
Slovakia	**50**	**54**	**57**	**46**
EU-25	50	54	56	(EU-15 48)
France	46	51	56	43
Czech Republic	**44**	**49**	**45**	**41**
Slovenia	**43**	**49**	**52**	**40**
Malta	**43**	**40**	**45**	**50**
Estonia	**41**	**48**	**52**	**31**
Cyprus	**41**	**43**	**52**	**42**
Sweden	39	44	48	37
Hungary	**39**	**42**	**49**	**45**
Finland	38	45	48	46
Latvia	**36**	**42**	**40**	**33**
UK	34	36	38	29
Austria	32	37	46	30

Source: Commission (2004b, pp. B34, C50; 2005a, p. 68; 2005c, p. 12).
Note: New Member States in bold.

about whether EU membership is 'a good thing' (see Table 1). On average, support for the EU dropped four percentage points to the 50 per cent mark between the spring survey recorded in *Eurobarometer 63* and the autumn survey of *Eurobarometer 64*. These two surveys, conducted either side of the referendums in France and the Netherlands, provide the basis for a discussion of public opinion in western Europe, where it ranges from a two-point improvement of Luxembourg's rating of EU membership to an eight-point drop in the Belgian ratings. The discussion of public opinion in the new Member States also compares developments in 2005 to the first *Eurobarometer* survey after accession, *Eurobarometer 62* from the autumn of 2004, and explores public opinion on the most salient questions related to European integration in 2005 in the new Member States: treaty ratification, accession to Schengen and EMU, and further enlargement.

I. Developments in the Old Member States

Until French and Dutch voters rejected the Constitutional Treaty, 2005 looked set to be an average year in the old Member States as far as political developments were concerned. Four general elections were held in the 15 old EU Member States in 2005 (see Table 2), only two of which led to a change of government (both were early elections). In addition to the two who lost elections, another two prime ministers were forced from office: one as a consequence of the referendum defeat, the other after a dismal result in regional elections. A few governments saw off votes of no confidence, some more serious than others. Across the old Member States, a number of ministers resigned for the normal variety of reasons, ranging from minor scandals to major policy disagreements, but there were few significant cabinet reshuffles. It was a quiet year for parliamentary enquiries about executive abuse of power, and outside Italy no ministers or party leaders were on trial. However, the French and Dutch referendums affected politics in most of the other old Member States in one way or another. Moreover, a number of party leaders, parties and alliances across western Europe revised their positions and strategies in 2005, some as the result of electoral defeats, others with a view to the next round of elections, and a few over genuine policy divisions.

Old Central Europe: Germany and Austria

Of all the EU Member States, *Germany* went through the most unexpected and significant political change in 2005 when Chancellor Gerhard Schröder called and lost a general election. The first surprise was that it was called at all. An election was due in 2006, and the German constitution barely permits early elections. The president can dissolve the Bundestag early only if the chancellor has lost his working majority, and this had happened on only two previous occasions. In 1972 it was uncontroversial. In 1982, when Helmut Kohl replaced Helmut Schmidt through a vote of no confidence and immediately contrived a defeat in a vote of confidence in order to bolster his majority through new elections, the constitutional court reviewed the decision and set stricter limits for early elections. When Schröder engineered a vote of no confidence against him on 1 July, the Social Democrat (SPD)–Green coalition still commanded a slim majority in parliament (almost half the coalition's deputies abstained

Table 2: Elections in the Old EU Member States in 2005, Votes in % and Seats in Absolute Numbers

	Denmark	Portugal	UK	Germany
The socialist left and greens	Unity List (E) 3.4/6; Socialist People's Party (SF) 6.0/11	Communists/Greens (CDU) 7.5/14; Left Bloc (BE) 6.4	Greens 1.0/0	Left Party 8.7/54; Greens 8.1/51
Social democrats	Social Democrats (SD) 25.8/47	**Socialist Party (PS) 45.1/121**	***Labour 35.2/356***	**Social Democrats (SPD) 34.2/222**
Centre parties and territorial parties	Radical Liberals (RV) 9.2/17; Centre Democrats (CD) 1.0/0; (KD) 1.7/0; ***Liberals (V) 29.0/52***		Liberals 22.0/62; Scottish National Party 1.5/6; * Welsh and NI parties 2.2/21	Free Democrats (FDP) 9.8/61
Conservatives and Christian Democrats	***Conservatives (KF) 10.3/18***	*Social Democratic Party (PSD) 28.8/75; Popular Party (PP) 7.2/12*	Conservatives 32.4/198	**Christian Democrats (CDU and CSU) 35.2/225**
The far right	Danish People's Party (DF) 13.3/24		UK Independence Party 2.2/0	National Democratic Party (NDP) 1.6/0

Sources: Knudsen (2005); Portugal's National Election Commission; Quinn (2006); Hough (2005); and the BBC. (In the German case the percentages refer to second votes).

Notes: Incumbent coalition parties in italics, new governing coalition in bold text.

* Plaid Cymru won 3 seats, the Democratic Unionists 9, Sinn Fein 5, the Ulster Unionists 1, and the Social Democratic and Labour Party 3 seats.

in the vote). It was therefore uncertain whether the constitutional court would permit elections to go ahead. President Horst Köhler agreed on 22 July to dissolve parliament, but two disappointed deputies (one SPD and one Green) took the case to court. The final obstacles on the path to the 18 September election were cleared with the court's ruling on 18 August.

The immediate trigger was the Social Democrats' defeat in the May regional election in North Rhine-Westphalia, a state that had long been an SPD stronghold. However, the coalition's small majority (reduced to four), the internal left-wing opposition in the SPD to the government's economic reforms, and the difficulties of governing with an upper house dominated by the opposition Christian Democratic Union (CDU)/Christian Social Union (CSU) and Free Democrats (FDP) all contributed.[1] A socialist left organization, Labour and Social Justice (WASG), which had been established in 2004 by trade unionists and dissident SPD left-wingers, formally became a political party in January 2005. However, Schröder may have gambled on his campaign skills paying off, particularly against an unprepared opposition that seemed to struggle to attract voters even as the governing parties lost support. The CDU/CSU chose CDU leader Angela Merkel as their candidate for chancellor only on 30 April, after speeding up the selection process with a view to possible autumn elections. European questions were of little consequence in the subsequent campaign, which focused on economic reform and unemployment. The only European question concerned Turkish membership of the EU, which the CDU/CSU opposed.

The second major surprise was the election result itself. In line with public opinion polls, the prevailing consensus after Schröder called the election was that Merkel would lead the CDU/CSU to victory and a coalition government with the FDP and become Germany's next chancellor. However, in the closing stages of the campaign the SPD made considerable gains on the CDU, and the result on 18 September was a hung parliament in the sense that neither of the two main coalitions commanded a majority of the seats. The CDU/CSU became the largest party (with 35.2 per cent of the vote), but did not poll as well as expected and ended up barely ahead of the SPD (34.2 per cent). Both Schröder and Merkel claimed victory on the night, and much of the press called a dead heat. The FDP performed surprisingly well (9.8 per cent). So did the Left Party, an electoral collation of the predominantly west German WASG and the Party of Democratic Socialism (PDS, the former east German communist party), which entered parliament with 8.7 per cent. On the other hand the Greens (9.1 per cent) were relegated to fifth place, dropping half a percentage point.

[1] See Hough (2005); the government lost its majority in the Bundesrat in February 2003, after the Lower Saxony election.

The final surprise was not that Merkel eventually became chancellor, but that she did so at the head of a 'grand coalition' of the CDU/CSU and the SPD; the only such coalition since the Kiesinger government of 1966–69. The FDP immediately rejected entering a 'traffic-light' coalition (i.e. the 'red' SPD, 'yellow' FDP and the Greens), and the Greens decided against a 'Jamaica' coalition (with the 'black' CDU/CSU and the FDP). This left little option but a grand coalition, which the two parties took nearly two months to negotiate. Nevertheless, after taking office on 22 November, Merkel established a very favourable reputation in other European capitals remarkably quickly, earning very favourable press reports of her role in helping brokering a compromise on the EU budget at the December summit.

Across the southern border, *Austria* had no general election in 2005 and the government did not fall. Nevertheless, the governing coalition changed as, to some extent, did the party system. The country began 2005 with a 'black–blue' majority coalition of the Austrian People's Party (ÖVP) and the Austrian Freedom Party (FPÖ), but ended the year with a 'black–orange' minority government made up of the ÖVP and the new Alliance for Austria's Future (BZÖ). In fact the government largely remained the same: when the FPÖ split, the rump party left the coalition but the leadership and several deputies formed the BZÖ and remained in government. Moreover, although the split technically meant that the coalition government lost its majority in both chambers of the Austrian parliament, most of the deputies that remained in the rump FPÖ continued to support the government.

The cause of this political turmoil was Jörg Haider's decision to re-enter national politics, which he did by heading a break-away group from the FPÖ that included most of the party leadership and half of the party's deputies. The new party emerged from a deep split in the FPÖ, which reflected both personalities and ideological divisions. The catalyst was the leadership's effort to expel the party's right-wing MEP, Andreas Mölzer, which reflected a deeper split among the FPÖ's regional party groups. The BZÖ was therefore generally welcomed as a more moderate right-wing party than the rump FPÖ, and considerably less eurosceptic. The summer opinion polls indicated that the new party enjoyed more popular support than the rump FPÖ. However, the BZÖ performed poorly in the three regional elections in October, and by the end of the year, it was polling well below the 4 per cent threshold for representation in parliament. The 2006 general elections will therefore be the test of whether Haider's new party heralds a change in the Austrian party system, or merely a small and temporary shock. In either case, the split has driven the FPÖ further to the right and into a more eurosceptic stance.

Neither Austria nor Germany was affected much by the French and Dutch referendums, at least in terms of the treaty ratification processes. Both chambers of the German and Austrian parliaments ratified the Constitutional Treaty in May. The German Bundestag approved the Treaty by 569 votes to 23 (with two abstentions), and the *Bundesrat* by 66 to nil (with three abstentions). The only German parliamentary party opposed to the Treaty was the PDS (which subsequently merged with WASG to become the Left Party), although one CSU deputy unsuccessfully brought the Treaty before the constitutional court, arguing that it undermined the constitution and demanding a referendum. Although the SPD had considered a consultative referendum, it needed the support of the CDU (which is opposed to the use of referendums) to enact the necessary constitutional change. By the end of the year President Köhler had yet to sign the Constitution, which was put on hold after the French and Dutch referendums. When the Austrian parliament ratified the Treaty in May, all but one deputy (from the FPÖ) voted in favour in the *Nationalrat*; in the *Bundesrat* the vote was 59 to three.

Meanwhile *Eurobarometer* recorded a 5 per cent drop in support for the EU over the summer in both countries, with 53 per cent of Germans and 32 of Austrians assessing EU membership as a good thing. This left Austria as the Member State with the lowest level of support for the EU, although this drop in support was not mirrored by a rise in opposition. All Austrian parties oppose Turkish membership of the EU, and Chancellor Wolfgang Schüssel promised a referendum on Turkish EU membership. Although the possibility of alternative forms of association were raised, in the end the Austrian position did not prove an obstacle to opening membership talks between the EU and Turkey in October (see also Lavenex and Schimmelfennig in this volume).

France and the Netherlands

If the most surprising development in domestic politics came in Germany, the biggest shocks undoubtedly came when French and Dutch voters rejected the Constitutional Treaty in referendums in May and June. Five weeks later, Luxembourg voters approved the Treaty (in Belgium the Treaty was subject to parliamentary vote). Although opinion polls had indicated for some time that the French referendum might not result in a 'yes' (a possibility that was foreshadowed in the 'petit oui' – the 'little yes' – in the Maastricht referendum in 1992), the double 'no' provided a shock for which the EU governments were hardly prepared. Neither referendum was obligatory. Especially in the Dutch case, even the decision to call a referendum came as a surprise, given that no national referendum had been held since the time of the Batavian Republic two centuries earlier.

In the *French* case, President Jacques Chirac overcame his initial scepticism toward a referendum partly because his rival in the Union for a Popular

Movement (UMP) Nicolas Sarkozy called for one, and Sarkozy had public opinion on his side (Marthaler, 2005). Moreover, it became increasingly difficult to resist a referendum once the British government announced its intention to hold one. From the very beginning, therefore, the politics of the French referendum on the Constitutional Treaty was inextricably linked to the 2007 presidential election. This was not only the case on the centre-right, but also on the left where Laurent Fabius, the deputy leader of the Socialist Party (PS), used his opposition to the Treaty to distance himself from party leader and 2007 rival François Hollande. The latter won the first round when an internal PS referendum in December 2004 resulted in a 'yes' (as did a Green Party referendum in February 2005; the Communists opposed the Treaty, as did the National Front), but Fabius persisted in campaigning for a 'no'. By the end of the year, however, the two main presidential contenders on the right were Sarkozy and the new Prime Minister, Dominique de Villepin, and on the left the race remained open.

The much-reported result on 29 May was a 10 per cent gap between the 'no' (54.7 per cent) and 'yes' (45.3 per cent) votes, and a clear defeat for the government. Prime Minister Jean-Pierre Raffarin's government already faced problems related to poor economic performance, and had seen the finance minister resign over a scandal related to public finance of his Paris apartment (this was the minister who had succeeded Sarkozy in 2004, when the latter resigned in order to lead the UMP). The 'no' campaign included parties from the far right as well as far left, and therefore focused on a range of issues from opposition to the government, defence of democracy and sovereignty, opposition to Turkish EU membership, and unemployment and threats to the French economic and social model. According to the *Flash Eurobarometer* survey (No. 171), four of the top five reasons reported for voting 'no' were related to the economy and economic or social policy in Europe. Opposition to the government ranked fourth, and opposition to Turkish membership seventh. Qvortrup's (2005) comparative analysis concluded that the result hinged on moderate social democrat voters, who turned against the Treaty in considerable numbers in both France and the Netherlands. In any case, the result was immediately linked to the government's unpopularity. It prompted Chirac to replace Raffarin with de Villepin, and recall Sarkozy to the cabinet as interior minister.

The French 'no' thus had important political consequences beyond its effect on the process of treaty ratification. In France, the campaign split the PS and divided the UMP, and affected the line-up for the 2007 presidential contest, which in turn has consequences for France's future European policy. During the referendum campaign de Villepin emerged as more economically protectionist than Sarkozy. Although the latter's popularity suffered from his handling of the suburban riots in October and November, Sarkozy seemed a marginally stronger contender by the end of 2005. On the left, the success of Fabius' rebel 'no' campaign in persuading a majority of PS supporters to vote against the Treaty left Hollande's authority seriously weakened and the party severely divided. Although the party congress in November saw the party's factions unite somewhat behind Hollande's leadership, the decision on a presidential candidate was postponed for one year. By the end of the year both Fabius and Hollande were trailing behind three other PS candidates in the polls, with Hollande's partner Ségolène Royal (the more Blairesque 'third way' candidate) clearly in the lead. On the European front, the referendum defeat gave Chirac stronger incentives to pursue the public dispute with Tony Blair over the EU budget, in an effort to isolate the British prime minister and shift the focus of debate from the Treaty to the budget. This Franco–British division in turn helped pave the way for Angela Merkel to emerge as the successful broker at the December summit.

If the French referendum was a political necessity (or 'politically obligatory', see Morel, 2005), the referendum in the *Netherlands* was much more a matter of political choice. There was less popular demand for a referendum, and it was hardly a political requirement. The initiative came from three centre-left deputies, in the form of a private members' bill. With the centre-left parties and the populist right List Pym Fortuyn (LFP) in favour, and the Christian Democrats (CDA) opposed, the decision had hinged on the Liberals (VVD). In 2003 the referendum question had got caught up in a challenge for the VVD leadership, and the party had opted to support a referendum. Van Holsteyn (2006) put the decision down to the confluence of several factors: the populist challenge to Dutch politics from the LPF; the consequent efforts by Labour (PvdA) and the VVD at 'renewal'; and the importance of the Constitutional Treaty. The result, however, was an even stronger rejection of the Treaty than the French verdict a few days earlier: 61.5 per cent 'no', and 39.5 per cent 'yes'.

Not only were the motives for the referendum different in the two cases, but so were the reasons for the 'no' vote and the political fallout. The Dutch 'no' campaign focused more specifically on the Treaty, and on the speed and cost of integration in particular, but also on opposition to the prevailing Dutch political elite in general. Both the far left and populist right, including the Groep Geert Wilders founded by an eponymous VVD defector, focused on protecting sovereignty and national identity, while the small religious parties focused on the Treaty's lack of reference to Christian values; and 'no' voters cited the cost, lack of influence and loss of identity as their principal motives (Harmsen, 2005). The *Flash Eurobarometer* survey (No. 172) similarly reported a lack of information, sovereignty, opposition to the national government, the cost of the EU, and general opposition to European integration as the principal motives. Although opposition to the government seems to have played a role in both countries, Dutch 'no' voters cited opposition to the Treaty itself more often than did French voters.

Although the referendum result in the Netherlands was seen as a defeat for the government, and its management of the 'yes' campaign was heavily criticized, the referendum had nothing like the impact it did in France on domestic politics. The government had already weathered a small crisis in March, when two ministers from Democrats 66 resigned over the direct election of mayors, but the party eventually voted to stay in the coalition with the CDA and VVD. With the PvdA and Greens equally committed to the Constitution, there was little political capital to be had by any of the major players from the 'no' result. Even the small parties on the far left, right and Christian flanks that opposed the Treaty barely benefited from it according to the opinion polls. The Dutch party system thus emerged less affected by their referendum than its French counterpart, even if the referendum hinted at the continued role of populist anti-elite politics of the LFP's kind in the Netherlands.

Unlike the French, but like some of the Dutch parties, the Luxembourg parties' decision to call the first national referendum in *Luxembourg* since 1937 was based more on a principled quest for public discussion and participation than on party politics (Qvortrup, 2005). Moreover, when the decision was made in 2003, popular opinion was overwhelmingly pro-Treaty as were all the parliamentary parties except for the far right Action Committee for Democracy and Fair Pensions (ADR). Prime Minster Jean-Claude Juncker and his ruling Christian Social Party (CSV) were firmly committed to the Treaty, as were the Democrats (his coalition partner until the 2004 election) and Labour (LSAP, his coalition partners since 2004). In the end, Juncker promised to resign in the event of a 'no' vote. The result, coming five weeks after the French and Dutch referendums, was a solid 56.5 per cent majority in favour, against a 'no' vote of 43.5 per cent. The 'no' campaign and 'no' voters focused on opposition to this specific Treaty, to further integration in general and to enlargement (Hausemer, 2005); the *Flash Eurobarometer* survey (No. 173) reports concern for employment and the economic situation as the main concerns of eurosceptic voters, followed by opposition to integration and Turkish membership. The effect on party politics was minimal, and at the end of the year Europe's longest-serving prime minister was still in office.

Meanwhile, at the time the referendum results from the three neighbouring states began to come in, the *Belgian* government was recovering from a near-constitutional crisis that saw the Francophone and Flemish parties push a dispute over reorganization of a bilingual electoral district to the brink. Prime Minister Guy Verhofstadt's four-party coalition of Francophone and Flemish liberal and social democratic parties came close to splitting along the linguistic cleavage that has threatened Belgian government stability repeatedly since the three main parties all split along linguistic lines in the late 1960s and 1970s. The dispute was eventually postponed rather than resolved, but not before Verhofstadt had called and won a vote of confidence in May. By comparison, European questions were uncontroversial. The process of treaty ratification got underway with the Senate's approval of the Treaty in April, and progressed through the summer and autumn with approval by the lower house, regional parliaments and linguistic community parliaments, concluding with the Flemish regional parliament's approval of the Treaty in February 2006.

Popular support for the Treaty in two of the three referendums ran far below broad support for EU membership as measured by *Eurobarometer*. Voters in Luxembourg continued to rate as the strongest supporters of the EU in 2005: the share reporting that EU membership is a 'good thing' rose two percentage points to 82 per cent. The three other states followed the EU-wide trend of a decline in support for the EU, down seven and eight points to 70 per cent and 59 per cent in the Netherlands and Belgium respectively, and down five points to 46 per cent in France. However, this still left the Netherlands and Belgium among the top five states in terms of support for the EU, which in turn is consistent with the low levels of party-based euroscepticism. In France, by contrast, support for the EU fell well below the EU average, but mirrored the referendum result. At least in the Netherlands and Luxembourg, support for the EU and support for the Constitutional Treaty were clearly different.

The Mediterranean States

Only one government in the old Member States apart from the German one was defeated at the polls in 2005: the Portuguese government lost office at the 20 February election. The other three Mediterranean states ended 2005 with more or less the same governments as they began the year: Spain's minority Socialist (PSOE) government led by José Luis Rodrigues Zapatero survived unscathed; in Greece Costas Karamanlis' New Democracy (ND) government survived a vote of no confidence; and although Silvio Berlusconi's centre-right government fell in the spring, the Italian prime minister reassembled his coalition and went on to weather other crises as the year progressed. None of the four saw crises over ratification of the Constitution, although the Portuguese referendum was postponed after the French and Dutch 'no' votes.

The *Portuguese* elections produced a clear change of government, with a majority centre-left government replacing a majority centre-right coalition. Nevertheless, the policy change was less dramatic than might be expected, as incoming Prime Minister José Sócrates selected a moderate cabinet including several non-party ministers. In late 2004 Portugal's Socialist President, Jorge

Sampaio, had called early parliamentary elections when the centre-right coalition of the Social Democratic Party (PSD) and Popular Party (PP) began to fall apart. In its present form the government was less than six months old: Prime Minister Santana Lopes had taken office when his more moderate predecessor José Manuel Barroso left to become President of the European Commission. Yet by December Lopes's more right-wing government was generally deemed a failure, in terms of coalition management as well as economic policy. As expected, the voters swung clearly against the government in the February 2005 election, giving the centre-left Socialist Party (PS) an absolute majority of the seats in parliament and allowing Sócrates (a centrist modernizer) to govern without support from the three small far-left parties. The new cabinet was even more centrist than generally expected, and included a non-partisan minister of finance (who resigned six months later) and a former centre-right party leader as foreign minister. The election of a centre-right president (former Prime Minister Anibal Cavaco Silva) in January 2006 looked set to reinforce this moderate tendency. Both centre-right party leaders resigned in the wake of the February election, Lopes to be replaced by the more moderate Luis Marques Mendes.

A referendum on the Constitutional Treaty was set for April 2005, after the three main parties reached agreement to this effect in late 2004 (the PS and PSD both support the Treaty, the PP is more eurosceptic but played down the issue when in office, and the Communists firmly opposed the Treaty). However, the constitution does not permit treaties to be put to referendum, and the Constitutional Court rejected the proposed question in December 2004. Like most other countries that had planned referendums in the second half of 2005, the Portuguese government put the ratification process on hold after the French and Dutch results.

Although it controls only a minority in parliament, *Spain*'s PSOE government was one of the most stable in the old Member States in 2005. With the main opposition party, the Popular Party (PP) adopting a confrontational stance, Zapatero's government relied on the support of two Catalan parties and the United Left. Devolution and local autonomy was the main political issue of 2005. A Basque Nationalist Party (PNV) proposal for greater devolution was overwhelmingly rejected by the Spanish parliament in January, generating some tension with one of the Catalan parties over devolution in general even though the plan was specific to the Basque country. The PNV nevertheless threatened a Basque referendum on the plan, running the risk of prompting a constitutional crisis, until the elections in April deprived the party of its majority in the regional assembly. By the end of the year, however, the Spanish parliament had approved proposals to grant Catalonia a degree of fiscal and legislative devolution. The proposal split the PSOE and drew strong opposition from the

PP (and prompted the head of the armed forces to mention the possibility of military intervention if autonomy was taken too far, which in turn forced his resignation and house arrest in early January 2006).

European integration proved a far less contentious political issue, for party politics as well as voters. In February Spain became the first country to see the Constitution approved in a referendum, with 76.7 per cent voting in favour (but with more than one in four voting 'no' in Catalonia and the Basque country). All the major parties supported the Treaty, which the Spanish parliament ratified by a vote of 311 to 19 in April. The process was completed when the Senate approved the Treaty in May, less than two weeks before the French referendum, unanimously with only one abstention.

Like its Spanish counterpart, the *Greek* government experienced relatively little trouble in 2005. Having won the March 2004 election after two decades of Socialist (Pasok) dominance, Costas Karamanlis's New Democracy (ND) remained in a strong position throughout 2005. In February 2005 a cross-party agreement saw Pasok's Karolos Papoulias elected (by parliament) to the largely ceremonial presidency. The main political controversy in 2005 centred on government moves on structural reforms, from privatization to labour law, which drew sharp criticism from Pasok and prompted ND to call a vote of confidence in June. The government won the vote, and despite this clash both main parties moved towards the political centre in 2005. George Papandreou had been chosen Pasok leader on a reformist platform shortly before the March 2004 election, and pursued a centrist and modernizing course in 2005 with a view to a more radical review of the party's policies and charter in 2006.

As in the other Mediterranean Member States, the Constitutional Treaty was uncontroversial in Greece. Although Pasok called for a referendum on the Constitution, this was primarily justified in terms of the need for public discussion. The Treaty was ratified by parliament with 268 votes to 17 in April, and the opposition's last effort to call a referendum was defeated in May.

After years of unprecedented stability, *Italy* saw a series of crises in 2005 that were more reminiscent of the 'first republic'. Prime Minister Bettino Craxi's reported reply to President Ronald Reagan's query in 1985 as to how his crisis was going – 'very well, thank you' – might not seem completely out of place two decades later. Prime Minister Silvio Berlusconi survived a severe defeat in the April regional election, the subsequent fall of the government, a central bank crisis, and the start of yet another corruption trial, and went on to secure constitutional reform on devolution, pass two controversial justice bills and change the electoral system back to proportional representation in time for the 2006 elections. Meanwhile, both the centre-left and centre-right parties and alliances positioned themselves strategically for the elections, altering the dynamics of the Italian party system in the process.

The governing Casa della Libertà, made up of Berlusconi's *Forza Italia*, the *Lega Nord* (LN), post-fascist National Alliance (AN) and the centrist Christian Democratic Union (UDC) and two small parties, suffered a sufficiently bad defeat in the regional elections in April 2005 to prompt the AN and UDC to call for an early general election. When this was not forthcoming, the UDC promptly withdrew from the coalition and caused the government's collapse. However, a similar Berlusconi government returned to office later the same month. The AN and UDC remained internally divided in 2005, and the LN remained the less integrated coalition partner (in June two LN ministers called for Italy to leave the euro). Nevertheless, the government pushed through several controversial bills, including a law on judicial reform that had been vetoed by the president in 2004, a law limiting the statute of limitations on some crimes and setting 70 as an age limit for sending first-time offenders to prison (broadly seen as an effort to prevent the incarceration of Cesare Previti, the prime minister's former lawyer), a bill increasing regional autonomy (strongly opposed by the left), and a return to proportional representation for general elections. The opposition claimed the latter was designed to limit the effect of the centre-right's expected defeat in 2006, and boycotted the vote. The government's second main crisis was the prolonged controversy about Central Bank Governor Antonio Fazio's alleged intervention against the foreign takeover of an Italian bank, which promoted the finance minister's resignation, government plans for a special law to fire Fazio, and a legal challenge by the European Commission before Fazio eventually resigned in December.

Meanwhile, the Italian centre-left regrouped with a view to the 2006 elections, uniting under the new label *Unione* and electing former Commission President Romano Prodi its candidate in the October 2005 primary. The new alliance united the four parties that fought and won the April regional elections, the Democrats of the Left (DS) and the more centrist Margherita, and two smaller centrist parties, with a range of smaller parties of the left and centre, including the communist and republican parties. Although Prodi won the primary with some three-quarters of the vote, the centre-left alliance entered 2006 at least as divided over policy and leadership as the centre-right, if not more so. By the end of 2005 polls indicated that the centre-left's lead in the race towards the April 2006 election was far from solid.

The increasingly eurosceptic messages coming from the *Lega Nord* notwithstanding, most Italian parties are solidly pro-EU. Berlusconi's government therefore had little or no trouble ratifying the Constitutional Treaty, which was approved parliament in January (436 to 28) and the Senate in April (217 to 16), the 'no' votes coming from the LN and the unreformed Communists (PRC).

Public opinion in Portugal and Italy took a clearer turn against European integration over the summer of 2005 than it did in Greece or Spain. With 66 per cent reporting (according to *Eurobarometer*) that EU membership is 'a good thing', unchanged from the spring, Spain ranked fourth among the 25 states in terms of support for the EU in the autumn of 2005. The equivalent percentage from Greece dropped only two points, whereas it dropped seven points in Portugal and six in Italy. This left Italy at the EU average, with 50 per cent approval of the EU, and Greece and Portugal marginally above this level at the 54 per cent mark. Spain thus saw little change, while Greece and Italy saw an increase in undecided or neutral voters, and Portugal a shift to the 'no' side. However, this is hardly reflected in the party systems, except at the flanks, and all three saw broad party support for the Constitutional Treaty.

The UK, Ireland and Scandinavia

All five governments in the EU's north-western corner were made up of the same parties at the end of 2005 as at the beginning of the year. The two elections, in Denmark and the UK, were won by the incumbent governments, and there were no major government crises in any of the five states. In fact, more than in any other part of the EU, the French and Dutch 'no' votes contributed to political stability in the north-west. Although the European question was not set to be critical in Ireland, Denmark and Finland, the question was more contentious in Sweden and Britain. Support for the EU declined in all five states, but Denmark and Ireland still score above the EU average.

As widely predicted, the British Labour Party won the May 2005 election and Prime Minister Tony Blair was returned with a comfortable, though substantially reduced, majority. The war in Iraq reduced Labour's popularity considerably, but the Conservatives proved unable to capitalize on this, leaving the Liberal Democrats and other smaller parties to perform well. As one election report summed it up: 'the unenthusiastic re-election of a Labour government, led by a widely distrusted prime minister, on the lowest winning plurality [*sic*] of the popular vote on record' (Quinn, 2006, p. 169). Having announced the previous year that he would seek a third term as prime minister, but not a fourth, the relationship between Blair and his expected successor, Chancellor [finance minister] Gordon Brown took centre stage. Through April the two successfully set aside their much-debated differences, and Brown took on a central role in managing the campaign. The Labour cabinet that took office after the 5 May election saw only a minor reshuffle.

The main political fall-out from the election was the Conservative Party leader Michael Howard's decision to stand down, after an interim period during which the party would adopt new rules for selecting its leader. The result of the contest came in December when the 'modern and radical' David Cameron was elected leader of the party, on a relatively vague but centrist platform that prompted comparisons with Tony Blair's election as Labour leader. However, as Cameron pledged that he would withdraw the Conservatives from the European People's Party (EPP)–European Democrats because it is excessively federalist, any centrist turn that the party might take did not look set to include a more pro-EU stance. Leaving the EPP would mean seeking to build alliances with other more eurosceptic centre-right parties, including the mainstream Civic Democratic Party in the Czech Republic, as well as more populist or far-right parties such as Italy's post-fascist National Alliance, and Poland's populist Law and Justice Party. Although the Conservatives have long opposed the euro and the Constitutional Treaty, leaving the EPP would underscore the party's euroscepticism to a new extent, and it could alter the party dynamics in the European Parliament if a new group were to be formed successfully.

The major challenge for Blair looked set to be the referendum the government had promised to hold on the Constitutional Treaty, expected in early 2006 after the completion of the UK's presidency. The possibility of a 'no' vote was frequently linked to speculation about when Blair would step down as party leader and prime minister, generating further media debate on the Labour leadership. In terms of purely domestic politics the French and Dutch 'no' votes clearly removed a controversial issue from the political agenda, and an issue on which the Conservatives would have been keen to compete with Labour. The UK was one of the first countries to put its ratification process on hold, suspending the ratification bill on 6 June, ten days before EU leaders agreed 'a period of reflection' at the June summit. The terrorist attacks on the London transport system on 7 July had far less impact on domestic party competition than the 11 September attacks on the USA in 2001 or the Madrid bombings of 11 March 2004, insofar as the Labour government and Conservative opposition have taken a similar line on the reaction and subsequent anti-terrorism bills (although in early 2006 the Conservatives and Liberal Democrats would take a more sceptical line with regard to proposals to ban 'glorification of terrorism').

In *Ireland* the Fianna Fail–Progressive Democrats coalition saw out its third year since the 2002 election (the coalition has been in office since 1997), suffering only minor scandals and more or less normal mid-term opinion poll lows. Some political re-alignment took place among the opposition parties with a view to the next election, as the Labour Party conference voted to form an electoral alliance with Fine Gael. Immediately after the French and Dutch referendums the government announced that it would proceed with the referendum on the Constitutional Treaty (following standard practice: Ireland has held six referendums on European integration since 1972), but these plans were postponed after the June summit. All the major parties are in favour of the Treaty: only Sinn Fein opposed it and prepared for a 'no' campaign.

The year 2005 was equally quiet politically in *Finland*, with Prime Minister Matti Vanhanen of the Centre Party doing well in the opinion polls. The only significant political development, a government reshuffle in September, was the consequence of a leadership change in one of the coalition members, the Social Democratic Party. The new SDP leader Eero Heinaluoma became minister of finance, prompting a reshuffle of several other government posts that hardly altered the political balance of the cabinet. Like Ireland, but despite a much higher level of popular euroscepticism, Finland features a remarkably pro-EU elite (Raunio, 2005). More to the point, consensual policy-making is the norm, particularly on foreign policy decisions. The main parties all support the Constitutional Treaty, and all agreed that the accession referendum on the EU in 1994 should be considered a special case. Only three small parties on the flanks (the True Finns, the Greens and the Christian Democrats) called for a referendum.[2] Parliamentary treaty ratification was planned for the autumn of 2005, but after the French and Dutch results and the ensuing 'pause for reflection', the government opted merely to present a report to parliament in November 2005. Finland remains very unlikely to use referendums on European integration in the near future.

Like the north-western Member States *Sweden* saw remarkable government stability in 2005 despite being run by a minority government. Göran Persson's Social Democrat (SAP) government relied on support from two smaller (and more eurosceptic) parties, the Greens and the Left Party, in what practically amounted to an informal coalition. The most critical change to the party system in 2005 came as an internal quarrel in the formerly communist Left Party, as a consequence of party leader Lars Ohly's reluctance to denounce communism. The party consequently lost a number of moderates to the Greens, and will be challenged in the 2006 election by the new Feminist Initiative, a party founded by former Left Party leader Gudrun Schyman (in 2006 the party would also attract a Liberal MEP). The far left part of the political spectrum was therefore relatively open at the end of 2005, with an election due in September 2006.

Like its Finnish counterpart, the Swedish government decided not to call a referendum on the Constitutional Treaty, but to ratify it in parliament. Cross-party consensus on ratification was reached in December 2004, with only the Greens and the Left Party demanding a referendum. However, the situation in the first half of 2005 was precarious both because the government relied on the two parties' support and because there is a considerable eurosceptic faction in the SAP. By the time the French referendum result came in, the eurosceptic SAP faction was collecting signatures to demand an internal party referendum on the

---

[2] Like its Norwegian, Danish and Swedish counterparts, the Finnish Christian party is a 'Christian people's party', or a peripheral protest party, rather than a catch-all Christian democratic party of the continental type (see Raunio, 2005).

matter, with a view to forcing through a national referendum on the Treaty. At the very least, therefore, the French and Dutch did not spare the SAP further internal debate. However, the suspension of the ratification process did not stop the eurosceptic June List, which had come in third place in the Swedish 2004 European Parliament election, from making good on its promise to field candidates in the 2006 general election unless a referendum was called.

The general election in *Denmark* was held on 8 February, and saw the ruling centre-right coalition of the Liberals and Conservatives returned to office. It was called early, but an election was due at some point in 2005. The minority coalition continues to rely on the support of the far-right Danish People's Party. On the government side, the election therefore made for continuity. On the opposition side, however, the Social Democrats saw their worst result since the 1973 'earthquake election', while the Social Liberals performed well. This was put down largely to the Social Democrats' failure to present a clear opposition to the government, leaving the Social Liberals as the main critics of, for example, tighter immigration policy (Knudsen, 2005; Pedersen, 2005). Social Democrat party leader Mogens Lykketoft promptly resigned. After a leadership battle that reopened the traditionalist left *v.* modernizers division, the former MEP and newly elected MP Helle Thoring-Schmidt took over the leadership, signalling some renewal of the party and its image. The far-left Socialist People's Party also changed leader, strengthening its recent development toward a less radical and more pro-EU stance.

Perhaps the most controversial development in retrospect, the publication of a dozen cartoons depicting the Prophet Mohammed in the newspaper *Jyllands-Posten* in September, was merely a minor controversy in Denmark during the autumn of 2005. However, the republication of the cartoons by a Christian Norwegian magazine in January 2006 would prove the catalyst of a major political controversy that extended across the EU and would draw comments from heads of state as well as the Commission.

Denmark was the only Scandinavian state to choose the referendum path towards ratification of the Constitutional Treaty. The Danish constitution requires referendums to be held on treaties that involve cession of sovereignty unless they are approved by a five-sixths majority in parliament, but during the last two decades a consensus has emerged among the main parties that referendums will be held on EU treaties (only Nice was ratified by parliamentary vote). Developments in 2005 were remarkable because all the five old parties (including the formerly eurosceptic Socialist People's Party) agreed not only on the referendum, but to recommend a 'yes'. This left only the Danish People's Party and the Christian Democrats (who fell below the 2 per cent threshold for parliamentary representation) on the 'no' side. Like most other states that had not ratified the Treaty by the time of the French 'no', Denmark suspended the ratification process.

All the five north-western EU Member States saw a swing in public opinion against EU membership as measured by *Eurobarometer*'s question of whether EU membership is a 'good thing'. The drop in support in Ireland (2 per cent), the UK (2 per cent) and Denmark (3 per cent) was less that the EU average, whereas the share of EU supporters dropped by 5 per cent in Sweden and 7 per cent in Finland. This left the UK (34 per cent), Finland (38 per cent) and Sweden (39 per cent) among the six Member States with the lowest support for EU membership; but Denmark was well above the EU average (56 per cent) and Ireland (73 per cent), second only to Luxembourg.

II. Developments in the New Member States

Political Life after Accession

2005 was the first full year of EU membership for the ten states that acceded on 1 May 2004. Across the region, it was less eventful than most of the preceding years: only one of the ten countries (Poland) had national-level parliamentary and presidential elections, and there was also generally greater governmental stability than in the previous year. This is not to say that the states concerned were not marked by bitter political disputes between governments and oppositions, but rather that these were of the same order as in the old EU Member States. No decisions were taken that were of great import to the future shape of their democratic governance.

In only two countries (Estonia and the Czech Republic) was the prime minister removed without losing a parliamentary election. In the *Estonian* case, the government of Prime Minister Juhan Parts of the Res Publica party resigned in March after a vote of no confidence in the justice minister, Ken-Marti Vaher, who was from the same party. The contentious issue was a proposal to introduce quotas at regional level for the number of civil servants who had to be prosecuted for corruption. Res Publica, a new party that had done unexpectedly well in the 2003 elections, left government, and Parts was replaced by Andrus Ansip, the economics minister and chair of the pro-market Estonian Reform Party. This had been the second largest party in the previous government. It retained the Estonian People's Union as a coalition partner, and brought the Estonian Centre Party back into government. The new government represented a slight shift to the right in economic terms, but did not otherwise mark a major shift in the direction of Estonian policy. The three governing parties performed well in local elections in October, thus strengthening the coalition's chances of surviving until the 2007 election.

In the *Czech Republic*, the young Social Democrat Prime Minister, Stanislav Gross, resigned in April 2005. He had held the premier's office for less than a year after his party colleague Vladimír Špidla (now EU Commissioner for Employment, Social Affairs and Equal Opportunities) had resigned in the wake of the Social Democrats' poor performance in the European Parliament elections. Gross had come under attack for suspected corruption due both to his property apparently exceeding his legal means, and because his wife had borrowed money from a friend who was later charged with fraud. The Social Democrats' coalition partner, the Christian Democratic Union-Czech People's Party, had withdrawn from the government at the end of March, which destroyed the government's wafer-thin majority. Although Gross's government survived a subsequent vote of no confidence proposed by the opposition Civic Democratic Party, this was due only to support from deputies of the Communist Party of Bohemia and Moravia, who were still a political pariah in the Czech Republic. Subsequently, the Social Democrats' other small coalition partner, the Freedom Union, also resigned from the government, which finally prompted Gross's resignation. The three former government parties then formed a new government, which bore a strong similarity to the old one. Gross was replaced by the Social Democrats' deputy chair, Jiří Paroubek, who made considerable strides in improving the Social Democrats' low support levels in the run-up to the June 2006 elections. President Václav Klaus, the founder and leading light of the opposition Civic Democratic Party, wielded some power in engineering Gross's resignation, but not even Klaus's augmentation of the significance of the largely ceremonial presidential office placed a serious question mark over the stability of the Czech political system.

What was noticeable in both cases was that the corruption issue, albeit in different manifestations, led to changes in the premiership, and it was also prominent in the *Polish* elections in September/October 2005 (and, indeed, in the parliamentary elections in the candidate state *Bulgaria* in June 2005). In *Slovakia* also, the minority government lost one of its four coalition partners after its party chair, the economics minister, was dismissed in the wake of accusations of improper financial dealings; the minister of labour, social affairs and the family resigned and the minister of agriculture was heavily attacked in connection with allegations of seeking personal gain from EU funds; and there were endless allegations that the government was being kept in office by independent deputies who had been 'bought'. The fight against corruption and the development of administrative capacity had been emphasized strongly by the European Commission throughout the accession negotiations, and might well have been an area where 'backsliding' took place once membership of the EU had removed the coercive potential of conditionality. However, rejection of corruption appeared to have been internalized as a value by politicians and voters in the post-communist accession states. There was a spreading belief that it should and could be countered, and this was the political agenda which resonated most strongly with disillusioned voters.

In the course of the year, there was only one change of head of state other than in Poland. László Sólyom, the nominee of the opposition Fidesz and Hungarian Democratic Forum parties, was elected president of *Hungary*. He gained 185 votes compared to 182 votes for the Hungarian Socialist Party's candidate, parliamentary speaker Katalin Szili. Although a two-thirds parliamentary majority is required in order to elect the president, the Constitution contains a 'tie-breaking' provision, whereby a simple majority of deputies voting suffices if no candidate reaches this threshold in the second ballot. The success of the opposition candidate was due to the fact that the smaller government partner, the Alliance of Free Democrats, did not support the socialist candidate.

Elsewhere in the new Member States, governmental politics were fairly stable, although the corruption issue was not absent. The four-party centre right government in *Latvia* successfully survived the year 2005 as the governing parties enjoyed a solid majority, and the only party change involved a merger between one of the governing parties (the Latvia's First Party) and the small Latvia's Way that was no longer represented in parliament. In neighbouring *Lithuania* the centre-left four party coalition government survived 2005, but in a far weaker condition than its northern neighbour. After a number of allegations of corruption, Viktor Uspaskich, whose Labour Party had enjoyed marked electoral success since its foundation in 2003, was forced to resign as economics minister in June, and the Social Democrat finance minister had resigned over a dispute about tax reform in May. However, the opposition proved unable to capitalize on this as even some of the opposition parties were accused of corruption in local politics. In *Slovenia* the four-party coalition led by the centre-right Slovene Democratic Party of Prime Minister Janez Janša also went through 2005 with no major misadventures, although the economic reforms that it proposed in the second half of the year drew considerable opposition.

The Polish Elections

Poland had, since a change in its electoral law before the 1993 elections, tended to display right/left alternation in coalition governments, with the left winning in 1993 and 2001, and the right in 1997. Presidential elections, which took place every five years, had produced a different sequence: when Lech Wałęsa's presidency ended in 1995, he was replaced by the Social Democrat (and ex-communist) Aleksander Kwaśniewski, who was re-elected in October 2000 with an impressive 53.9 per cent of the vote in the first round. In autumn 2005, both parliamentary and presidential elections took place in quick succession for the first time, with the parliamentary elections on 25 September followed by the first and second rounds of the presidential contest on 9 and 23 October. This meant that the parliamentary contest was far more personality-led than usual, since the parties' presidential candidates inevitably became the focal point for electoral coverage (Szczerbiak, 2005).

The results of the parliamentary election showed a degree of stabilization in the Polish party system, since the six parties that crossed the 5 per cent threshold to enter the *Sejm* (lower chamber of parliament) were the same as had been successful in 2001 (see Table 3). However, this fact belied the turbulence that Polish parliamentary politics had faced over the previous four years. The centre-left government elected in 2001 had replaced a highly unpopular centre-right government, and yet itself lost popularity very quickly, both because of its inability to produce quick solutions to problems of economic hardship, and because it became tainted by corruption scandals. The Polish Peasant Party left the government in March 2003. A year later, the previously rather disciplined post-communist Democratic Left Alliance split, leading to a change of prime minister after EU accession and an expectation that there would be early elections (which did not, in fact, happen).

The disarray on the left made it highly likely that the new government would be a centre-right coalition between Civic Platform and Law and Justice, excluding both the left of centre parties (if they made it into parliament) and the maverick eurosceptic right represented by Self-Defence and the League of Polish Families. Civic Platform and Law and Justice represented the two kinds of right-of-centre parties common in the post-communist world. Civic Platform was economically liberal, and in the European Parliament belonged to the European People's Party; Law and Justice was a traditional and

Table 3: Polish Parliamentary Election, September 2005

Party	% Vote	Sejm Seats	Sejm Seats (2001)	Senate Seats	Senate Seats (2001)
Law and Justice (PiS)	27.0	155	44	49	0
Civic Platform (PO)	24.1	133	65	34	0
Self-Defence	11.4	56	53	3	2
Democratic Left Alliance (SLD)	11.3	55	216	0	75
League of Polish Families (LPR)	8.0	34	38	7	2
Polish Peasant Party (PSL)	7.0	25	42	2	4
Other parties*	11.2	2	2	5	17

Source: IFES Election Guide, available at «http://www.electionguide.org».
Note: * Includes seats reserved for ethnic minorities.

© 2006 The Author(s)
Journal compilation © 2006 Blackwell Publishing Ltd

conservative party with a more reserved attitude to radical economic reform, which belonged to the more marginal Union for Europe of the Nations. The two parties together gained a firm majority in the 460-seat *Sejm*, elected by proportional representation, and an even larger majority in the 100-seat Senate, elected on a majoritarian principle.

That the centre-right coalition was not eventually formed was in part a result of the impending presidential election. The two most popular presidential candidates, Civic Platform leader Donald Tusk and the mayor of Warsaw Lech Kaczyński for Law and Justice, represented the potential coalition partners, meaning that, in the wake of the parliamentary election, the two parties were in competitive mode. Their only major competitor who, after announcing his candidacy in June, had for a time led in opinion polls, was the *Sejm* speaker, Włodzimierz Cimoszewicz, who ran as an independent but was identified with the Democratic Left Alliance. However, Cimoszewicz lost support after his integrity was questioned in a parliamentary commission enquiring into another alleged scandal, and he withdrew his candidacy ten days before the parliamentary election.

Civic Platform's tactic after coming second in the parliamentary election was to demand that Law and Justice's leader, Jarosław Kaczyński, became prime minister. Since his twin brother Lech was the party's presidential candidate, it was hoped that the prospect of having an identical pair of politicians as prime minister and president might dampen Lech Kaczyński's chances in the presidential race. Aware of this possibility, Law and Justice chose another nominee, Kazimierz Marckinkiewicz, to be premier. While Civic Platform's Tusk had a narrow lead in the first round of the presidential election, he was overtaken convincingly by Kaczyński in the second round (see Table 4). This was because Kaczyński was strongly supported by voters of the candidate who had come third, Self-Defence's Andrzej Lepper, and was able to tap into the fears of many voters that Tusk's liberal economic policies would benefit only the better off.

The consequence of the presidential rivalry between the two leading parties was that Law and Justice ended up forming a minority government on its own, largely using non-party experts to fill economic roles. Civic Platform finally withdrew from talks on a coalition when, with support from Self-Defence, Law and Justice had its candidates elected as speakers of both the upper and lower chambers of the parliament, meaning that one party held all four high-profile posts in Polish politics.

From an EU viewpoint, this was a far from ideal scenario. Law and Justice was more eurosceptic than Civic Platform; Kaczyński was more oriented towards Washington, whereas Tusk looked to Brussels; and the government's minority status opened up the alarming prospect of its relying for support on the two

Table 4: Polish Presidential Election, October 2005

Candidate	% Vote First Round	% Vote Second Round
Donald Tusk (Civic Platform)	36.3	46.0
Lech Kaczyński (Law and Justice)	33.1	54.0
Andrzej Lepper (Self-Defence)	15.1	
Marek Borowski (Social Democratic Party of Poland)	10.3	
Others (8)	5.1	

Source: IFES Election Guide, available at «http://www.electionguide.org».

more eurosceptic parties in parliament. Polish politics was also left with two other problems. One was that the government's weak parliamentary base led to months of speculation about whether there might be new elections. The second was the voters' clear disillusionment with politics and political corruption as a whole. While Poland had, throughout its post-communist history, been plagued by some of the lowest electoral turnouts in central and eastern Europe, 2005 produced record lows for both the parliamentary and the presidential elections. The EU's largest new Member State was, therefore, scarcely providing a model likely to encourage further European integration.

The EU Issue in Domestic Politics

The European Commission's *Eurobarometer* polls showed reasonable levels of support for EU membership in the new Member States. There had been a noticeable increase in support for membership in the first *Eurobarometer* poll conducted after enlargement in autumn 2004, followed by slight regression during 2005 (see Table 1). Surveys conducted in October and November 2005 showed that, in the EU-25 as a whole, 50 per cent of respondents thought that their country's membership was 'a good thing'. However, while only three new Member States – Lithuania, Poland and Slovakia – were above average on this indicator, neutral stances were more common than a belief that EU membership was 'a bad thing', and they exceeded even the belief that it was 'a good thing' in Hungary, Slovenia, Latvia and Estonia. Opposition increased significantly only in Latvia. The increase in ambivalent views on the EU was not illogical: membership brought an increasing awareness of the complexity and diversity of the EU's functions.

Only one of the ten new Member States had shown an increase in support for the EU in all three surveys since accession, and this pattern was repeated when respondents were asked whether their country had benefited from being a member of the EU. This was important because the country concerned was Poland, which was not only as populous as all nine other new members together, but had also since the late 1990s been the most conspicuously eurosceptic. The politicization of the EU at the level of party competition did not, therefore, necessarily accord with citizens' perceptions of what had happened since accession.

The new Member States were fairly acquiescent participants in the area of EU politics that, elsewhere in the EU, was profoundly affected by domestic politics and the decisions of national electorates: the Constitutional Treaty. Having taken voters to the ballot box in two successive years for the EU accession referendums and the European Parliament elections, most were content to have the Treaty ratified by parliament. Lithuania and Hungary had been the first EU members to accomplish this in late 2004, and they were followed in 2005 by Slovenia, Slovakia, Latvia, Cyprus and Malta, the latter two voting after the French and Netherlands referendums had made the issue largely academic. The parliamentary votes were generally very strongly in favour. The narrowest margin was Cyprus's 30 to 19 in favour, which was a consequence of the strong communist left faction in parliament. Malta, which was traditionally the country most polarized on EU issues, and which had had the closest accession referendum, was perhaps surprisingly the only state where parliament passed the Treaty unanimously. This was not because of a reduction of euroscepticism in Malta, but rather a reflection of the bipolar party system, which meant that once the two parliamentary parties had agreed to support the Treaty (albeit with some reservations), there were no small maverick parties in parliament to add any 'no' votes.

Referendums had been considered necessary only in the two more eurosceptic states, Poland and the Czech Republic, where at least one major party was opposed to the Treaty. In both cases, it was originally expected that the referendums would be held to coincide with national elections: the October 2005 presidential election in Poland and the June 2006 parliamentary election in the Czech Republic. However, since neither had been fixed by June 2005, both were put on hold pending further developments. In either case, the outcome would be hard to predict. While parts of the political elites in the new Member States are developing more nuanced views of certain aspects of the Treaty, particularly where the 'flat tax' issue is concerned, the public, as indicated by the *Eurobarometer* polls, has generally become slightly more positive about the EU since enlargement.

Three other accession-related issues also affect the new Member States. Joining Schengen has been the least politicized; subject to positive Schengen evaluations, they should be able to lift border controls with the Schengen area in 2007. Public opinion has been more concerned with the issue of free movement of labour, objecting to the 'second-class citizenship' implied by the transition periods imposed by most of the old Member States.

Greater national differences are to be found on the question of joining the euro area. By the end of 2005, seven of the new Member States had joined ERM II, which precedes a period of at least two years before joining economic and monetary union. Only the largest three new Member States – the Czech Republic, Hungary and Poland – have yet to reach a decision on the matter. In the minds of many voters, adopting the euro is linked to the very emotive issue of price rises. By autumn 2005, *Eurobarometer* data suggested that the percentage of citizens expecting positive consequences from the introduction of the euro in their country had decreased since autumn 2004 from 44 per cent to 38 per cent, while those expecting negative consequences increased from 41 per cent to 46 per cent. Resistance to the euro was strongest in the three Baltic states: Estonia, Latvia and Lithuania. While this may be linked to fears of loss of sovereignty after their very negative experiences in the Soviet Union, it should also be noted that, despite substantial 'catching up' in the case of Estonia, living standards still remained low by EU standards in all three.

Finally, citizens of the new Member States are particularly strong supporters of continuing the enlargement process. The autumn 2005 *Eurobarometer* showed that for 12 possible future Member States, accession enjoyed stronger support among those who had themselves joined the EU in May 2004. As in the old Member States, support was strongest – two-thirds or more – for the prosperous possible candidates, Switzerland, Norway and Iceland, and weakest – at 40 per cent or below – for Albania and Turkey. Generally, however, the difference in support between old and new Member States was strongest in the case of states that formerly belonged to the Warsaw Pact or Yugoslavia, ranging from 11 percentage points higher in the new Member States for Bosnia and Herzegovina (50 per cent support from new Member States, and 39 per cent from old Member States) to 23 percentage points higher (70 per cent support from new Member States compared to 47 per cent in old Member States) in the case of Croatia, which happens to be very familiar as a popular holiday destination for many central Europeans. There is also a striking difference in support for Ukrainian membership, which citizens of new Member States rank four percentage points higher than for Romania, whose accession is imminent. This particular support for Ukrainian membership can in part be explained by the fact that more than half the citizens of the new Member States are Poles, and Poland shares a lengthy land border with Ukraine and therefore has economic and security interests in furthering the democratic stabilization of their neighbour.

In the course of 2005, the popular preferences for future enlargements in the new Member States were also mirrored by diplomatic efforts of states such as

Hungary and Slovakia to secure the opening of negotiations with Croatia. The EU's post-communist neighbours are of far more immediate political concern to the governments of central and eastern Europe than to old EU Member States. At neither popular nor governmental level is there any interest in the new EU in 'shutting the door behind them' now that they have joined, thereby keeping the economic benefits of enlargement to themselves. This may be regarded as an ultimate sign of the success of the EU's enlargement project.

Key Reading

Harmsen (2005), Hausemer (2005), and Marthaler (2005) comment – respectively – on the referendums in the Netherlands, Luxembourg, and France. Hough (2005), Pedersen (2005), Quinn (2006), and Szczerbiak (2005) analyse the elections in Germany, Denmark, the UK and Poland, respectively.

References

Commission of the European Communities (2004a) *Flash Eurobarometer* Nos 171, 172, 173, 175b (Brussels: CEC).

Commission of the European Communities (2004b) *Eurobarometer Spring 2004* (Brussels: CEC).

Commission of the European Communities (2005a) *Standard Eurobarometer 62, Autumn 2004* (Brussels: CEC).

Commission of the European Communities (2005b) *Standard Eurobarometer 63, Spring 2005* (Brussels: CEC).

Commission of the European Communities (2005c) *Standard Eurobarometer 64, Autumn 2005: First Results* (Brussels: CEC).

Harmsen, R. (2005) 'The Dutch Referendum on the Ratification of the European Constitutional Treaty, 1 June 2005'. EPERN Referendum Briefing Paper No.13, Sussex European Institute.

Hausemer, P. (2005) 'Luxembourg's Referendum on the European Constitutional Treaty, 10 July 2005'. EPERN Referendum Briefing Paper No.14, Sussex European Institute.

Holstyen, J.J.M. van (2005) 'To Refer or Not to Refer, That's the Question: On the First National Referendum in the Netherlands'. ECPR conference paper, Budapest 8–10 September.

Hough, D. (2005) 'The German Bundestag Election of September 2005'. EPERN Election Briefing No. 23, Sussex European Institute.

Knudsen, A.C.K. (2005) 'The Danish General Election of February 2005'. EPERN Election Briefing Paper No.19, Sussex European Institute.

Marthaler, S. 'The French Referendum on the Ratification of the European Constitutional Treaty, 29 May 2005'. EPERN Referendum Briefing Paper No.12, Sussex European Institute.

Morel, L. (2005) 'Le choix du référendum: Leçons françaises, l'émergence d'un référendum politiquement obligatoire'. ECPR conference paper, Budapest 8–10 September.

Pedersen, K. (2005) 'The 2005 Danish General Election: A Phase of Consolidation'. *West European Politics*, Vol. 28, No. 5, pp. 1101–8.

Quinn, T. (2006) 'Choosing the Least-Worst Government: The British General Election of 2005'. *West European Politics*, Vol. 29, No. 1, pp. 169–78.

Qvortrup, M. (2005) 'The Revolt of the Masses or Elites? Three Referendums on the European Constitution Treaty in 2005'. School of Economics and Political Sciences Working Papers, GOV2205-5, University of Sydney.

Raunio, T. (2005) 'Hesitant Voters, Committed Elite: Explaining the Lack of Euro-sceptic Parties in Finland'. *European Integration*, Vol. 27, No. 4, pp. 381–95.

Szczerbiak, A. (2005) 'Europe and the September/October 2005 Polish Parliamentary and Presidential Elections'. EPERN Election Briefing Paper No. 22, Sussex European Institute.

JCMS 2006 Volume 44 Annual Review pp. 199–212

Economic Developments in the Euro Area

AMY VERDUN
University of Victoria

Introduction

The year 2005 was characterized by turmoil for the Member States of the euro area. The Stability and Growth Pact (SGP) was revised at the March European Council. By June the French and Dutch had voted down in a referendum the draft Treaty establishing a Constitution for Europe. In the autumn spiking oil prices, following the hurricane season (in particular Hurricane Katrina that hit the American city of New Orleans), led to concerns about stifling the prospects of a precarious recovery of the euro area economy and those of others. In December the European Central Bank (ECB) raised its interest rate by 25 basis points – changing its rate for the first time since 2003. These developments came against the background of a seemingly poorly performing euro economy (compared to others) and the mid-term review of the Lisbon agenda (see Howarth in this issue).

Reflections on the performance of the euro area economy come amidst mounting speculation about whether the United States' (US) current account deficit and indebtedness are sustainable in the long run, and what implications any corrections might have on the relationship between the euro and the dollar. In addition, during 2005 the economies of China and India gained further in strength, suggesting that for the foreseeable future the world will be characterized by multiple poles of economic strength.

This review looks at the economic development in the euro area by highlighting a few core characteristics and discusses some policy areas more closely.

The first section provides some key economic performance indicators. The second discusses developments surrounding the SGP, particularly the March reform. Next, the review examines the policy of the ECB, before reviewing the external dimension of the euro. It closes with a brief summary and outlook for 2006.

I. Main Economic Indicators

In September, the International Monetary Fund (IMF) reported that the average rate of *economic growth* for advanced economies in the years 2004 and 2005 remained largely unchanged, from the previous forecast, at respectively 3.3 per cent and 2.5 per cent annual change of gross domestic product (GDP) (IMF, 2005; see also Table 1). The euro area, however, continues to show a weaker than average performance compared to the advanced economies as a whole (lagging behind by about 1 per cent, i.e. 2.0 per cent (2004) and 1.2 per cent (2005)). Not surprisingly, the euro area performed worse with regard to other leading nations. For example, GDP in the United States was 4.2 per cent (2004) and 3.5 per cent (2005), and even Japan, which had experienced slow growth in the previous decade, stood at 2.7 per cent (2004) and 2.0 per cent (2005). Furthermore, even the EU as a whole performed better than the euro area, 2.5 per cent (2004) and 1.6 per cent (2005).

Table 1: Overview of World Economic Outlook Projections in Annual % Change

		Projections		
	2003	2004	2005	2006
World output	4.0	5.1	4.3	4.3
Advanced economies	1.9	3.3	2.5	2.7
United States	2.7	4.2	3.5	3.3
Euro area	0.7	2.0	1.2	1.8
Japan	1.4	2.7	2.0	2.0
United Kingdom	2.5	3.2	1.9	2.2
Canada	2.0	2.9	2.9	3.9
Other advance economies	2.5	4.4	3.2	3.9
Central and eastern Europe	4.6	6.5	4.3	4.6
Commonwealth of Independent States	7.9	8.4	6.0	5.7
China	9.5	9.5	9.0	8.2
India	7.4	7.3	7.1	6.3
European Union	1.3	2.5	1.6	2.1

Source: IMF (2005).

In December the Organization for Economic Co-operation and Development (OECD) estimated euro area GDP growth for 2005 at only 1.4 per cent, compared with 3.6 per cent for the US, 2.4 per cent for Japan and 3.0 per cent for Canada (OECD, 2005). As was the case last year (Grimwade, 2005, p. 183) the large economies of the euro area were still underperforming (Germany and Italy) or not performing much above the average (France). The OECD estimated the growth in GDP at market prices in 2005 for Germany at 1.1 per cent, France 1.6 per cent, and Italy even as low as 0.2 per cent. The countries in the EU-15 not part of the euro area did a little better. For example, growth in the United Kingdom (UK) was estimated at 1.7 per cent, Denmark at 3.0 per cent and Sweden at 2.4 per cent of GDP at market prices. Table 2 sets out the latest estimates of the European Commission for GDP growth in the euro area plus Denmark, Sweden and the UK and the forecast for 2006.

Table 2: Annual Average % Change in GDP at 1995 Prices for the EU-15, 1991–2006

	1991–2000	2001	2002	2003	2004	2005	2006
Euro area Member States:							
Belgium	2.1	1.0	1.5	0.9	2.6	1.4	2.1
Germany	2.1	1.2	0.1	−0.2	1.6	0.8	1.2
Greece	2.3	4.6	3.8	4.6	4.7	3.5	3.4
Spain	2.8	3.5	2.7	3.0	3.1	3.4	3.2
France	2.1	2.1	1.2	0.8	2.3	1.5	1.8
Ireland	7.1	6.2	6.1	4.4	4.5	4.4	4.8
Italy	1.6	1.8	0.4	0.3	1.2	0.2	1.5
Luxembourg	5.5	1.5	2.5	2.9	4.5	4.2	4.4
Netherlands	2.9	1.4	0.1	−0.1	1.7	0.5	2.0
Austria	2.6	0.8	1.0	1.4	2.4	1.7	1.9
Portugal	2.9	2.0	0.5	−1.2	1.2	0.4	0.8
Finland	1.8	1.0	2.2	2.4	3.6	1.9	3.5
Euro area	2.2	1.9	0.9	0.7	2.1	1.3	1.9
Non-euro area Member States of the EU-15:							
Denmark	2.6	0.7	0.5	0.6	2.1	2.7	2.3
Sweden	2.0	1.0	2.0	1.5	3.6	2.5	3.0
UK	2.5	2.2	2.0	2.5	3.2	1.6	2.3
EU-15	2.2	1.9	1.1	1.1	2.3	1.4	2.0

Source: Commission (2005a).

The *employment* situation also continued to improve, as had been the case in 2004. Stronger economic growth, in particular in the latter part of 2005, contributed significantly to the improved employment performance and forecast. Table 3 again shows stronger employment performance for the non-euro area Member States than those in the euro area. In the case of employment, the trend is even stronger than with regard to GDP growth. Again the difference is caused mostly (but not only) by poor performance of the larger Member States. Note the continuing buoyancy of Ireland, but also the strong performance of Austria and the Netherlands. High unemployment still exists in Germany, France, Spain and Greece. The situation in Germany looks to improve slightly next year.

Looking at the harmonized index of consumer prices, we find that *inflation rates* in the countries of the euro area continue to diverge a little, but still remain low (the average at about 2.3 per cent with the maximum at just over 3.7 per

Table 3: % Share of the Civilian Labour Force Unemployed in the EU-15, 1991–2006

	1991–2000	2001	2002	2003	2004	2005	2006
Euro area Member States:							
Belgium	8.5	6.7	7.3	8.0	7.9	8.0	7.9
Germany	7.7	7.4	8.2	9.0	9.5	9.5	9.3
Greece	9.5	10.8	10.3	9.7	10.5	10.4	10.0
Spain	16.0	10.8	11.5	11.5	11.0	9.2	8.5
France	10.7	8.4	8.9	9.5	9.6	9.6	9.3
Ireland	11.1	3.8	4.3	4.6	4.5	4.3	4.4
Italy	10.4	9.1	8.6	8.4	8.0	7.7	7.6
Luxembourg	2.5	2.1	2.8	3.7	4.8	5.3	5.6
Netherlands	5.1	2.2	2.8	3.7	4.6	5.1	4.9
Austria	3.9	3.6	4.2	4.3	4.8	5.0	5.0
Portugal	5.6	4.0	5.0	6.3	6.7	7.4	7.7
Finland	12.5	9.1	9.1	9.0	8.8	8.4	7.8
Euro Area	9.6	7.9	8.3	8.7	8.9	8.6	8.4
Non-euro area Member States of the EU-15:							
Denmark	6.6	4.3	4.6	5.6	5.4	4.6	4.2
Sweden	7.6	4.9	4.9	5.6	6.3	6.8	5.9
UK	7.9	5.0	5.1	4.9	4.7	4.6	4.9
EU-15	9.2	7.2	7.6	7.9	8.1	7.9	7.7

Source: Commission (2005a).

cent (Spain) and the minimum at 1.1 per cent (Finland) (Commission, 2005a; see also Figure 1). Inflation in the euro area peaked in September of 2005 (2.6 per cent) in response to the higher oil prices in the wake of Hurricane Katrina, but came down nicely (2.5 per cent in October, 2.4 per cent in November, 2.2 per cent in December 2005 (Eurostat, 2006)).

If we compare the inflation performance with those in the rest of the EU we find that inflation is still diverging among both euro area Member States, the three 'outs' and the new Member States (see Table 4). Inflation in the non-euro area Scandinavian states is low. Those that experienced high inflation rates in 2005 are new Member States eager to join the euro (Estonia and Latvia), but also Greece and Spain, with the latter experiencing higher than average growth rates (on the policies towards EMU of the new Member States, see Johnson in this volume).

Turning to *public finances*, the situation in the EU seemed to have stabilized somewhat. In particular the deficit situation was subject to considerable scrutiny in 2005, because of the reforms in the SGP. Compared to the situation in 2004 in which the average deficit in the euro area was 2.5 per cent, the situation in 2005 had worsened mostly because of the performance of a small group of countries. With the weighted average deficit at 3.0 per cent, it is clear that some members are above the threshold, and in some cases by quite a margin. Greece continued to be a concern with its deficit at 5.7 per cent. Germany and France were also still above the 3.0 ceiling and were both estimated by the Commission by the end of 2005 to be hitting 4.1 per cent, albeit on a down-ward trend (see Table 5). However, all other Member States are closer to the

Figure 1: Inflation in the Euro Area

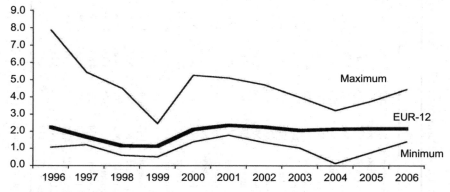

Source: Commission (2006).

Table 4: Harmonized Consumer Price Index, Annual % Change

	1991	1992	1993	1994	1995	1996	1997	1998	1999	2000	2001	2002	2003	2004	2005	2006
Belgium	N/a	2.25	2.49	2.39	1.27	1.78	1.50	0.91	1.13	2.68	2.44	1.55	1.51	1.86	2.53	2.60
Czech Rep.	N/a	N/a	N/a	N/a	N/a	9.09	8.01	9.69	1.81	3.94	4.55	1.42	-0.06	2.56	1.58	2.90
Denmark	2.16	1.95	0.91	1.81	2.05	2.08	1.96	1.29	2.06	2.73	2.26	2.42	1.96	0.92	1.70	2.00
Germany	N/a	N/a	N/a	N/a	N/a	1.21	1.53	0.60	0.64	1.39	1.90	1.36	1.04	1.78	1.94	1.64
Estonia	N/a	N/a	N/a	N/a	N/a	19.80	9.27	8.79	3.10	3.94	5.62	3.59	1.39	3.03	4.11	3.30
Greece	N/a	N/a	N/a	N/a	8.90	7.87	5.46	4.51	2.16	2.88	3.66	3.92	3.46	3.01	3.49	3.10
Spain	N/a	N/a	4.87	4.63	4.58	3.56	1.87	1.77	2.23	3.48	2.83	3.59	3.10	3.05	3.38	3.27
France	3.40	2.42	2.21	1.74	1.79	2.08	1.28	0.67	0.56	1.83	1.78	1.94	2.17	2.34	1.90	2.09
Ireland	N/a	N/a	N/a	N/a	2.80	2.15	1.26	2.13	2.46	5.27	3.98	4.72	4.00	2.31	2.18	2.50
Italy	6.22	4.98	4.51	4.17	5.39	3.98	1.90	1.97	1.65	2.60	2.33	2.60	2.82	2.26	2.20	2.13
Cyprus	N/a	N/a	N/a	N/a	N/a	N/a	3.32	2.34	1.14	4.86	1.98	2.79	3.96	1.90	2.04	2.10
Latvia	N/a	N/a	N/a	N/a	N/a	N/a	8.06	4.29	2.13	2.64	2.53	1.95	2.94	6.19	6.90	6.00
Lithuania	N/a	N/a	N/a	N/a	N/a	24.70	10.27	5.39	1.46	1.07	1.55	0.34	-1.08	1.17	2.66	2.80
Luxembourg	N/a	N/a	N/a	N/a	N/a	1.16	1.38	0.97	1.02	3.78	2.40	2.06	2.54	3.23	3.76	4.45
Hungary	N/a	N/a	N/a	N/a	N/a	23.49	18.46	14.22	9.97	9.96	9.08	5.24	4.68	6.77	3.49	2.00
Malta	N/a	N/a	N/a	N/a	N/a	N/a	3.92	3.70	2.29	3.04	2.51	2.61	1.94	2.72	2.53	2.60
Netherlands	3.16	2.83	1.62	2.14	1.38	1.43	1.86	1.78	2.03	2.34	5.11	3.87	2.24	1.38	1.50	2.04
Austria	3.08	3.48	3.16	2.70	1.62	1.78	1.16	0.82	0.51	1.96	2.30	1.70	1.30	1.95	2.11	2.10
Poland	N/a	N/a	N/a	N/a	N/a	N/a	14.97	11.79	7.18	10.08	5.33	1.94	0.70	3.60	2.17	2.30
Portugal	11.43	8.86	5.93	4.97	3.97	2.93	1.89	2.22	2.17	2.80	4.41	3.68	3.26	2.51	2.13	2.70
Slovenia	N/a	N/a	N/a	N/a	N/a	9.91	8.34	7.91	6.12	8.95	8.56	7.46	5.69	3.66	2.46	2.50
Slovakia	N/a	N/a	N/a	N/a	N/a	5.78	6.00	6.69	10.45	12.20	7.16	3.50	8.43	7.47	2.80	3.60
Finland	4.54	3.25	3.33	1.61	0.40	1.07	1.22	1.34	1.32	2.94	2.67	2.01	1.30	0.14	0.77	1.40
Sweden	8.74	1.30	4.81	2.88	2.70	0.96	1.81	1.03	0.54	1.30	2.67	1.93	2.34	1.02	0.82	1.36
UK	7.54	4.24	2.53	1.98	2.73	2.49	1.81	1.56	1.35	0.80	1.22	1.27	1.36	1.34	2.05	2.22
EUR-12	4.32	3.77	3.38	2.83	2.55	2.25	1.68	1.16	1.13	2.12	2.36	2.27	2.08	2.14	2.17	2.16
EU-25	N/a	3.97	3.43	2.84	2.98	3.07	2.57	2.10	1.60	2.44	2.52	2.12	1.94	2.15	2.16	2.22
EUR-15	5.17	4.05	3.43	2.80	2.78	2.42	1.71	1.31	1.16	1.91	2.20	2.08	1.95	1.95	2.14	2.18

Source: Commission (2006).

Table 5: Net Lending (+) or Net Borrowing (-) as a % of GDP in EU-15, 1991–2006

	1996–2000	2001	2002	2003	2004	2005	2006
Euro area Member States:							
Belgium	−1.4	−0.5	0.1	0.6	0.0	0.1	0.0
Germany	−1.7	−1.5	1.3	−2.9	−3.8	−4.1	−3.7
Greece	−5.2	−3.4	−4.1	−6.1	−4.9	−5.7	−6.6
Spain	−2.6	−1.2	−0.9	−0.5	−0.3	0.0	−0.1
France	−2.6	−1.7	−1.4	−1.5	−3.2	−4.1	−3.7
Ireland	2.1	2.5	4.4	0.8	−0.4	0.2	1.4
Italy	−3.0	−1.7	−0.8	−3.2	−2.7	−3.2	−3.2
Luxembourg	3.6	3.5	6.1	6.5	2.1	0.2	−1.2
Netherlands	−0.2	0.6	2.1	−0.2	−2.0	−3.2	−2.1
Austria	−2.3	−2.2	−1.5	0.1	−0.4	−1.2	−1.0
Portugal	−3.3	−2.7	−2.9	−4.2	−2.8	−2.9	−3.0
Finland	1.3	2.2	7.1	5.2	4.3	2.5	2.1
Euro area	−5.1	−1.3	0.1	−1.8	−2.5	−3.0	−2.7
Non-euro area Member States of the EU15:							
Denmark	1.2	2.3	3.3	2.6	1.4	1.2	2.9
Sweden	1.2	2.5	5.1	2.5	−0.3	0.2	1.6
UK	−0.3	1.0	3.8	0.7	−1.7	−3.3	−3.2
EU-15	−1.6	−0.7	1.0	−1.2	−2.2	−2.9	−2.6

Source: Commission (2005a).

3.0 per cent ceiling, although the Italian deficit performance started to attract attention again in early 2006. The situation on the deficits was the key subject of the reforms of the SGP discussed in detail below.

II. Reform of the Stability and Growth Pact

The Stability and Growth Pact (SGP) was created in 1997 to serve as a disciplining mechanism once Member States were in the third stage of EMU (Heipertz and Verdun, 2004, 2005). The SGP[1] specifies the fiscal policy framework set out in Article 104 of the Treaty Establishing the European Community (TEC).

[1] The legal text of the SGP consists of (1) Resolution of the European Council on the Stability and Growth Pact (OJ 1997, C 236/1); (2) Council Regulation No. 1466/97 of 7 July 1997 on the strengthening of the surveillance of budgetary positions and the surveillance and co-ordination of economic policies (OJ 1997, L 209/1 as amended by Council Regulation 1055/105 of 27 June 2005); and (3) Council Regulation No. 1467/97 on speeding up and clarifying the implementation of the excessive deficit procedure (OJ L 209/6 as amended by Council Regulation 1056/2005).

Since the start of stage three of EMU on 1 January 1999, attention has been paid to how the SGP would be implemented. In the 2001 and 2002 so-called 'early warnings' were given, and the excessive deficit procedure was started against some Member States such as Portugal, Germany and France, that were running deficits in excess of 3 per cent of GDP. These Member States were supposed to correct the excessive deficits within a year, which Portugal did, but Germany and France did not. In 2003 the Commission proposed that the next step of disciplinary action, which envisages the imposition of sanctions, be taken against France and Germany, but the Council of Ministers of Economic and Financial Affairs (Ecofin) decided on 25 November 2003 not to adopt the Commission proposal. Instead, it decided that application of the SGP in the cases of France and Germany be interrupted. This decision effectively put the excessive deficit procedure for these two countries into limbo.

The Commission challenged Ecofin's decision before the European Court of Justice (ECJ). In July 2004 the ECJ ruled that the Council indeed *had the right* not to adopt the Commission's proposal, but it *could not* adopt provisions on its own without a proposal by the Commission (see Dougan, 2005, pp. 93–5). In the light of the resulting difficult political situation, it was considered necessary to review the SGP, which eventually happened in the spring of 2005.

Critics had been making the case that the SGP was too rigid. It put too much emphasis on the needs of the euro area to be protected against free-riding behaviour of some Member States, which happens if they run excessive deficits, at the expense of allowing Member States the flexibility and autonomy to take fiscal measures aimed at stabilizing their domestic economies. These observers became more vocal in 2003–04 and argued that the SGP should be relaxed (Enderlein, 2004). The principles of the SGP, however, are firmly embedded in the Treaty on European Union, and the SGP provisions in a sense are merely a clarification of the provisions in the Treaty. Hence, it was not a feasible option to abandon the SGP altogether, but rather to make sure that a reformed SGP would make for better compliance and greater sensitivity to some of the Member States' difficulties.

A review of the SGP was initiated in September 2004 and was concluded in the spring of 2005 and the final regulations were adopted in June 2005 (Almunia, 2005). The preventive arm of the SGP has been strengthened by making the rules more differentiated and focused on the medium term. The new provisions seek to pay proper attention to the fundamentals of fiscal sustainability when setting budgetary objectives. More attention will be paid to the debt level than was the case before. In the future, the medium-term budgetary objective of a Member State will be determined by its current debt ratio and potential economic growth. This means in practice that Member States with a combination of low debt and high potential economic growth should be allowed to run a small deficit over the medium term, whereas those with high debt and low potential growth will have to keep a balanced budget or a surplus. The preventive arm of the SGP is further strengthened by the Member States' commitment actively to consolidate public finances under favourable economic conditions. Furthermore, it has been envisaged that the Commission may act and give 'policy advice' if this consolidation does not occur often enough.

The revised SGP includes provisions that seek to facilitate the choices of Member States that are considering going through major structural reforms. The new SGP allows Member States to be given more flexibility if major structural reforms have direct long-term cost-saving effects and verifiably improve fiscal sustainability. In this way, the new rules have tried to encourage the Lisbon agenda reforms, whilst still aiming at fiscal discipline. The timing of some corrective measures has also been extended. The one-year deadline for the correction of an excessive deficit has been extended by an additional year, as it is very difficult to correct a deficit within only one year.

Since 2003 there have been numerous cases of opening an excessive deficit procedure against Member States. Some, such as the Netherlands, had been opened and were closed. By the end of 2005 procedures were ongoing in at least five euro area countries: Greece, France, Germany, Italy and Portugal (second time). The new SGP gives them a little more time. In some circumstances that should enable them to argue why they need more room for manœuvre. Nevertheless it is expected that it will still be difficult for these countries to bring down their deficits or to argue for a prolonged period of deficits exceeding the reference value of 3 per cent of GDP.

III. Policies of the European Central Bank

The ECB sets the monetary policy for the entire euro area. Since its creation, the ECB has taken the euro area as a whole as its reference point. In determining policy, the Member State economies are weighted proportionally to their economic size in the euro area economy. The ECB has typically kept interest rates unchanged even when commentators have pointed to weak economic growth (and argued that the ECB should reduce rates), or called on the ECB to increase interest rates to increase the value of the euro, as was the case in 2002. In 2005 there was not that much pressure on the ECB regarding the value of the euro, compared to earlier years, even though there was still pressure on the ECB to lower rates (or not increase rates) in order to improve the prospects of economic growth. The ECB did not respond to these demands.

Even though the ECB values proportionally the Member States' economies in determining its policy, the effect of the single interest rate has been divergent. In some countries, such as Ireland, the ECB's interest rate was generally seen as too low. In others, such as Germany, the interest rate was seen as too high. Nevertheless, as we saw in 2004, economic growth and inflation rates were not wildly out of sync with one another (see Table 2 above).

In 2004 and during almost all of 2005 the ECB kept rates unchanged. Only on 1 December 2005 did it increase interest rates by 25 basis points (a second 25 basis point increase occurred on 2 March 2006). As a result, the key interest rate in the euro area in April 2006 is 2.5 per cent compared to a primary credit rate of 5.25 in the US.

The ECB has focused on pursuing monetary policy with a view only to maintaining price stability. It has unilaterally explained that price stability means maintaining inflation at or below 2 per cent over the medium term. It has refused to deal with matters related to economic growth, employment, or economic activity more generally, or the costs associated with keeping interest rates relatively high to secure low inflation. Instead it focuses merely on low inflation, arguing that low inflation ultimately leads to growth (Trichet, 2006).

IV. External Dimension of the Euro

The most immediate external dimension of the euro concerns those EU Member States that wish to join EMU. Along with having to meet the SGP targets, the EMU aspirants must join the exchange rate mechanism (ERM)-II, under which their currencies have to stay within 15 per cent (plus or minus) of the agreed parity for two years. The new Member States are working on meeting those criteria, just as euro area Member States did before joining EMU (see Johnson in this volume).

The euro lost considerable value against other major currencies during 2005. At the beginning of 2005 there were real concerns, carried over from 2004, that the euro was overvalued and was disrupting the competitiveness of the euro area economy. As the year progressed and the euro fell, however, these concerns became less vocal. Towards the end of 2005, the concern was less with the euro than with whether the US dollar could be facing a major depreciation in value.

The value of the euro remains an issue of much discussion as it has fluctuated quite considerably in value. Following its introduction at $1.17 it fell to $0.825 on 26 October 2000. Between summer 2001 and late 2004 it rose, peaking at $1.36 on 28 December 2004. In 2005 the euro was initially still quite high at around $1.30, but roughly stabilized around $1.20 (see Figure 2). Even though significant currency fluctuations occurred in the mid- to late-1980s, fluctuations of this magnitude (one could say of 30 per cent in the first few years) led to considerable concern about the external value of the euro.

Figure: US–Euro Exchange Rates January 1999–January 2006

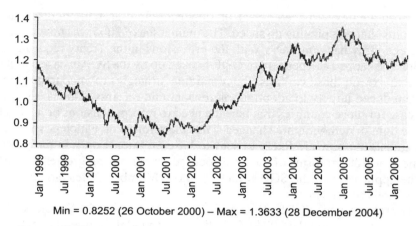

Min = 0.8252 (26 October 2000) – Max = 1.3633 (28 December 2004)

Source: European Central Bank.

During 2005, however, the fluctuation *vis-à-vis* the US dollar was more in the 10 per cent range, which is much more common. Indeed the relevance of currency fluctuations depends largely on the size of the import/export sector of the euro area economy with the countries outside that area. Consequently, as the Member States of the euro area trade considerably more with each other than those outside the euro area, the effect of a high or low euro may not in fact be as influential on the economy as the symbolism of the fluctuation.

V. EU Politics in 2005 and the Dutch and French Referendums

The rejection of the Treaty establishing a Constitution for Europe in referendums in France and the Netherlands pointed to the symbolic role of the euro in domestic politics (on the referendums, see Taggart in this volume). The referendums are interesting for developments in the euro area in a number of ways. First, the euro figured in the 'no' campaigns of both countries. In the Netherlands the 'expensive euro' was used as an argument. In France the left-of-centre parties argued that the EU was synonymous with neo-liberalism (or 'Anglo-Saxon' market mechanisms). Moreover, in Italy in spring 2005, some argued that Italy should leave the euro area. These statements were mostly received with some ridicule as it was quickly pointed out that the Italian government would have to pay much more to service its large debt (over 100 per cent GDP) if it had to borrow in the marketplace without the support of the other EU Member States.

Conclusion

The euro area experienced a year of slow economic growth amidst a global economy that was picking up speed. The main issue of 2005 was how to get the euro economy back on track. With the provisions in the Treaty requiring that deficits be capped at 3 per cent of GDP, backed up by the SGP in case countries were to exceed those ceilings, the remaining strategies to encourage growth were reduced largely to adopting microeconomic reforms. This is especially the case for those countries that face the need to reform pensions or healthcare in the light of demographic changes. Thus the reforms on which governments are embarking now are likely to start to have an impact only in the years to come. The 2005 reforms of the SGP focused on permitting greater flexibility in the application of the SGP's rules for those Member States embarking on these kinds of reform.

The reform of the SGP had become necessary following the November 2003 Council decision and the 2004 ECJ ruling that found the Council conclusions illegal. It is as yet unclear what the impact of the revised SGP will have on the governance of EMU.

During 2005 the ECB pursued monetary policy very much in line with what it had done in the first years of its existence. It strongly signalled its commitment to price stability by leaving interest rates largely unchanged throughout 2005, with the exception of December 2005 when it raised its rate in response to the inflationary pressures resulting mainly from higher fuel prices.

The outlook for 2006 is that it is generally believed that the economy is picking up, even in the larger economies of the euro area. The ECB's policies are – predictably – still predominantly focused on containing inflation. In its statement in April the ECB signalled a possible increase in interest rates foreseen for July. All in all the euro area economies are seeking ways to increase their economic growth. Those countries with excessive deficits have been given some more flexibility under the SGP, but it still has some teeth. How the reformed SGP is applied will be something to watch in 2006.

Key Readings

Commission (2005b) offers an oversight of the EU economy until October 2005 and gives a balanced view of the challenges and opportunities that have faced the EU in 2005 and those that lie ahead. This particular issue is devoted to 'globalization'.

de Grauwe (2005) offers an overview of the issues related to EMU from an economic perspective, providing various models and analytical tools to study the issues at stake in the creation of EMU.

Hosli (2005) provides a brief overview of the history and policies of EMU, the structure of the ECB and the role of the euro in the international system.

Howarth and Loedel (2005) give a general introduction to the ECB's history, design, organization and governance. It offers various theoretical approaches to the ECB, a review of national perspectives on central bank independence and accountability. It also reviews its first years of operation.

OECD (2005) offers an oversight of the economic situation and the policies of the euro area to 13 June 2005.

References

Almunia, J. (2005) 'Fiscal Discipline and the Reform of the Stability and Growth Pact'. Speech 05/404, Warsaw 30 June.

Buti, M. and Pench, L. (2004) 'Why Do Large Countries Flout the Stability Pact? And What Can Be Done About It?'. *Journal of Common Market Studies*, Vol. 42, No. 5, pp. 1025–32.

Commission of the European Communities (2005a) *Economic Forecasts*, Autumn. Directorate-General for Economic and Financial Affairs, Brussels.

Commission of the European Communities (2005b) 'The EU Economy 2005 Review' *European Economy,* No. 6, November.

Commission of the European Communities (2006) 'Harmonised Index of Consumer Prices'. Available at «http://www.europa.eu.int/comm/economy_finance/indicators/key_euro_area/keyeuroarea_en.htm».

Dougan, M. (2005) 'Legal Developments'. *JCMS Annual Review,* Vol. 43, pp. 89–107.

Enderlein, H. (2004) 'Break It, Don't Fix It'. *Journal of Common Market Studies*, Vol. 42, No. 5, pp. 1039–46.

Eurostat (2006a) 'Euro-indicators News Release'. 34/2006, 16 March.

Eurostat (2006b) 'Harmonised Consumer Price Index'. Data provided by the Commission services, DG Ecofin. Also available at «http://epp.eurostat.cec.eu.int/».

Grauwe, P. de (2005) *Economics of Monetary Union*, 6th edn (Oxford: Oxford University Press).

Grimwade, N. (2005) 'Developments in the Economies of the "Fifteen"'. *The European Union: Annual Review 2004/2005,* Vol. 43, pp. 181–99.

Heipertz, M. and Verdun, A. (2004) 'The Dog that Would Never Bite? On the Origins of the Stability and Growth Pact'. *Journal of European Public Policy*, Vol. 11, No. 5, pp. 765–80.

Heipertz, M. and Verdun, A. (2005) 'The Stability and Growth Pact – Theorizing a Case in European Integration'. *Journal of Common Market Studies,* Vol. 43, No. 5, pp. 963–84.

Hosli, M.O. (2005) *The Euro: A Concise Introduction to European Monetary Integration* (Boulder, CO: Lynne Rienner).

Howarth, D. and Loedel, P. (2005) *European Central Bank. The New European Leviathan?* 2nd edn (Basingstoke: Palgrave).

IMF (2005) *World Economic Outlook* (Washington DC: International Monetary Fund).

OECD (2005) *OECD Economic Survey of the Euro Area* (Paris: Organization for Economic Co-operation and Development).

Trichet, J.-C. (2006) 'Press conference'. 6 April, available at «http://www.ecb.int/ press/pressconf/html/is060406.en.html».

Developments in the Economies of Member States Outside the Euro Area

DEBRA JOHNSON
Hull University

Context

Real world gross domestic product (GDP) growth in 2004 was over 5 per cent, the fastest growth since the early 1970s. Despite higher oil prices, the external economic environment continued to be positive in 2005 with world GDP growth registering 4.3 per cent (or 4.9 per cent excluding the European Union). Growth was distributed across all regions, but the United States and the emerging economies of India and China were the main drivers. This was propitious for the 2004 accession states in their first full year of EU membership as it helped them sustain their main export markets, both within the EU and outside. Indeed, the outlook was sufficiently bright that the European Commission revised its forecasts marginally upwards between spring and autumn 2005 (Commission, 2005). US growth remained healthy, reaching 3.5 per cent in 2005, supported by strong private consumption and favourable financial circumstances. However, the US's twin deficits (budget and trade) cast doubts over the long-term sustainability of its economic performance. The Japanese economy, bolstered by rebounding domestic demand, continued to show signs of pulling out of the economic doldrums in which it had been becalmed for several years. Elsewhere in Asia, despite a slight easing of growth from 7.8 per cent in 2004 to 7.2 per cent in 2005, the economy remained strong. The Chinese economy, which grew by over 9 per cent in 2005, continues to act as a very significant growth pole in the region. The Commonwealth of Independent States and oil-producing developing countries generally continued to benefit from higher oil prices. Although growth in Latin America decelerated somewhat in 2005, its 4 per cent growth was still very favourable compared to the stuttering performance of the late 1990s and early 2000s. African growth, however, continued to accelerate as a result of higher commodity prices and growth elsewhere.

Rising oil prices remain the biggest risk to the stability of the world economy. So far, the world's main economies have remained robust, despite high oil prices. Oil prices in real terms remain far below their peak in the oil shock of the late 1970s (35 per cent below, according to the Commission) and the oil intensity of most importing countries' economies has decreased significantly since then. Other potential risks for the world economy include a worsening of the geopolitical situation, perhaps through a major act or acts of terrorism, further instability in the Middle East, or disruption arising from a possible bird 'flu pandemic.

I. Overall Economic Performance of the Non-Euro Area Member States

Economic growth in the euro area in 2005 was 0.8 percentage points below growth in 2004 – indeed growth rates in most euro area countries slowed in 2005. However, the situation was more mixed in Member States outside the euro area. The majority of the 2004 accession states experienced stronger growth in 2005, partly as a result of ongoing transition and partly in response to accession. In all cases of slower growth in the accession states, the deceleration was less than 0.5 percentage points, except in Poland, which at the beginning of 2005 was still feeling the effects of the slowdown that began at the end of 2004. However, by the second half of 2005, Polish growth rates had begun to pick up again.

In all cases except that of Malta, however, growth in the non-euro area was higher than that in the euro area, in many cases twice as high or more (see Table 1). This continued the trend of the 2004 accession states growing more quickly than the EU-15 which began in the mid-1990s when the immediate chaos following the onset of transition was over and the effects of economic reform were starting to be felt. The tendency has also been for those three EU-15 states that did not join the euro area to grow more quickly than euro area members. As long as these three states continue to outperform the euro area, it will prove extremely difficult for the governments of these three countries to persuade their population (should they attempt to do so) to join the euro area.

The main economic drivers behind growth of the euro-outsiders varies. Growth in Denmark, Lithuania, Cyprus and Slovakia was largely driven by domestic demand, whereas in the Czech Republic external demand was the crucial factor. For the UK and Hungary, reduced domestic demand (especially private consumption) was at least partially offset by improvements in external

Table 1: Real GDP Growth (% Annual Change), Non-Euro Area

	1996–00	2001	2002	2003	2004	2005 Estimate	2006 Forecast
Cyprus	3.6	4.1	2.1	1.9	3.8	3.9	4.0
Czech Rep.	1.5	2.6	1.5	3.2	4.4	4.8	4.4
Denmark	2.9	0.7	0.5	0.6	2.1	2.7	2.3
Estonia	5.6	6.5	7.2	6.7	7.8	8.4	7.2
Latvia	5.4	8.0	6.4	7.2	8.3	9.1	7.7
Lithuania	4.2	7.2	6.8	10.5	7.0	7.0	6.2
Hungary	4.0	3.8	3.5	2.9	4.2	3.7	3.9
Malta	4.5	0.2	0.8	−1.9	0.4	0.8	0.7
Poland	5.1	1.0	1.4	3.8	5.3	3.4	4.3
Slovakia	3.7	3.8	4.6	4.5	5.5	5.1	5.5
Slovenia	4.4	2.7	3.5	2.7	4.2	3.8	4.0
Sweden	3.2	1.0	2.0	1.5	3.6	2.5	3.0
UK	3.2	2.2	2.0	2.5	3.2	1.6	2.3
Euro area	2.7	1.9	0.9	0.7	2.1	1.3	1.9

Source: Commission (2005).

demand. For Estonia and Slovenia, growth demonstrated a healthy balance between the two.

Labour market conditions generally improved in 2005, both within and outside the euro area. Indeed, apart from Hungary and Sweden, the unemployment rate fell in all the euro-outsider countries in 2005 (see Table 2) and the employment rate rose, albeit moderately in most cases. The unemployment rate showed wide variation within the outsider countries, ranging from 4.6 per cent – the second lowest rate in the EU as a whole – in the UK and Denmark to the two Member States with the highest unemployment in the EU – Poland and Slovakia – with rates of 17.8 per cent and 16.7 per cent respectively.

Given the continuing high levels of growth in the 2004 accession states, bigger falls in unemployment and/or increases in employment could have been expected. That this has not happened is attributable to a number of factors. Economic transition is not complete and productivity improvements and restructuring mean that output can increase without necessarily resulting in the creation of new job opportunities. Moreover, labour market rigidities continue to cause problems in several of the 2004 accession states, with wide differences in regional employment levels within states, indicating sub-optimal labour mobility and reports of skills shortages signifying a mismatch between the supply of and demand for labour.

Table 2: Unemployment (as a % of the Civilian Labour Force), Non-euro Area

	1996–2000	2001	2002	2003	2004	2005 Estimate	2006 Forecast
Cyprus	5.0	4.4	3.9	4.5	5.2	4.9	4.8
Czech Rep.	6.4	8.0	7.3	7.8	8.3	7.9	7.5
Denmark	5.1	4.3	4.6	5.6	5.4	4.6	4.2
Estonia	10.5	11.8	9.5	10.2	9.2	7.2	6.0
Latvia	15.6	12.9	12.6	10.4	9.8	9.7	9.4
Lithuania	13.9	16.4	13.5	12.7	10.9	9.0	8.1
Hungary	8.0	5.6	5.6	5.8	6.0	7.0	6.9
Malta	6.4	7.6	7.7	8.0	7.6	7.2	7.1
Poland	12.6	18.5	19.8	19.2	18.8	17.8	16.8
Slovakia	14.5	19.4	18.7	17.5	18.2	16.7	16.2
Slovenia	7.0	5.8	6.1	6.5	6.0	5.8	5.7
Sweden	8.0	4.9	4.9	5.6	6.3	6.8	5.9
UK	6.4	5.0	5.1	4.9	4.7	4.6	4.9
Euro area	9.8	7.9	8.3	8.7	8.9	8.6	8.4

Source: Commission (2005).

In 2004, several of the 2004 accession states, including the Czech Republic, all three Baltic states, Poland and Hungary, experienced significant increases in inflation (see Table 3). Indirect taxation changes required by the accession process had been responsible for some of the acceleration in price rises. However, this effect was due to fall out of the statistics in 2005 with the potential for inflation to return to its longer-term trends. Indeed, this appears to have happened in some states, but in others inflation continued to gather pace. Indeed, in Latvia, where inflation was relatively moderate in the three years prior to 2004, inflation has risen to such an extent that it could well compromise that country's aspirations to adopt the euro. In the majority of euro-outsiders, however, inflation appears reasonably well-contained given the upward pressure from oil and energy prices and the potential for strong wage demands in the face of buoyant economic activity.

II. Economic Developments in the Old Euro-outsiders

The United Kingdom

Although UK real GDP growth in 2005 of 1.6 per cent was half the growth rate of 2004 and the lowest in the UK since 1992, growth remained above that of

Table 3: Inflation, Non-Euro Area

	1996–2000	2001	2002	2003	2004	2005 Estimate	2006 Forecast
Cyprus	–	2.0	2.8	4.0	1.9	2.3	2.1
Czech Rep.	6.5	4.5	1.4	−0.1	2.6	1.7	2.9
Denmark	2.0	2.3	2.4	2.0	0.9	1.7	2.0
Estonia	8.8	5.6	3.6	1.4	3.0	4.1	3.3
Latvia	–	2.5	2.0	2.9	6.2	6.8	6.0
Lithuania	7.7	1.3	0.4	−1.1	1.1	2.6	2.8
Hungary	15.1	9.1	5.2	4.7	6.8	3.7	2.0
Malta	–	2.5	2.6	1.9	2.7	3.1	2.6
Poland	–	5.3	1.9	0.7	3.6	2.2	2.3
Slovakia	8.2	7.2	3.5	8.4	7.5	2.9	3.6
Slovenia	8.2	8.6	7.5	5.7	3.6	2.6	2.5
Sweden	1.1	2.7	2.0	2.3	1.3	2.4	2.2
UK	1.6	1.2	1.3	1.4	1.3	2.4	2.2
Euro area	1.7	2.4	2.3	2.1	2.1	2.3	2.2

Source: Commission (2005).

the euro area. Business and financial services were among the best performing sectors, whereas growth in other services slowed and manufacturing output declined.

The slowdown was largely the result of sluggish domestic demand, particularly of slower private consumption growth, which was less than half the levels of 2004 and which has, in recent years, been the major factor behind growth. After several years of rampant house prices, the housing market slowed considerably from 2004 and, at times, seemed to be teetering on the brink of an early 1990s-style collapse – a spectre which appears to have passed with the onset of a moderate recovery in the housing market. Higher house prices had given homeowners the confidence to spend, a situation that was reversed when the housing market seemed more uncertain. This, plus successive, albeit small, interest rate increases, encouraged households to show more caution in the face of rising debt levels, and the savings ratio even rose slightly.

The other components of domestic demand also slowed in 2005. Despite high corporate profitability, healthy equity markets and low real interest rates, investment was muted in 2005. Given the favourable business conditions, the most plausible explanation for subdued investment is general uncertainty about the macroeconomic environment both home and abroad.

The UK economic slowdown would have been greater in 2005 were it not for the performance of the public sector and changes in external demand. Public consumption growth has not been robust, but public investment growth has picked up sharply in line with the government's plans for long-term improvement in public services. In fiscal year 2005–06, the budget deficit increased to 3.4 per cent from 3.2 per cent the previous year. Revenue was restrained because of the impact of lower economic activity on indirect taxes – although this effect was offset to some extent by the impact of higher oil prices on the offshore tax take. After several years of a negative contribution to GDP, the impact of the external sector on growth was neutral in 2005. This was possible because of continuing improvements in the performance of exports, which grew 4.6 per cent in 2005, together with lower import levels, a phenomenon that accompanied lower domestic demand.

Inflation in 2005, driven on by high oil prices in particular, exceeded the Bank of England's target of 2 per cent. However, inflationary expectations are being constrained by confidence in the monetary policy framework. This small increase in inflation, which is forecast to be temporary in any case, shows no sign of resulting in higher wages or wage demands. Given the continuing good performance of the UK's labour market, where unemployment in 2005 was the second lowest in the EU behind that of Ireland, ongoing stable and moderate wage growth is an important achievement.

The consensus among economic forecasters is that the slowdown in UK economic activity is a temporary blip rather than the onset of recession or something more serious (HM Treasury, 2005). The expectation is that domestic demand will continue to drive growth, but that this growth will be better balanced with more support from investment and public consumption, on the one hand, and even a small positive contribution from external demand, on the other. The risks to this largely positive scenario for the UK stem from a mixture of external factors such as further oil price increases, a downturn in the US, a setback in the shaky euro area recovery or a major geopolitical disruption and internal factors such as a sharp deterioration in the housing market or the need for drastic fiscal contraction.

Denmark

The pick-up in Danish economic activity that began in 2004 continued into 2005 with GDP growth registering 2.7 per cent, compared to 0.6 per cent and 2.1 per cent in 2003 and 2004, respectively. The main drive behind growth has been private consumption, itself stimulated by gains in real disposable income arising from falling unemployment, tax cuts, low interest rates and the booming housing market, also boosted by low interest rates. Fixed investment is also growing strongly. Export growth has also been strong but any positive impact on GDP has been offset by similarly strong increases in growth-induced imports.

Danish public finances are among the EU's strongest, resulting in a public sector surplus approaching 3 per cent in 2005. Underpinning these healthy public finances were buoyant economic growth and significant additional revenues from activities of the oil and gas industry in the North Sea.

In 2004, inflation was unusually low as a result of tax cuts and low import prices. Rising energy prices contributed to a moderate increase in prices in 2005. In the longer term, the tightening of labour markets could place upward pressure on inflation through higher wages, but there was little evidence of this occurring in 2005.

Sweden

The slowdown in growth that began towards the end of 2004 continued into early 2005, but this trend was reversed from the second quarter and growth for 2005 as a whole reached 2.5 per cent. Investment remained strong throughout the period, but exports and domestic consumption showed temporary signs of weakness, although they later rallied to lead the recovery. Consumption benefited from a coincidence of factors that increased real disposable income, including lower income taxes, expansionary monetary policy and an improving labour market. Domestic demand growth, particularly private consumption and increasing construction activity, is forecast to be central in driving growth above 3 per cent in 2006. The contribution to GDP growth from exports will be offset by the higher levels of imports needed to satisfy buoyant domestic demand.

The labour market showed signs of improvement in 2005. Following declines during the previous two years, employment growth resumed in 2005. This improvement is forecast to continue as high levels of labour productivity growth ease, but strong domestic demand persists. These factors are also forecast to herald a slow decline in unemployment from 2005 onwards. Hitherto, relatively weak developments in the labour market, despite oil price rises, have helped the downward trend in inflation. However, a tightening labour market creates the conditions for higher wage settlements. Along with expansionary monetary policy and a relatively weak krona, this has the potential to boost inflationary pressure.

Public sector finances remain in good shape. In 2005, Sweden's budget surplus was around 1.5 per cent of GDP. Despite planned increases in public consumption, the budget is expected to continue to register surpluses because of higher tax revenues, lower debt repayments and larger dividends from government owned companies.

III. Economic Developments in the New Member States

Poland

Recovery from the slight deceleration in Polish growth that began towards the end of 2004 did not really get into full swing until the second half of 2005, with the result that annual GDP growth in 2005 was 3.4 per cent, down from 5.3 per cent in 2004. The initial main driver behind growth was net exports, but a gradual improvement in private consumption and investment also played a part.

Investment was sluggish in the first quarter of 2005. This was the result of delayed decisions arising from uncertainties about the outcome of parliamentary and presidential elections later in the year and difficulties in absorbing EU funds. However, political uncertainties had been resolved by the end of the year and investment prospects are promising given strong levels of corporate profitability, extremely low interest rates and emerging capacity constraints. Limited real wage growth and pension indexation are expected to contribute to growth in household consumption. However, the increased imports associated with improvements in domestic demand limit the contribution of net exports to GDP growth, despite the strong performance of Polish exporters.

The performance of Poland's external sector is noteworthy. Despite the disappointing performance of the euro area economies, Poland's most significant export market, Polish exports to the EU have held up well. Moreover, Poland is regaining market share in the east, especially in Ukraine and Russia and is performing well in international agricultural markets. This positive export performance has taken place despite ongoing zloty appreciation since mid-2004. These trends resulted in a narrowing of the current account deficit in 2005. However, it is likely to widen once more as a result of higher oil prices and the growth of imports associated with higher domestic demand.

Although labour market conditions have improved since mid-2004, Poland's employment rate is among the lowest in the EU and unemployment, which by December 2005 had fallen to 17.8 per cent, remains the EU's highest. Despite periods of strong growth, unemployment has remained persistently high because of continuing restructuring in heavy industry and agriculture. Accordingly, economic activity has tended to absorb productivity improvements rather than unemployed labour. Nevertheless, unemployment is falling slowly, a process that is helped by falling participation rates resulting from early retirements and an increase in those in higher education.

The subdued labour market has helped contain inflation by moderating wage demands. Price increases peaked in 2004, averaging 3.6 per cent for the year as a whole, but fell back again in 2005 as the one-off inflationary effect of EU accession fell out of the index. Despite higher energy prices, inflation for 2005 was moderate and below the government's target of 2.5 per cent, and by November 2005, Poland was once more complying with the Maastricht reference value for inflation.

The most significant recent economic development in Poland is the apparent turnaround in its public finances. Methodological changes have resulted in substantial data revisions, notably the downwards revision of the 2004 deficit from 4.8 per cent of GDP to 3.9 per cent. The Central Bank estimates that, in 2005, the deficit fell to 3.3 per cent of GDP, considerably lower than originally forecast (National Bank of Poland, 2006). There has been uncertainty over the implementation of the 2005 budget and increases in permanent spending could occur if certain bills successfully pass through the legislative process. On the face of it, however, Poland's fiscal problems have improved more rapidly than many commentators anticipated. Continuation of current trends would increase the chances of Poland's meeting the Maastricht fiscal convergence criteria sooner rather than later. However, this outcome remains far from guaranteed.

Hungary

During 2004 and 2005, Hungarian GDP growth became more balanced. After relying almost entirely on buoyant domestic demand based on unsustainable increases in public spending and private consumption in previous years, growth was led by exports and investment. Despite an apparent slowdown in the first quarter of 2005 arising from weak growth prospects in the EU, Hungary's main export market, growth picked up again in the second quarter as a result of strong growth in gross fixed capital formation, particularly from large-scale public infrastructure projects. In the end, real GDP growth in 2005 was 3.7 per cent.

The favourable inflation trend that began towards the end of 2004 continued into 2005. Wage increases moderated and the forint appreciated. The intensification of competition arising from EU accession also kept prices down.

Hungary's labour market problems persist. Although employment rose slightly in 2005 and the unemployment rate is below the EU average, despite increasing from 6 per cent to 7 per cent in 2005, there is much scope for improvement in labour markets. Participation rates in particular are low, the result, according to the OECD (2005), of labour taxes that dampen the demand for labour and of disincentives to enter the labour market inherent in social welfare schemes. Labour mobility generally is limited, and the available skills do not match the skills demanded by employers in key areas.

Hungary's official target date for euro area entry is 2010, but significant improvements will have to be made in its fiscal position if this target is to be met. Hungary has missed its deficit target by a wide margin for each of the past four years. In 2005, the original deficit target was 3.6 per cent of GDP but the final outcome was over 6 per cent. The 2006 budget does not create confidence that budgetary problems will be rectified swiftly, given proposed tax cuts equivalent to about 1 per cent of GDP and the absence of plans to tackle underlying problems leading to expenditure overruns. In order to meet the Maastricht targets, large infrastructure projects need to be reclassified as off-budget financing, but this will not be acceptable to Eurostat. Moreover, Hungary's fiscal problems risk pushing it through Maastricht's 60 per cent debt ceiling. In short, tough and unpopular decisions need to be made if Hungary is to meet the Maastricht criteria.

The immediate outlook for Hungary is continuing, sustained growth at similar levels to those of 2005. Infrastructure projects will continue to fuel investments and the external outlook appears steady. Moderate private consumption should continue and will receive a slight boost from reductions in the highest rate of VAT. In the medium to longer term, if the 2010 euro area target entry date remains, fiscal policy will have to tighten considerably.

Czech Republic

The Czech economy continues to exhibit strong growth, reaching 4.8 per cent for 2005 as a whole. Positive external sector developments underpinned the buoyant economy. As well as driving GDP growth, vigorous export growth helped push the trade balance into surplus for the first time since 1991 and made a substantial contribution to narrowing the current account deficit. Exports have been helped by accession to the EU and have benefited particularly from improvements in the Czech Republic's two main export markets, Germany and Slovakia, and by the rediscovery of markets to the east. Exports were also boosted early in 2005 with the onset of production by the export-oriented Toyota Peugeot Citroën joint venture, the biggest ever greenfield investment by a foreign multinational in the Czech Republic.

Buoyant export demand has persisted despite continuing appreciation of the koruna. The strong currency, along with intensifying competition arising from accession and falling food prices, helped keep inflation down to 1.7 per cent for the year as whole. Energy prices did, however, push inflation up towards the end of the year.

Private consumption growth, driven largely by improvement in demand for durable consumer goods, accelerated and also made a contribution to GDP growth. However, it was still relatively sluggish by the standards of a few years earlier. Following a decline in 2004, public consumption barely expanded in 2005 and gross fixed capital formation growth was almost half that of 2004, although investment in capital equipment did accelerate.

The Czech Republic's labour markets have been helped by strong economic performance. In 2005, the trend of falling and flat employment was reversed and unemployment registered a modest fall to 7.9 per cent. One obstacle to a greater fall of unemployment was the mismatch between the skills and occupational make-up of the unemployed and the areas of increased labour demand, namely civil engineering, construction and assembly work, manufacturing associated with foreign direct investment (FDI), education, real estate and public administration. The upshot was an increase in the number of long-term unemployed.

Strong growth performance, along with lower debt service obligations, also helped the government's budget position. Revenues grew about three times faster than expenditures. Consequently, the final budget deficit of 3.2 per cent of GDP significantly exceeded the convergence programme target of 4.7 per cent. Despite major improvements in public finances in 2004 and 2005, doubts remain about their sustainability.

In 2005, the government approved a joint document by the Ministry of Finance, the Ministry of Industry and Trade and the Czech National Bank (Ministry of Finance of the Czech Republic, 2005) which recognized these doubts and recommended that the Czech Republic should not seek ERM-II membership in 2006 on the grounds that it was far from guaranteed that the Czech Republic would fulfil the eligibility criteria for euro membership after two years within ERM-II. Although the prospects for compliance with the monetary criteria were promising, the fiscal prospects were more uncertain. Reference was also made to the need to improve flexibility of the labour market and the economy in general for euro area membership to be successful.

Although forecast to come in below 2005 levels, prospects for economic growth in 2006–07 remain strong. Net exports are expected to remain a major driver, but domestic demand will play a bigger role with private consumption stimulated by improvements in labour markets and with investment benefiting from greater absorption of EU funds. An increase in public consumption is also forecast.

Slovakia

In 2004, domestic demand, particularly investment and private consumption, replaced net exports as the main factors behind Slovakia's impressive growth. Domestic demand continued to drive the economy forward in 2005 with GDP growth reaching 5.1 per cent for the year as a whole.

Strong private consumption has been helped by real wage increases and by significant growth in employment coupled with unemployment falling below 17 per cent. These labour market improvements were themselves helped by buoyant economic activity. However, not all regions of Slovakia have benefited from labour market improvements. Eastern Slovakia, for example, suffers from poor infrastructure and unemployment of around 20 per cent.

Domestic demand is expected to remain the main economic driver through into 2007 when growth is forecast to be over 6 per cent. However, by then the contribution of net exports should pick up as new export capacity starts production. Indeed, Slovakia, with its large-scale production facilities owned by VW, Peugeot-Citroën and Hyundai Kia, is well on its way to producing more cars per head than any other country in the world.

The contribution of the external sector to GDP growth was negative in 2005 as a result of the acceleration of private consumption, which sucked in imports, and the high level of capital goods imports needed to support investment. Consequently, the current account deficit widened in 2005 to over 5 per cent of GDP compared to 3.4 per cent in 2004. The export growth alluded to above should begin to reverse the situation on the current account in 2006–07.

According to the national euro changeover plan approved by the government in July 2005 (National Bank of Slovakia, 2005), the objective is to join ERM-II by June 2006 with a view to euro area entry by 1 January 2009. This requires Slovakia to fulfil the Maastricht convergence criteria. Rather unexpectedly, Slovakia in fact joined ERM-II in November 2005, eight months ahead of schedule. The immediate prospects for inflation are good. Following the inflationary surges of 2003 and 2004, inflation fell back to 2.9 per cent in 2005 from 7.5 per cent in 2004 as a result of an appreciating currency and as the previous year's increases in indirect taxes and administered prices fell out of the figures. Energy prices and demand pressures could put upward pressure on this indicator in the future. On the fiscal side, helped by economic growth and by lower interest payments on public debt, the actual deficit in 2005 was 3.3 per cent of GDP compared to a forecast outturn of 4 per cent. Pension reforms may increase the deficit in the future.

Slovenia

Slovenian growth decelerated slightly to 3.8 per cent in 2005 from the 4.2 per cent of 2004, the highest level for five years. Domestic demand played an important role in this continuing growth. Private consumption was helped by improvements in the labour market, including a rise in employment and a fall in unemployment to below 6 per cent, lower interest rates and significant increases in real wages. Increased investment made a contribution to growth, but it increased less rapidly than in the previous two years, despite vigorous construction activity, partly because of destocking.

Exports continued to grow more quickly than imports. Indeed, considering the ongoing restrained growth in Slovenia's main European trading partners, exports held up well. Moreover, Slovenia's exports regained markets in CIS states and in former Yugoslav Republics, particularly Serbia, Montenegro and Croatia. In general, accession to the EU has afforded Slovenia better access to many third-country markets to the benefit of its exports. The deficit on the current account declined slightly in 2005, but this trend is expected to be reversed in 2006 given the expected rise in imports to accompany strong private consumption and investment.

In January 2005, the government adopted a *Masterplan for the Euro Changeover* (Bank of Slovenia, 2005) which sets out the main practical steps that need to be taken for the successful introduction of the euro. As a member of ERM-II since June 2004, the government anticipates entry into the euro area by January 2007, provided it satisfies the Maastricht criteria. Despite the uncertainties created by oil prices, inflation continued to decline from its peak of 8.6 per cent in 2001 to 2.6 per cent in 2005. This was achieved by adjusting excise duties to mitigate the effects of oil price increases, by regulating price rises and because of the accession-induced intensification of competition. Although upside inflationary risks remain from oil and commodity prices, Slovenia looks set to satisfy the Maastricht inflation criteria. Notwithstanding the major revision of the deficits for the previous five years to bring Slovenian practices into line with Eurostat rules, the 2005 budget deficit still fell to 1.7 per cent of GDP. In order to prepare for demographic changes and to improve the business environment, the government is pushing forward reforms in health, tax and social welfare and prospects for achievement of Maastricht's fiscal criteria are also positive.

Estonia

Revised figures indicate that Estonian GDP growth in 2004 was 7.8 per cent, much higher than the original estimate of 6 per cent. Growth in 2005 was even stronger at 8.4 per cent. This growth was well balanced, driven by both domestic and external demand. On the domestic demand side, personal and public consumption growth was strong, but both were outdone by investment, especially by investment in construction which was boosted by a credit-driven housing boom. The contribution of net exports to growth turned from negative in 2004 to positive in 2005. Exports generally performed well, but technology exports were particularly healthy and tourism proved to be buoyant.

The strong economy underpinned improvements in the labour market. There was a modest increase in employment in 2005 and average unemployment was an impressive two percentage points below the average for 2004. Reports of labour shortages even began to emerge during the course of the year. As yet, labour market improvements have not resulted in inflationary wage demands; aggregate real wages matched but did not exceed the productivity increases experienced during the year. There was, however, some inflationary pressure during 2005, mostly from energy prices and from administered price rises. Inflation reached 4.1 per cent in 2005, but is forecast to decline over the following two years.

Control over inflation is important because of Estonia's aspirations to adopt the euro in January 2007. Certainly, Estonia looks well placed to meet the fiscal convergence criteria. The final budget surplus for 2005 looks certain to be over 1 per cent – despite a supplementary budget in October 2005 which raised expenditure by the equivalent of 1.3 per cent of GDP. This performance was assisted by strong economic growth and an efficient tax collection system. Overall government debt levels remain at an extremely low 5 per cent of GDP.

Latvia

In 2005, for the second year in succession, Latvia's economy was the fastest growing in the EU with real GDP growth registering 9.1 per cent. This was made possible because domestic demand grew 10.8 per cent, only slightly below the unprecedented 11.1 per cent of 2004. Moreover, the relatively large negative contribution from net exports became neutral as exports began to grow more quickly than imports. Nevertheless, trade and current account balances remained significantly in deficit. Domestic demand remained strong because favourable credit conditions, improvement in labour markets and increases in real disposable income arising from real wage increases spurred on private consumption. Investment was driven by the credit conditions, by strong demand for equipment and by a continuing construction boom. Inward FDI in 2005 was also at its highest level since the onset of transition.

Strong growth has resulted in a marginal boost to employment and a slight fall in unemployment. The limited impact on labour markets of these elevated growth rates is attributable to continuing productivity growth, a trend that is forecast to continue into 2006 and 2007. Consequently, Latvian unemployment will continue to fall, but only gradually.

Latvia has also been at the top of the EU's inflation league since mid-2004, and price rises continued to gather pace in 2005. Inflation for the whole year was 6.8 per cent, but prices were running nearly 7 per cent higher in December 2005 than in December 2004. A combination of high oil prices, rapidly increasing food prices and steeply rising administratively regulated prices for goods, such as natural gas and postal services, created this inflationary pressure. So far, real wage increases have been sustainable because of the above-mentioned productivity improvements but the danger of overheating remains if strong demand continues to push output.

Inflation currently poses the main danger to Latvia's aspirations to adopt the euro by January 2008. The lat became a member of ERM-II on 1 May 2005, just four months after it was pegged to the euro. Latvia is well on course to satisfy euro area membership requirements in relation to interest rates and the fiscal criteria, but the ongoing strong growth forecast for 2006 and 2007 on the back of continuing trends in domestic and external demand could make it difficult to put the inflation genie back into the bottle.

Lithuania

As in 2004, Lithuania grew at an impressive 7 per cent in 2005. Domestic demand remained the main driver for growth. Private consumption growth of 8.2 per cent, helped by labour market improvements, real wage increases and availability of credit, made a key contribution to economic activity. However, despite a temporary slowdown in the first half of 2005, investment growth of 10.1 per cent for the year as a whole spearheaded the growth push for 2005. External demand continued to exercise a negative influence on Lithuanian economic activity but less so than in previous years. Although import growth remained strong at 11.5 per cent (down from 14.8 per cent in 2004), export growth accelerated from 4.2 per cent in 2004 to 10.7 per cent in 2005. Exports benefited from continuing strong demand in EU markets and greater demand from CIS countries to the extent that the impact of the sharp drop in electricity exports from the Ignalina nuclear power station was neutralized.

Helped by several years of strong growth, Lithuania's labour markets are showing significant signs of improvement. After a temporary setback in 2004, employment growth resumed in 2005 and unemployment fell almost two percentage points to 9 per cent, continuing the steady fall in joblessness from its 2001 peak. The tightening of labour markets is such that shortages are starting to appear in some sectors and wage growth is rather strong. These trends are reinforced by emigration and by the structural nature of unemployment which means that the available labour supply is not necessarily able to meet labour demand.

Tight labour markets pose problems for inflation which, although still within acceptable limits at 2.6 per cent in 2005, has been gradually picking up for some time. In 2005, the acceleration in price rises stemmed from rising energy, health, transport and food prices. Potential further energy price rises plus possible wage-induced pressure continue to pose inflationary risks.

Following its June 2004 entry into ERM-II, Lithuania is targeting euro area entry for 1 January 2007. Although the budget deficit rose from 1.4 per cent of GDP in 2004 to 2 per cent in 2005 as the result of higher pensions and public sector wage increases, the budget deficit remains largely under control and is a beneficiary of the robust economic growth which has been keeping government tax revenues high. General government debt remains well within the Maastricht criteria.

Malta

Malta has experienced the most sluggish growth of all the 2004 accession states in recent years and continues to do so. In the first quarter of 2005, earlier trends appeared to be continuing but growth picked up again and registered 0.8 per cent in 2005, compared to 0.4 per cent in 2004, according to the European Commission (Commission, 2005).

The Maltese government (Central Bank of Malta, 2005) is more bullish than the Commission about the Maltese economy, claiming that private consumption improved somewhat from its erstwhile negative contribution to growth and benefited from small increases in disposable income and slight labour market improvements. Investment has been the most dynamic component of domestic demand as a result of large-scale infrastructure projects financed by the EU's structural funds and by grants from the Italian government, also for big infrastructure projects. Investment's contribution will decline as these projects near completion. Public consumption growth has been restrained because of spending cuts. The government has also introduced revenue-enhancing measures in an effort to meet the deficit target in its 2005 convergence programme (Maltese Ministry of Finance, 2005).

The budget deficit has indeed been falling, but the process has been adversely affected by low GDP growth. The deficit fell from 5.1 per cent of GDP in 2004 to 4.2 per cent in 2005. The 2005 budget includes expenditure cuts and revenue-enhancing measures, but lower than forecast growth is an obstacle to the achievement of deficit targets in the 2005 convergence programme. Malta joined ERM-II in May 2005, but remains a long way from satisfying the Maastricht convergence criteria because of government debt levels that approach 80 per cent of GDP.

The contribution of the external sector to growth has been negative and, although the prospects for exports are improving along with the fortunes of the semi-conductor industry, which accounts for 60 per cent of manufacturing exports, and the tourism sector, imports will also accelerate as a result of the increase in consumption.

Cyprus

The strong growth (3.8 per cent) experienced by Cyprus in 2004 carried over into 2005. The main drivers behind growth continued to be private consumption and investment, but their contribution was more muted than in 2004. Despite this, real GDP growth in Cyprus in 2005 was similar to that in 2004 because of a small increase in public consumption, which had declined in 2004, and a boost in external demand. Buoyant GDP has helped reverse the gradual increase in unemployment taking place since 2002 with joblessness falling to 4.9 per cent in 2005 from its peak of 5.2 per cent in 2004.

The external sector benefited in particular from growth in tourism arrivals of over 6 per cent. The recovery in tourism, following the disastrous falls in the early 2000s, had begun in a modest way in 2004, but picked up significantly in 2005. Import growth moderated in 2005 with the result that the negative contribution of external demand to growth in 2004 became positive in 2005. However, the current account deficit still remained around 5.8 per cent of GDP.

In May 2005, Cyprus acceded to ERM-II. It is performing well on all the convergence criteria except for public debt. Interest rates fell both before and after ERM-II entry, thereby helping maintain the growth momentum. The exchange rate has been relatively stable, albeit with a slight tendency towards appreciation. This has helped restrain the inflationary pressures which have arisen because of higher energy prices as did wage moderation in the public sector. Overall, inflation for 2005 as a whole averaged 2.3 per cent compared to 1.9 per cent the previous year. The public sector deficit fell to 2.8 per cent of GDP in 2005 from 4.1 per cent in 2004. This improvement resulted from a combination of a 17 per cent increases in revenues, which had been boosted by increased economic activity, compared to a 7 per cent expenditure increase. Despite this progress in public sector finances, public debt still remained ten percentage points above the Maastricht convergence ceiling.

References

Bank of Slovenia (2005) *Masterplan for the Euro Changeover.*
Central Bank of Malta (2005) *Quarterly Review,* Vol. 38, No. 4.

Commission of the European Communities (2005) 'Economic Forecasts: Autumn 2005'. *European Economy,* No. 5/2004.

HM Treasury (2005) *Forecast for the UK Economy: A Comparison of Independent Forecasts.* Available at «http://www.hm-treasury.gv.uk/media/4CA/35/ forecast211205.pdf».

Maltese Ministry of Finance (2005) *Update of the Convergence Programme, 2005– 2008.*

Ministry of Finance of the Czech Republic, Ministry of Industry and Trade of the Czech Republic and the Czech National Bank (2005) *Assessment of the Fulfilment of the Maastricht Criteria and the Degree of Economic Alignment of the Czech Republic with the Euro Area.*

National Bank of Poland (2006) *Inflation Report.* January.

National Bank of Slovakia and the Ministry of Finance for the Slovak Republic (2005) *The National Euro Changeover Plan.*

OECD (2005) *Economic Survey of Hungary* (Paris: OECD).

Chronology: The European Union in 2005

ULRICH SEDELMEIER
London School of Economics and Political Science

ALASDAIR R. YOUNG
University of Glasgow

At a Glance

Presidencies of the EU Council: Luxembourg (1 January –30 June) and the United Kingdom (1 July–31 December).

January

18 Council dropped excessive deficit proceedings against France and Germany.

February

1 Slovenia ratified the Constitutional Treaty.

8 Danish election.

9 Commission launched social agenda for 2006–10.

11 Commission green paper on an EU approach to managing economic migration.

16 Kyoto Protocol to the United Nations Convention on Climate Change entered into force.

20 Spanish referendum on the Constitutional Treaty (favourable).

20 Portuguese elections.

| 21 | First bilateral ENP action plans adopted by EU (with Israel, Jordan, Moldova, Morocco, Palestinian Authority, Tunisia, Ukraine). |
| 22 | EU–US Leaders' Meeting, Brussels. |

March
| 22–23 | European Council. Mid-term review of Lisbon process and agreed reform of the Stability and Growth Pact. |

April
6	Italy completed ratification of Constitutional Treaty.
19	Greece ratified Constitutional Treaty.
25	Accession treaties with Bulgaria and Romania signed.
28	WTO finds EU sugar regime incompatible with WTO rules.

May
5	UK elections.
10	EU–Russia summit, Moscow.
11	Slovakia ratified Constitutional Treaty.
23	Commission communication on European space policy.
25	Austria ratified Constitutional Treaty.
27	Germany ratified Constitutional Treaty.
27	Framework agreement on relations between the Commission and European Parliament concluded.
29	French referendum on the Constitutional Treaty (negative).

June
| 1 | Dutch referendum on the Constitutional Treaty (negative). |
| 1 | Commission framework strategy on the provision of effective legal protection against discrimination. |

| 2 | Latvia ratified Constitutional Treaty |

7   Commission action plan for improving research in the nanosciences and nanotechnologies (2005–09).

13   Council conferred official language status on Irish.

15   Commission imposed fine of €60 million on Astra Zeneca for abuse of dominant position.

16–17   European Council. Ratification of the Constitutional Treaty suspended during period of reflection.

20   EU–US summit, Washington, D.C.

21   Council agreed reform of CAP financing.

27   Reform of Stability and Growth Pact formalized.

29   Commission report on promoting the life sciences and the biotechnology sector.

30   Cyprus ratified Constitutional Treaty.

July

5   Commission adopted strategic guidelines for rural development, 2007–13.

6   Malta ratified Constitutional Treaty.

7   London bombings.

September

1   Commission communication on a common agenda for the integration of third-country nationals in the EU.

5   EU–China summit, Beijing.

7   Council and Parliament directive on the recognition of professional qualifications.

7   EU–India summit, New Delhi.

13   ECJ judgment on the use of criminal law for EC objectives.

14–16   UN world summit.

18   German elections.

25   Polish parliamentary election.

27   Commission proposed scrapping 68 legislative proposals.

29   Tenth social dialogue summit.

October

4   EU–Russia summit, London.

11   Council code of conduct to improve the consistent implementation of the Stability and Growth Pact and the guidelines for stability and convergence programmes.

3   Accession negotiations with Turkey opened.

4   Accession negotiations with Croatia opened.

4–5   Risk capital summit.

9 and 23   Polish presidential election.

10   Negotiations on a stabilization and association agreement with Serbia and Montenegro formally opened.

12   Council adopted directive on procedures for admitting third-country nationals for the purposes of scientific research.

26   Council and Parliament adopted directive to facilitate cross-border mergers.

27   Informal meeting of Heads of State and Government at Hampton Court Palace.

November

9   Commission adopted enlargement strategy paper.

21   Council authorized Commission to start negotiating a stabilization and association agreement with Bosnia and Herzegovina (started 25 January 2006).

24   Council political agreement to reform the common organization of the sugar market.

30   Council agreement on EU counter-terrorism strategy.

December

1   Council adopted directive on minimum standards for procedures for granting and withdrawing refugee status.

1   Council and Parliament agreement on a regulation allowing EU-based companies to produce copies of patented medicines under licence for export to developing countries without the authorization of the patent holder.

1   European Central Bank raised the euro interest rate 25 basis points.

8   Commission communication on EU–Latin American relations.

12   Cars 21 report on improving the competitiveness of the EU automobile industry.

13–18   Sixth WTO ministerial conference, Hong Kong.

14   Solana proposals related to the 'EU's rapid expansion in crisis management and its increasingly important role in the world'.

15   Parliament adopted the 2006 budget.

15–16   European Council. Agreed financial framework for 2007–13; candidate status for Macedonia; strategy for Africa.

21   Commission policy plan on legal migration.

23   Commission guidelines on regional aid (for 2007–13).

Index

Note: Italicized page references indicate information contained in tables.